EMPLOYMENT AND EQUILIBRIUM

EMPLOYMENT
AND
EQUILIBRIUM

A THEORETICAL DISCUSSION

BY
A. C. PIGOU, M.A.

SECOND (REVISED) EDITION

AUGUSTUS M. KELLEY · PUBLISHERS
FAIRFIELD 1978

 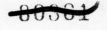

First edition 1941
Second revised edition 1949
(London: Macmillan & Co. Ltd., 1949)

Reprinted 1978 by

Augustus M. Kelley · Publishers
Fairfield, New Jersey 07006

By arrangement with Macmillan & Co. Ltd.

Library of Congress Cataloging in Publication Data

Pigou, Arthur Cecil, 1887-1959.
    Employment and equilibrium.

    (Reprints of economic classics)
    Reprint of the 1949 ed. published by Macmillan, London.
    Includes index.
    1. Economics. 2. Equilibrium (Economics)
I. Title.
HB171.P58   1977   330.1   76-52397
ISBN 0-678-01224-5

PREFACE

THE " objective " of this book is a set of interrelated problems which bear on the behaviour, not of particular parts of economic systems, but of economic systems as wholes. Many of these problems were brought into the forefront of economic discussion by the late Lord Keynes' book on *The General Theory of Employment, Interest and Money*. Whatever may be thought of the value of his criticisms upon other people, or of the solutions which he himself offered, the author of that book rendered a very great service to economics by asking important questions. When once that has been done, the task of answering these questions is often a relatively pedestrian one. In this field, therefore, Keynes was a true pioneer.[1]

After dealing in Part I with definitions and some other preliminary matter, I try in Part II to elucidate the conditions necessary in order that an economic system may be in what I shall call short-period flow equilibrium, examining under this general heading the " classical view " and the relation in various circumstances between equilibrium and what has come to be spoken of as " full employment ". Part III is devoted to a discussion of the relation, as between two economic systems, of differences in the state of several important determining influences to differences in aggregate

[1] I have not, either here or in the body of the book, altered anything that was said about Keynes in the first edition. Since the calamity of his death I have tried, very inadequately, in the 1947 *Proceedings of the British Academy*, to pay my tribute to his memory.

employment, together with studies of various kinds of "multiplier". Finally, Part IV is concerned with what happens when economic systems are in disequilibrium, in the course of movement, it may be, from one equilibrium situation to another. The whole book is abstract, in the sense that, with a view to concentrating attention upon what are conceived to be essentials, many of the characteristic circumstances of real life are ignored.

The book is addressed to professional economists. I have tried, however, so to arrange it that at least the main drift shall be intelligible to lay readers who care to take trouble. Parts I, II and IV may perhaps have interest for them even though the severer argument of Part III has not. Since the problems dealt with are in essence problems of equilibrium and maximum and minimum problems, a completely non-mathematical treatment of them is impossible. Moreover, in view of the fact that four variables are usually involved, the mathematics cannot be translated into graphs. I have, therefore, been obliged, from time to time, to write out in the text algebraic formulae. To understand the significance of these, the reader needs to be acquainted with the meaning of the symbols used in the differential calculus ; *but with nothing more*. He is not asked to follow mathematical manipulations, though sometimes, when the answers to the questions cannot readily be found by unaided common sense, he is asked to accept the conclusions to which such manipulations lead. A few manipulations are given in footnotes ; and the results of a large number, all referring to Part III, have been brought together in an Appendix.

In preparing the first edition I owed much to Prof. Dennis Robertson, who read, in their earlier stages, drafts of a large part of the book, and made valuable comments. Also to Mr. Sraffa, to whose critical judgment I submitted it at a later stage, and who, instead of, as I had expected, blowing it sky-high, encouraged me to go on. The tables in the Appendix were worked out and very carefully checked by Mrs. Glauert. To her, too, my best thanks are due.

The most important alteration in this edition is the substitution of the present Chapters III and IV for the former Chapter III in Part II. This removes, as is shown in the new Chapters, a serious mistake. The other changes have to deal with minor matters, but are, I hope, improvements. Some passages, *e.g.* Chapter I of Part I, have been incorporated from my *Theory of Unemployment,* which is out of print. The book is still, I feel, defective in many ways. In 1940 I made excuses by reference to the preoccupations of war. Now that these are ended, I can only invoke the gathering stupidity of age.

I trust that these explanatory remarks will not be taken to imply that the subject-matter treated here consists of mathematical frills, about which " literary " economists need not trouble themselves. The problems tackled are *fundamental economic problems,* with which every economist, whether in this way or in some other way, *must* trouble himself.

A. C. P.

King's College
  Cambridge
  August 1947

CONTENTS

PRELIMINARY   PAGE 1

PART I
SOME PROBLEMS OF DEFINITION

CHAP.

I. EMPLOYMENT AND UNEMPLOYMENT   9

II. REAL AND MONEY INCOME   18

III. MONEY INCOME AND MONEY STOCKS   20

IV. INVESTMENT AND SAVING   28

PART II
FLOW EQUILIBRIUM

I. THE MEANING OF FLOW EQUILIBRIUM   39

       Note   47

II. THE RELEVANT QUANTITIES AND FUNCTIONS   48

III. THE ECONOMIC SYSTEM IN SHORT-PERIOD FLOW EQUILIBRIUM   66

IV. STABILITY CONDITIONS   73

V. THE DETERMINATION OF CERTAIN SIGNS OTHERWISE THAN FROM STABILITY CONSIDERATIONS   81

VI. THE CLASSICAL VIEW   85

VII. MARSHALL ON THE RATE OF INTEREST   99

VIII. THE SIZES OF AVAILABLE REAL INCOMES AND THE PROPORTIONS SAVED   103

IX. THE SPECIAL CASE OF LONG-PERIOD FLOW EQUILIBRIUM   123

       Note   135

PART III

DIFFERENCES AMONG POSITIONS OF SHORT-PERIOD FLOW EQUILIBRIUM

CHAP.   PAGE
I. INTRODUCTORY   139
II. THE FORMAL TECHNIQUE   144
III. THE MODELS   150
IV. MODEL I (A)   155
V. MODEL I (B)   168
VI. MODEL II   170
VII. MODEL III   177
VIII. EMPLOYMENT MULTIPLIERS   181
IX. MONEY MULTIPLIERS   190
X. THE CASE OF A BANKING POLICY THAT KEEPS
     THE RATE OF INTEREST CONSTANT   194
XI. UNEMPLOYMENT BENEFIT   198
XII. PERIODS OF PRODUCTION   205
XIII. MONOPOLISTIC POLICY   208

PART IV

DISTURBANCES OF SHORT-PERIOD FLOW EQUILIBRIUM

I. INTRODUCTORY   213
II. DOMINANT FACTORS OF CHANGE   215
III. TRANSITIONS BETWEEN POSITIONS OF EQUI-
      LIBRIUM   223
IV. TRANSITIONS BETWEEN POSITIONS OF DIS-
      EQUILIBRIUM   230
V. THE EVALUATION OF MULTIPLIERS   232
VI. CUMULATIVE MOVEMENTS   235
APPENDIX   245
INDEX   279

PRELIMINARY

§ 1. In popular discussions it is often tacitly assumed that the question why such and such an amount of unemployment exists at a particular time can be answered by naming some single " cause " : high direct taxation; the absence — or presence — of a protective tariff; the presence in office of a Socialist government — or a Conservative government; the return to the gold standard; or whatever the cry of the moment may be. No reflective person is entrapped by these crudities. He recognises, perforce, that not one, but many, factors are at work. For him, as a plain man, such unemployment as prevails at any time is the consequence of a large number of separate causes, each of which is responsible for a part of it ; responsible in the sense that, if it were removed, that part of unemployment would disappear, and if it is not removed, no matter what else is done, that part will not disappear. This view, though, of course, a great improvement on any " single cause " theory, is, none the less, seriously misleading. The unemployment that exists at any time is not the summed effect of a number of causes acting independently : it arises because a number of factors are balanced against one another in a particular way. To speak of the state of one of these factors as *the* cause, or even as *a* cause, is arbitrary ; for that factor might remain as it is and yet the relevant part of unemployment disappear, provided that the state of one or more of the others was modified. When a ship is too low in the water, this effect is a combined result of the weight of the cargo

and of the capacity of the ship. If the capacity of the
ship is taken as given, the excess weight of the cargo
is called the cause ; but, if the weight of the cargo is
taken as given, the inadequate capacity of the ship is
called the cause. In truth neither of these things taken
by itself is the cause, but the maladjustment between
them. The evil will be cured if the maladjustment is
removed either by decreasing the cargo in sufficient
measure or by enlarging the ship in sufficient measure,
or by decreasing the cargo and enlarging the ship in
such measures that adjustment between them is attained. The effects of the various relevant factors in
promoting unemployment are thus, in general, not independent of one another. We cannot say that A is
responsible for so much and B for so much. For A is
responsible for different amounts according to the state
of B. If both A and B are removed together, the
quantitative result will not be equal to the sum of the
result of removing A while B is left and of removing
B while A is left. It may even happen that, in a
situation where, by reducing both of two causal factors,
we should lessen unemployment, by reducing one while
the other is not reduced, we should make unemployment
larger. Thus, if, in an industry where the method of
engaging labour is of the casual type, the wage-rate is
held artificially high and also some physical barrier
hinders workpeople from entering the industry from
outside, to remove the barrier while leaving the arti-
ficial rate would add nothing to employment there
and might draw people to unemployment there away
from employment elsewhere. What we are confronted
with, therefore, is not a sum of separate causes of unemployment, each accountable for so much of it, but
rather a system of interconnected *factors* jointly responsible for the whole of it.

§ 2. The purpose of this book is to elucidate certain dominant characteristics of that system. In order that this may be done in a clear way, many important aspects of reality are deliberately ignored. For a full concrete study of what happens in the actual world a number of other elements would need to be brought into account. But this does not mean that we shall be engaged on merely academic exercises. The study of the behaviour of model aeroplanes in a wind tunnel is, in a sense, unrealistic. But, none the less, it makes it easier to understand the behaviour of actual aeroplanes. Here, too, though the actual world is not the direct object of our analysis, that analysis will, it is hoped, enable us to see clearly some of its essential characteristics.

§ 3. Throughout the book the following general assumptions are made. First, our world, or country, is conceived as perfectly isolated and self-contained — a closed economic system. Secondly, labour is perfectly homogeneous, or, what comes to the same thing, its several kinds and qualities can be represented by an appropriate number of homogeneous units, in such wise that we may speak unambiguously of a quantity of labour. Thirdly, the stock of fixed capital is homogeneous, consisting of a large number of precisely similar structures. Fourthly, the fact that fixed capital wears out and may become obsolete, which implies that prime costs include some allowance for depreciation, is ignored. Fifthly, labour is completely mobile ; which implies that money rates of wages are everywhere the same. Finally, money wages are used exclusively in buying consumption goods.

§ 4. Further, our task being to study industrial activity as a whole, it is necessary, in order to avoid intolerable cumbersomeness, to abstract from the de-

tailed circumstances of individual industries. One way
of doing this would be to work with a model containing
only one kind of commodity, a kind which, once it had
been constructed, could be directed at choice to the uses
of consumption or of investment, just as grain can at
choice be eaten or used for seed. The chief objection
to this plan is that under it it would be impossible to
take any account of the characteristic implications of
monopoly or imperfect competition. When a single
kind of commodity only is being produced it is immaterial whether monopoly exists or not ; for a monopolist will find his best advantage in acting according
to the rules of competition. There will be no point,
for example, in a monopolistic landlord keeping production below the competitive level, because, since no
other commodity except the one he is producing exists,
he would have no chance, by doing so, of obtaining better
terms of exchange. Another plan would be to work
with a model in which two commodities are being produced, one a consumption good, the other a capital or
investment good. In this sort of model there would,
indeed, be scope for monopolistic bargaining between
the producers of the two kinds of goods. But imperfect
competition, as it appears in actual life, would still be
excluded. This plan also is, therefore, not satisfactory,
and it is necessary to search further.

§ 5. Mr. Harrod, in his book on *The Trade Cycle*,
has made use of a model in which there are many sorts
of consumption goods, but these are related to one
another in a special way. First, each sort has exactly
the same period of production ; which period cannot
be altered. Secondly, for every sort, the demand and
also the supply conditions are exactly similar in form,
so that relative values cannot change, whatever happens
to the demand or supply function of investment, to the

rate of money wage, or to anything else. Thirdly, in each industry all the producing firms are similar or similarly situated.[1] With this construction it is, of course, *possible* for perfect competition to prevail everywhere. But it is now also possible for imperfect competition — some degree of monopolistic power — to be exercised in respect of all consumption goods. Mr. Harrod postulates that the same degree — whether a nil degree or any other — of monopolistic power is exercised in all of them. I shall take over this device, with the addition that there are also a number of different kinds of investment goods, in respect of which too monopolistic power may be exercised. I allow, moreover, that, while the degree of monopolistic power exercised in respect of all kinds of investment goods must be the same, it need not be the same as the degree exercised in respect of consumption goods.

§ 6. In a world constructed on this plan and subjected to the conditions assumed in § 3 I propose to investigate the general problem of what Keynes calls " employment as a whole ". As was forecast in the second paragraph of this chapter, great violence is being done to realities. But the reader is asked not yet to abandon the hope which the end of that paragraph suggested. Whether and in what degree a study of simplified models throws light on problems of real life can only be decided by trial. After, not before, trial has been made, will come the time to pass judgment.

[1] This condition is necessary ; for otherwise there need not be a single value of one good in terms of other goods ; there might be different values per unit of the one good coming from different firms.

PART I

SOME PROBLEMS OF DEFINITION

CHAPTER I

EMPLOYMENT AND UNEMPLOYMENT

§ 1. THE volume of *employment* in any occupation over any assigned period can be defined unambiguously as the number of man-hours of work performed during that period. It is recognised that the quality of the men at work may vary from time to time and also the energy with which they perform their work. But this does not spoil the statistical measure any more than the fact that the quality and age distribution of the persons constituting a community varies prevents us from stating unambiguously the number of the population.

§ 2. *Unemployment*, however, is not an equally clear-cut conception. If it meant simply the number of man-hours that exist over a period, during which people are *not* employed, it would be so. But nobody seriously proposes to define unemployment in such a way as to make a man unemployed during the whole of the time (*e.g.* while he is asleep at night) that he is *not* employed. A man is only unemployed when he is *both* not employed and *also* desires to be employed. Moreover, the notion of desiring to be employed must be interpreted in relation to established facts as regards (1) hours of work per day, (2) rates of wage and (3) a man's state of health.

Thus, first, if the normal hours of work in a particular factory are eight, and a specially strong man would have liked to be at work for nine, nobody would say that he is, therefore, "unemployed" for one hour a day. In fact, for the purpose of measuring unemployment, the normal hours of work per day must be taken as given. This must be done even when the normal hours are different at different seasons of the year, as they are in the building trade. Awkward questions may, indeed, arise if this line of thought is pursued to its logical conclusion. Thus, obviously, it is in substance much the same thing whether a cotton mill closes three days a week or cuts down its daily hours from eight to four. If the idleness due to the former act is to be called unemployment, it is arbitrary to refuse that name to the idleness due to the latter. But, if we do not refuse it, we are not interpreting the notion of desiring to be employed in relation to established facts as regards hours of work.

Secondly, desire to be employed must be taken to mean desire to be employed at current rates of wages in an establishment not engaged in an industrial dispute. A man is not unemployed because he would like to work if the current wage were £1000 a day but does not so like when the current wage is 12s. a day. There are here, of course, certain ambiguities about the meaning of current rates of wage. If the wage in a man's own town is 12s. a day, whereas in another town it is 15s., a man is not unemployed if he stays in his own town and refuses to work because the wage there is not 15s. The same thing is true if a man of poor quality, such that the current rate for one of his ability is 10s., refuses to work for that, because the current rate for stronger men is 12s.

Thirdly, desire to be employed means desire subject to the facts of a man's own health. A man is not unemployed because he desires to work but is prevented from doing so by sickness. In the terminology current in England that type of non-employment is carefully separated from unemployment.

§ 3. We thus conclude that the number of persons unemployed at any time is equal to the number of persons who desire employment in the above sense — the number of would-be wage-earners — *minus* the number of persons employed. The task of obtaining a correct record of the difference between these two numbers is rendered difficult by the fact that some persons, who are not in fact desirous of employment in our sense, are, nevertheless, enumerated as though they were. It is well known that casual labourers often do not desire, and do not offer themselves for, work on more than three or four days in a week. Moreover, it is alleged that some men on occasions, possibly even for considerable periods, prefer to draw unemployment pay rather than make difficult efforts to find a job, particularly if this would require a shift in dwelling-place and, still more, a shift in occupation. Such men do not in fact desire employment in any effective sense; and yet in current statistics they are always classed as unemployed. With a well-organised system of Employment Exchanges, reasonable rules about conditions of benefit and rates of benefit not too high relatively to normal wages, they can sometimes be disentangled as a result of their declining unfilled vacancies. In periods of depression, however, there are unlikely to be any vacancies for them to decline. In these conditions the fact that they do not desire employment does not cause them to act otherwise than they would do if they did desire it ; and, since it is impossible to look directly into people's minds, there are, therefore, no means of discovering or enumerating them. When records are based on the number of persons eligible for benefit under Unemployment Insurance schemes, and when the test of eligibility is such as to include persons who *were* desirous of employment at some date in the past but are not necessarily so desirous now, there is further scope for the type of error we are here considering. Before the amendment of the Insurance Act in 1931 there were a number of persons recorded as unemployed who did not in fact desire employment. Thus in the *Labour Gazette* of November 1930 we read : " If the average rate of exit (from the Insurance scheme) experienced during the three years 1925–28 had continued during the subsequent two years, while the number of new entrants remained the same, there would have passed out of the Insurance scheme approximately 185,000 males and 130,000 females, who are now included in the figures for July 1930 ".[1] It appears further that the number in insurance in the northern section of this country took a spurt upwards in 1929–30. The *Labour Gazette* writes : " This change in the trend is attributable in the main to the retention within the scheme of unemployment insurance, in areas where unemployment has been heavy, of numbers of persons who would have passed out of the scheme if the changes in the conditions for the receipt of benefit introduced by the Unemployment Insurance Act, 1930, had not been made ".[2] Under the technique of the English scheme, as it then stood, women who had married and in effect withdrawn from industry, were, nevertheless, legally entitled to claim benefit for a considerable period, and a fair number of them did so. These women were clearly not would-be wage-earners and not unemployed in the terms of my definition. For the purposes of a general view, however, the proportion of " unemployment " that is affected by difficulties of this character is too small to make unemployment as here defined

---

[1] *Loc. cit.* p. 397.　　　　　　[2] *Loc. cit.* p. 399.

seriously different from unemployment as recorded in British official statistics.

§ 4. With this definition it is plain that one very important type of cause, namely alterations in the rate of wages offered by employers, coming about while other things remain the same, may affect employment and unemployment in different degrees. They will affect them in equal degrees if, and only if, they leave the number of men who desire to be employed unaltered. It may happen, however, if the rate of wage is raised, that a few men, who, at the lower rate, would have been in retirement, living on pensions or on their savings or with friends, and a few who would have been engaged in non-wage work, will become seekers after wage work. *Per contra*, it may happen that a rise in the rate of wage, if the effort demand of workers for stuff is inelastic, may cause some men to seek employment on fewer days in the week. But the generality of occupations in the real world are so organised that men cannot do that except on pain of dismissal, so that this point is not practically important. Of more weight is the tendency of a rise in the rate of wage, by enabling the husband to support his family without his wife working, to cause a certain number of women to withdraw from the labour market. This tendency and the tendency for men to be drawn back from retirement, and so on, work in opposite directions. In any event neither tendency is likely to manifest itself on a large scale. It is not probable, therefore, that on this account the amount — or the proportion — of unemployment caused by a rise in the rate of wages will be appreciably different from the amount, or proportion, of employment that is destroyed.

§ 5. It should be noted further that in certain conditions a given reduction in the number of persons employed is associated with an equal transfer of persons from inside the class of would-be wage-earners to outside that class, and so leaves the number of unemployed, in my sense, unaltered. This will happen if women, who have been employed, leave their jobs on marriage, and the vacancies that their withdrawal creates are not filled because acceptable candidates are not available. In times of general depression, however, it is very improbable that vacancies thus created will remain unfilled for any appreciable period. In England in the slump following the 1914-18 war domestic service was probably the only large-scale occupation in which unfilled vacancies played any significant part. In such circumstances withdrawal from employment by particular persons merely means the entrance into employment of others. The volume of employment is not affected. The voluntary idleness of A is a substitute for, not an addition to, the involuntary idleness of B. Thus this type of reaction is not likely to prove practically important in bad times. In good times it conceivably might do so. But even then its scope is probably not great.

§ 6. In sum, then, we may conclude that the number of would-be wage-earners and the number of persons employed are in the main independent of one another, so that, if the first decreases or the second increases in a given measure, the number of persons unemployed, in the sense of my definition, will decrease in an approximately equal measure. In this book I shall take the number of would-be wage-earners in a given situation as a fixed datum, so that the quantity of unemployment and the quantity of employment are simple complements of one another. It is obvious, of course, that, if the number of the would-be wage-earning population expands and employment remains unchanged, the absolute and the proportionate quantity of unemployment must both increase. If employment grows with population, the absolute quantity of unemployment will increase, but the proportionate quantity will remain constant.

§ 7. From the way of approach that we have been following so far, a careless reader might perhaps be led to suppose that the *aggregate quantity* of unemployment prevailing at any time is all that really matters. This is, of course, not so. The extent of the social evil that unemployment carries with it depends in great measure upon the size of the lumps in which it is served out to individual unemployed men. With even distribution an average of 6 per cent unemployment over the year would mean that everyone was involuntarily idle for about one work-day in every three weeks, or, say, for a spell of four or five days once every quarter. Plainly this would not be a very serious matter. If the idle days could be foreseen and arranged for beforehand, the net subjective cost, even though there were no unemployment pay contributed by other people, might well be nil. Even 10 per cent unemployment evenly distributed only means a little over five weeks a year of holidays without pay for everybody — a serious matter no doubt, for some poor men, but not a devastating calamity. In real life, however, unemployment is not distributed evenly over everybody. While leaving the larger part of the wage-earning population untouched or but lightly touched, it falls with tremendous force on a relatively small group. Thus, under the instructions of the Ministry of Labour, 1 per cent sample inquiries were held on March 18 and September 16, 1929 — in each of which months the aggregate percentage of unemployment was 10 per cent — into the period of unemployment of men then unemployed.

Averaging the two sets of numbers, which are fairly close, we obtain the following table:[1]

	Men.		Women.
	All Industries.	All Industries other than Coal Mining.	All Industries.
	%	%	%
Less than 3 months .	30·8	33·5	51·1
3-6 months . .	29·5	31·3	30·9
6-9 ,, . .	20·2	20·95	11·65
9-12 ,, . .	14·5	11·95	5·55
12 months or more .	5·0	2·3	0·8

Thus, even apart from coal mining, two-thirds of the men unemployed had been out of work for more than three months and more than one-third for over six months. Among the women unemployed nearly half had been out of work for over three months and one-fifth for over six months. In a sample count taken on February 2, 1931, the situation was not substantially different.[2] Nobody can suppose that, with a distribution of this sort, the leisure associated with unemployment is an asset to be weighed against the loss of what work would have produced. It is an aggravation, not a mitigation, of the social loss involved. Moreover, we have so far spoken only of the direct and contemporaneous loss. There is much more than this. If a man is subjected to unemployment for a long period of time injurious reactions to his industrial and human quality are almost certain to result. It is not merely that technical skill deteriorates through lack of practice. The habit of regular work may be lost and self-respect and self-confidence destroyed, so that, when oppor-

---

[1] *Labour Gazette*, June 1930, p. 7.
[2] Report of the Royal Commission on Unemployment Insurance [Cmd. 4185], p. 76.

tunity comes again, the man, once merely unemployed, is found to have become unemployable. Meanwhile his home life may have suffered shipwreck and the atmosphere in which his children are growing up may have been poisoned. Evils of this kind do not follow from small doses of unemployment spread over many men, even though the aggregate amount is large. They are the fruit, in the main, of large concentrations of unemployment upon a small number of especially unfortunate people. This subject does not fall within the ambit of our present study. But that must not be taken to imply that the author does, or that anybody else should, regard it as unimportant.

CHAPTER II

REAL AND MONEY INCOME

§ 1. SINCE the concepts of saving and (or) investment will play an important part in our study, and since these concepts depend in some measure on the mother concept, income, we require, at the outset, clear ideas about what income — real and money — is to mean.

§ 2. Our drastic assumption, for the purposes of this book, that capital goods do not decay, do not suffer destruction either through lapse of time or through catastrophes, such as fire and earthquake, and do not become obsolete, gets rid of the main difficulties that are entailed in finding a definition for real income in actual life. For us, real income in any year is, in principle, simply the sum of the services of factors of production, whether directed towards consumption goods or towards additions to the stock of capital, which are rendered against money payment. Services rendered gratis are not counted in real income, and money payments which are made otherwise than against the services of factors of production, such as a son's allowance from his father, War Loan interest paid out of taxation and (some) pensions, are not counted as money income. Thus money income is the counterpart of and payment for all the services that constitute real income, *i.e.* all those that are, in the conditions of the time, rendered against money. This broad statement needs qualification in detail, but it is adequate for the present purpose.

§ 3. There is, indeed, a difficulty. When a piece of work is proceeding, the manual wage-earners engaged on it are, for the most part, paid weekly and the salary earners monthly or quarterly. But the entrepreneurs (or shareholders) do not become possessed of any income for their services until the product they helped forward is sold. Thus, of the money income that is actually being received by factors of production in any period, part is the value of elements in the real income of that period, part the value of elements in the real income of earlier periods. The money income of any period, therefore, though it may be defined as the money value of *some* corresponding real income, cannot be defined as the money value of the real income that comes into being in that same period. The only way to make money income the value of real income then coming into being would be to define entrepreneurs' money income at any time, not as what they actually receive then, but as what is accruing to them then. This would entail, in periods of fluctuation, the size of the actual money income of any period being dependent upon events which were to happen *subsequently* ; a defect which puts that device out of court.

§ 4. In stable conditions, however, *i.e.* so long as what I shall presently call " flow equilibrium " is being maintained, this difficulty is not active, but only latent. For, since successive periods are alike, the money value of the real income received in any one of them is necessarily *equal* to the money value of the real income accruing in that period. Hence, for conditions of flow equilibrium, the discrepancy of dates between the emergence of real income and of associated parts of money income is immaterial.

CHAPTER III

MONEY INCOME AND MONEY STOCKS

§ 1. FOR a full clarification of our ideas, what was said
in the last chapter needs a supplement. The picture
which most of us have in mind when we think about
economic processes — whether or not we proceed so far
as a study of causal relations — is, I imagine, something
like this. Annual real incomes consist of a succession
of outputs, which come into being, are consumed or
worn out, and presently disappear, or, more strictly,
lose their quality as economic goods.   Annual money
incomes, on the other hand, are not a succession of
different entities ; they are, apart from additions and
subtractions which are made from time to time, a succession of appearances of the same entity, namely, a
stock of money, which constitutes annual money income
again and again. Two stages, as it were, are set. On
the one an endless procession of different men marches
past constantly ; on the other a stage army, varying
occasionally in numbers, but for the most part consisting of a single set of men, marches through, marches
off, and then marches on again. On the one stage many
armies succeed one another, on the other the same army
" circulates ".   Each £, that has become income on
one day, subject, as I have indicated, to withdrawals
sometimes being made and new entrants sometimes
arriving, reappears as income at a later day ; and so
on for ever.

§ 2. If money consisted solely of pieces of metal or bank-notes that were physically distinguishable, each, for example, being marked with a different number, this picture would represent the facts quite accurately. The circulation of money would be just as " real " a thing as the circulation of motor-cars, each piece having a perfectly definite history, capable in principle of being precisely known. Some things about these histories we could learn from general common-sense considerations. Thus a piece of money, after appearing as income once, does not appear again till some finite interval has elapsed. It would be impossible for it to reappear instantaneously ; for to be received as income and to depart out of income without the lapse of *any* time would mean not to be received at all. It is theoretically conceivable that, for every piece of money in existence, the interval between successive income appearances might be the same. But, of course, in fact this could not be so. There must be differences both in the intervals between the receipts of different pieces as income and their expenditure, and also differences in the intervals between their expenditure and their reappearance as income. First, different pieces accruing as income on the same day are expended after many different intervals. Thus consider a number of men, each of whom has no outgoing of expenses in connection with earning his income, has an annual income of £365 and, expending this regularly, so arranges things that the last instalment is always exactly used up when the next one falls due. Suppose that one of these men receives his income weekly as wages. The £'s that accrue to him as income must, on the average, be expended $3\frac{1}{2}$ days later. In contrast suppose that another of the men is paid a quarterly salary ; his income must on the average be expended $1\frac{1}{2}$ months after being received.

Secondly, when money is expended by anybody, it sets out on a journey, at the end of which — unless before the end it is drawn out of circulation — it becomes income a second time. That part of it which is devoted to the direct purchase of factor services reaches the end of its journey at the same moment that it begins it. The rest does other work on the way, achieving, say, the purchase of a piece of real property, or a security, or an article standing in a shop, or a raw material passing forward to a later stage of manufacture.[1] Thus, of the money that is expended, different pieces reappear as income, some after short, others after moderate, others after long intervals.

§ 3. This kind of qualitative knowledge we could obtain, as I have indicated, from ordinary common sense. But, with our separate money pieces physically distinguishable, statistical technique could carry us much further. Each £, whenever it appeared as income, would be marked in and its number recorded. This recording would be carried out over a large number of years, so that we could be sure of not missing £'s that made very slow journeys. When the enquiry was closed down, it would be easy to count how many of the grand total of £'s that we knew to be in existence had not appeared as income at all — like motor-cars locked away permanently to escape licence duty — how many had appeared once, how many twice, and so on. No £ could have appeared an infinite number of times. The £'s that had not appeared at all we might call, if we liked, hoards of idle money ; the remainder would be active money, or money standing in the income-expenditure circuit. Our tables would then tell us

[1] The intermediate transfers, not being expenditure on the services of factors of production, and so not being income, the total expenditure of all sorts on a representative day is, of course, much larger than the income received on that day.

how many pieces of active money there were, so that, if we knew how many pieces of money there were altogether, we could, of course, infer the number that were idle. The tables would also tell us how many pieces had circulated with each several frequency per year, any £ appearing once in an observation period extending, say, over five years being set down as a £ with a frequency of one-fifth of an appearance per year. We might further, if we liked, use our records to trace the complete path of particular individual pieces of money, setting out the intervals between the several income appearances of each one of them.

§ 4. The whole of the foregoing discussion has been carried through on the hypothesis that money consists of separate distinguishable pieces. In actual fact the main part of a modern country's money consists of credit balances in the books of banks, plus overdraft facilities. It is thus not made up of physical units that are capable of circulating in any literal sense. When A draws a cheque in favour of B for £1000 in payment for services rendered, and B subsequently draws a similar cheque in favour of C, the *same quantity of money* has, indeed, passed in both transactions, but it would be nonsense to say that the *same money* has passed. This clearly renders impossible the sort of statistical check-up described in § 3. About that there can be no question. But does the dominance of bank money do more than this ? Does it render useless the whole idea of monetary circulation ? Clearly it means that circulation is no longer, for the main part of money, a physical fact. Is it a fact in any sense ?

§ 5. It may be suggested that, though any specified unit of bank money, which appears in one man's income now, is not *physically* identical with any specified unit that appears presently in another income, it is *causally*

C

identical; is linked to it, not, indeed, by material structure, but by causal descent. If we accepted this idea, we might *represent* each separate £ of bank deposits by a separate piece of paper held in the banks and moved about from one account to another; thus treating bank money *as if* it were split up into separate physical units in the same way that coins and notes are in fact split up. This, however, is a very dubious device. For, if C's income comes in part from A and in part from B, how much of C's payment to D is to be reckoned as coming from the one or from the other of these two sources? Presumably, we shall have to say that C's payment to D is made in equal proportions out of A money and B money. But this is an arbitrary convention, not verifiable matter of fact. The concept of causal identity cannot, therefore, help us.

§ 6. Again, it may be suggested that, while bank money itself clearly cannot circulate, *command* over it can be transferred from one person to another, and so can pass out of one income, via expenditure, to be presently reincarnated in another income. The transfers are effected by means of tickets (cheques), which, in general, carry command over the sum of money inscribed on them once only. They carry command, not over this or that piece of money, but over stipulated quantities of money. They resemble, not cloak-room tickets referred to such-and-such named bags, but rather ration cards referred to such-and-such *quantities of* meat or sugar; not theatre tickets assigning so many specified seats, but railway tickets assigning so many unspecified ones. In these conditions it is plain that investigations of the type illustrated in § 3 are impossible. None the less, command over bank money in a sense *does* circulate. Furthermore, if we know, for any country, what the aggregate money income for any given period, and also what the stock of money, *i.e.* bank money plus currency outside the banks, over the average of that period has been, we are free to say, if we will, that this stock during the period has had a defined average income velocity per (say) year; this velocity measuring the average money income per year divided by the average money stock. Alternatively, we may say that the money stock has had a defined average period of income circulation in fractions of a year, namely, the average amount of the money stock divided by the average money income per year. This is, of course, the reciprocal of the average annual income velocity of circulation. In this country in 1938 the income velocity of money, as found roughly by dividing notes outstanding with the public plus the current and deposit accounts of the London clearing banks into estimated national income was 1·71. In 1946, when spending was discouraged by controls, restrictions and propaganda, the corresponding figure was 1·36. The data for calculating these figures are given in the *Annual Abstract of Statistics, 1935–46*.

§ 7. This purely arithmetical relation is *prima facie* so barren — promises such little help for analysis — that we are bound to ask whether it is possible to conceive of the circulation of command over money in some more useful way. There is one conception which deserves to be considered. Had bank money consisted of physically distinguishable pieces, it might have been found that some of these units during a given (substantial) period never stood in what we may call the income-expenditure circuit and so never entered into income, while the rest were all the time held in the circuit. The income velocity of the money so held is, we might suppose, kept approximately constant, being determined by such things as the length of the intervals at which the incomes earned by various classes of people are handed over, business habits and so on. The quantity of money in the circuit can be increased either by money which already exists outside it or by newly created money being passed into it. In like manner, when money income is cut down, this is accomplished by money being drawn out of the circuit, whether the money so drawn out continues to exist as money or is absorbed in the repayment of debts to banks. Since money does not in fact consist of distinguishable physical pieces, this line of approach, as I have just been describing it, is, of course, barred for the actual world. May it not be, however, that in any period some only of the total money stock is *relevant to* money income, and the rest not relevant ? This is the idea underlying the attempts, which some writers have made, to distinguish the money stock into active deposits and inactive deposits. Only active deposits are relevant, in the sense that changes in their amount will be reflected in changes in money income, while the quantity of inactive (sometimes called savings) deposits may vary to any extent and yet the level of money income remain unaltered. Now, if the quantity of money held in the two sorts of deposits could be ascertained by means of some objective sign, if, for example, all balances on current account were active deposits, and all balances on deposit at notice were inactive, we should have firm ground under our feet. But in fact no objective sign is available. When it is asked how much of the total stock of money is relevant in the above sense, the answer is not subject to statistical test, and is in fact a guess.

§ 8. Even so, however, to distinguish between relevant and irrelevant money — the counterpart of the distinction, in a world of physically distinguishable money pieces, between money standing in and money standing outside the income-expenditure circuit — may perhaps eventually prove useful. For, though we can only make rather a vague guess at how large the stock of relevant (active) money at any time is, we may, on certain occasions, be able to say that the relevant (active) stock has been increased, whether at the expense of the irrelevant (inactive) stock or through a new creation of money, by some roughly ascertainable amount ; or conversely. I have spent a considerable time in trying to elucidate the problem of income fluctuations with the help of this conception, but the result so far has not been satisfactory.

CHAPTER IV

INVESTMENT AND SAVING

§ 1. REAL investment in any period is that part of real income which consists of additions to fixed capital, working capital (goods in process) or liquid capital (goods in stores and shops), including any addition to liquid capital that may be made, so to speak, involuntarily, *e.g.* when shopkeepers accumulate stocks of unsold goods on account of a sudden falling-off in demand. This agrees with Keynes' definition : " Net investment equals the net addition to all kinds of capital equipment, after allowing for those changes in the value of the old capital equipment which are taken into account in reckoning net income ",[1] *i.e.* income *simpliciter* as defined in the last chapter but one. Real saving consists of the excess of real income over real consumption. Since real income is evidently the sum of real consumption and additions to capital, real investment and real saving, regarded as aggregates, are thus identical.[2]

§ 2. What has been said implies, of course, that

[1] *General Theory*, p. 75.

[2] It is customary to mean by consumption the receipt of something by a consumer, as distinct from a trader, so that a Rolls-Royce car sold to a private customer is " consumed ", while one sold to a garage is not. This usage rests, of course, upon convention, and, particularly when we remember that houses sold to private persons are reckoned as additions to capital, is logically indefensible. In practice (except in the case of houses) the distinction between consumption and investment is made to turn on whether what is purchased is expected to yield money income to the purchaser. It is, however, immaterial where precisely the line is drawn, provided that throughout any given argument it is drawn in the same place.

the quantity of labour devoted to investment and the quantity devoted to saving are also identical. But, it should be noted, the quantity of labour devoted to consumption is not the same thing as the quantity of labour directly serving consumption ; nor is the quantity of labour devoted to investment the same thing as the quantity of labour engaged in making particular items of capital, whether fixed, working or liquid. All labour except that engaged in rendering direct services to consumers is devoted to creating elements which at the time belong to capital. It follows that the specific units of labour that are directly serving consumption at any time constitute only a small part of the total quantity of labour that is being *devoted* to consumption. We must then regard as devoted to consumption in any period all the labour that is engaged (i) in rendering direct services to consumers, (ii) in replacing consumption goods that are being currently consumed, and (iii) in maintaining capital equipment intact — an item, which, since we are here ignoring the fact that capital wears out and may become obsolete, does not concern us. The quantity of labour devoted to investment is the total quantity of labour employed minus the quantity devoted to consumption.

§ 3. We have agreed that money income must be defined as the money value of a corresponding real income, though this corresponding real income is not likely to be the real income that comes into being in precisely the same period as the money income to which it corresponds. Now, while it is usual for an individual to speak of himself as investing when he buys an already existing security, or piece of real property, aggregate money investment in any period is always defined as the money value of a similarly corresponding aggregate real investment. If then money saving is defined, in like manner, as the money value of real saving, aggregate money saving and aggregate money investment in any period must be identical. This follows directly from the fact that aggregate real saving and aggregate real investment are identical.

§ 4. It is important to be clear about the implications of these definitions when people or governments borrow from the banks. Everybody agrees that money so borrowed only becomes income when it is paid out, for services rendered, to factors of production. But what happens then ? Suppose, first, that it is paid out direct in hiring new labour to create additions to capital. Total money investment and total money income are then enlarged in equal degrees. We have, in conformity with our definitions, to say that total money saving has also been enlarged in that degree. How can this be ? The answer is implicit in the argument of § 2. Saving is defined as the excess of total income received over income received for services in providing for consumption. It follows at once that saving is enlarged by the amount of the payments made to the newly engaged men. Suppose, secondly, that the new money is paid out in purchase of consumption goods already in existence and held by shopkeepers. In this case nothing happens, either to money income or to money investment, till the shopkeepers in turn directly or indirectly expend the new money in hiring factors of production to replace their stocks of consumption goods. When they do this the situation is essentially the same as when a government hires additional factors of production direct.

§ 5. This matter may be approached from another angle thus. Money saving, as ordinarily understood, is the excess of money income over expenditure on consumption goods. Is money saving so defined equal to money investment ? Provided that shopkeepers maintain exactly the *value* of their stocks, *i.e.* make neither money investment nor money disinvestment, it is plain that money saving in this meaning is identical with money saving as defined in § 3 ; in which case it is obviously equal to money investment, as there defined. But suppose that the value of shopkeepers' stocks is increased by, say, £1000. Obviously money investment is increased by that amount, no matter in what way the extra value of stocks comes into being. What, then, happens to money saving as ordinarily understood ? If the increase in the value of stocks has been brought about by the shopkeepers increasing the value of their expenditure on factor services by £1000 and not altering the value of their sales, the income of the factors is increased by £1000, none of which — since the shopkeepers, *ex hypothesi*, do not increase the value of their sales — is spent on consumption goods. Hence aggregate money saving is enlarged by the same amount as aggregate money investment. If the value of the stocks has been increased by £1000 because the public have saved £1000, and shopkeepers, refusing to lower their prices, have piled up stocks, this extra £1000 worth of stocks is an addition to investment ; so that once more, money saving, as ordinarily understood, and money investment are equal. It follows that in all circumstances aggregate money saving, in the sense of value of real saving, and aggregate money saving in the sense of excess of money income over expenditure on consumption goods, *i.e.* as ordinarily understood, are identical ; and *both* are necessarily equal to aggregate money investment.[1]

---

[1] This does *not* imply, it need hardly be said, that the money saving undertaken by a particular individual is necessarily equal to the money investment undertaken by him. For money saving by one individual may

§ 6. Now the plain man — and I myself in this matter for some time was a plain man — does not like this. He wants a definition of money saving that will make the existence of a difference between money saving and money investment possible; and that even though the total stock of money income is held constant. One of his reasons for this is a bad one. He knows that he individually is able to save money, *i.e.* to withhold part of his money income from expenditure on consumption goods, and yet is under no obligation to invest money, even in the sense of buying from somebody else already existing securities, *a fortiori* in the sense of engaging factors of production to make additions to the physical stock of capital. There is nothing to prevent him from saving part of his, say, year's money income by accumulating it as an addition to his stock of currency or his bank balance, without making any money investment at all. From this he is apt to infer that what he individually is free to do the community as a whole must be free to do also. But that is the fallacy of composition. In fact, though A's saving is equal to his investment plus the increase in his stock of money, every £ which he adds to that stock in a given instant implies an equivalent cut in somebody else's money income. Hence, since saving is equal to money income minus expenditure on consumption goods, it implies an equivalent cut in somebody else's saving. It follows that, whatever addition is made to aggregate money saving in any instant, aggregate money investment is enlarged

entail equivalent dissaving either by other individuals, to whom it is lent for purchasing consumption goods, or by other individuals, in whose incomes it causes an equivalent contraction, while leaving their expenditure on consumption goods intact. Thus, if A reduces his purchases of B's services by £100, and B thereupon borrows £100 from A and continues consuming as before, B's dissaving cancels A's saving, so that net saving is nil: and, in like manner, net investment is nil. Aggregate money income meanwhile is down by £100.

by the same amount. That is to say, the two aggregates are equal to one another.[1]

§ 7. But the plain man has a second reason for wanting a definition of money saving that will allow aggregate money saving and aggregate money investment to be different. He feels that to treat as money investment an increase in the money value of traders' stocks, when these have been piled up, so to speak, involuntarily, in consequence of a slump in demand, is paradoxical, and even savours of sharp practice. One may well sympathise with this feeling. The sense of paradox is, however, mitigated when we reflect that our definitions, though they make actual money saving equal at any moment to actual money investment, do not imply that the amounts of money investment and of money saving that people set out, or intended, to make at that moment, must be equal to one another. Thus, when consumers save £1000, and dealers, maintaining their prices, pile up in consequence £1000 worth of stocks, their actual investment is £1000, but their intended investment is nothing; so that saving, while equal to actual investment, exceeds intended investment by £1000. But, in any event, the fact that a definition has, *prima facie*, paradoxical implications, is not a sufficient reason for rejecting it, if on the whole it proves more convenient than others.

§ 8. Thus the plain man's attitude cannot, I think, be successfully defended by argument. But it is, none the less, an important fact. It grows out of a sort of instinct. It is a *cri de cœur* demanding that what looks like a road towards understanding economic processes shall

---

[1] This is, of course, not inconsistent with the fact that an *attempt* on the part of all the individuals in a community to save more money than they invest pushes up the value of money in terms of commodities, and so, while leaving the physical stock of money unaltered, increases the real value of that stock.

not be blocked at the start. This is not a demand to be disregarded if by any means a way to satisfy it can be found.

§ 9. Prof. D. H. Robertson has proposed a definition of money saving, the acceptance of which would allow the plain man's desire to be satisfied. He conceives of time as divided into a succession of very thin slices. The money income received in time-slice 1 becomes, so to speak, ripe for use in time-slice 2. Such part of it as is expended in that time-slice on consumption and investment together, plus any further money that is so expended, must be equal to the payment made in that time-slice for the services of factors of production, and so to the money income of that time-slice. But the total of money so expended, and, therefore, the income of time-slice 2, need not be equal to, but may either exceed or fall short of the income that becomes ripe for use in time-slice 2, *i.e.* the money income of time-slice 1. Prof. Robertson defines money saving in time-slice 2 as the excess of money income in time-slice 1 over money expended for consumption in time-slice 2 ; which implies that saving minus investment in time-slice 2 equals the excess of money income in time-slice 1 over money income in time-slice 2. Obviously on this definition money saving is not necessarily equal in any time-slice to money investment.

§ 10. Plainly Prof. Robertson's conception is watertight in point of logic. But how far is it applicable to the facts of real life ? There are two difficulties. First, if it is to be applicable, time-slices must exist so thin that no money income received in any time-slice can be expended, and so become income again, within the same time-slice. This condition is implicit in the concept of money income received in one time-slice becoming " ripe for use " in another. But there is no logical reason why my receipt of £100 or of a cheque giving command over £100 should not *synchronise* with my disbursement of another £100 or of another cheque giving command over that same amount. Indeed, even though I hold normally a stock of money balances up to half or more than half of my annual money income, provided that my receipts and expenditure of income are equal and take place at constant rates, there is no firm ground for denying that the *whole* of the income of each instant is expended at that same instant. Thus, it is not, I think, possible to prove that in the conditions of real life *any* length of time-slice can be found short enough to satisfy Prof. Robertson's requirement.

§ 11. But, secondly, even if we waive this point and allow that some sufficiently thin time-slice does in fact exist, there is still a difficulty. Prof. Robertson's definition has, indeed, now a precise content. The sufficiently thin time-slice being called a " day ", we can, without any ambiguity, define money saving in day n, whether investment is taking place or not, as the excess of income in day $(n - 1)$ over expenditure on consumption in day n. By doing this, we shall leave ourselves free to deny that money saving and money investment *must be* equal. But will not excess of saving over investment in day n be then simply a *name* for the excess of income in day $(n - 1)$ over income in day n ? There seems little to be gained in providing such a name.[1]

§ 12. If the view set out in the last section is

---

[1] If we define saving and investment in Prof. Robertson's way, it is natural to conceive money hoarding in any time-slice as the excess of saving over investment in that time-slice ; so that hoarding, like excess of saving over investment, is merely a name for the excess of income in one time-slice over income in the next. Prof. Robertson, however, does not conceive money hoarding in this way. He writes : " A man is said to be *hoarding* if he takes steps to raise the proportion which he finds existing at the beginning of any day between his money stock and his disposable income " (*Economic Journal*, 1933, p. 400). Thus for him hoarding is defined as what might perhaps be

accepted, since it is very unlikely that anything superior to Prof. Robertson's structure will be devised, the plain man's desire to preserve the possibility of inequality between aggregate money saving and investment must be left unsatisfied. He may perhaps be rendered less unwilling to allow this by the following reflection. When the economic system is in equilibrium — the short-period flow equilibrium that I shall describe in the next chapter — saving and investment are, on Prof. Robertson's definition, and indeed on any reasonable definition, necessarily equal to one another. It is only when the system is in disequilibrium that Prof. Robertson's definition makes them unequal, while mine makes them equal. In disequilibrium, however, processes, which Prof. Robertson, with his definition, envisages as following from a difference between saving and investment, are equally well described, with my definition, in a manner to be explained in Part IV, Chapter III, § 8, as a consequence of the disequilibrium between the demand and supply of labour for investment. This fact, as it seems to me, removes any advantage which Prof. Robertson's definition appears at first sight to have as regards periods of disequilibrium ; while the disadvantages inherent in it, which have been described above, remain. Definitions are, of course, matters of convenience rather than of principle ; but convenience is important. For my part then, I shall henceforward define money saving as the value of real saving ; a definition which, as we saw above, makes aggregate money saving and aggregate money investment necessarily equal.

called a decision to hoard. This may properly rank as a cause of the deficiency of the income of time-slice 2 below that of time-slice 1, and not merely as a name for that deficiency. It corresponds to the cause behind what is called in Part III of this book a downward or a leftward swing in the money income function.

PART II

FLOW EQUILIBRIUM

CHAPTER I

THE MEANING OF FLOW EQUILIBRIUM

§ 1. WHEN economists speak of equilibrium between demand and supply there is one thing that never is, or at least never should be, meant. That is equality between the quantity of anything that is bought in any place and period and the quantity that is sold. These two quantities in all circumstances, whether there is equilibrium of any kind or not, are necessarily equal; for the simple reason that every purchase *is* a sale looked at from the other side : a circumstance which is, of course, perfectly compatible with the quantity of anything purchased by a particular individual being different from the quantity sold by *him*. Thus, if, as I have done, we define money investment in such a way that the definition itself compels aggregate money saving and aggregate money investment to be equal, it is nonsense to speak of this equality being "brought about" by equilibrating or any other forces.[1] This sort of tautological equality has nothing whatever to do with equilibrium.

§ 2. This false equilibrium being thus ruled out of

[1] Very surprisingly, so practised an economist as Mr. Harrod seems to have nodded over this point. In his book on *The Trade Cycle*, having employed definitions for aggregate saving and aggregate investment, which, from the meaning of the words, make them equal, he writes : " The principle that the amount of saving undertaken is accommodated to the amount of net investment through changes in the level of income is called the multiplier . . . changes in the amount of net investment *elicit* [my italics] the necessary changes in the amount of saving through variation in total activity and income " (p. 74). Mr. Harrod's argument in this field is further defective in that, by a loose use of language, he makes a sum of money *equal to* a quantity of goods (p. 61).

D

account, there are still two senses of equilibrium between demand and supply that need to be distinguished. The first is equality between the quantity, which, at the ruling price, demanders would like to buy and the quantity which, at that price, suppliers would like to sell ; the second is equality between the quantity which, at the ruling price, demanders would like to buy, and the quantity which would make price equal to the marginal cost of production. Under perfect competition these two senses of equilibrium come to the same thing ; the quantity which the suppliers wish to sell at the ruling price *is* the quantity which makes price and marginal cost of production equal. But under monopoly this is not so. The monopolist *represents* the sellers, so that, when *he* decides to sell, they presumably desire to sell. But this quantity is not the quantity which makes price equal to marginal cost of production. In accordance with a familiar formula, it is the quantity which makes price multiplied by $\left(1 - \dfrac{1}{\eta}\right)$ equal to marginal cost of production, where η is the elasticity of demand in respect of the quantity of the commodity affected that is being produced.[1] As regards single commodities, the second definition is the one usually adopted, so that equilibrium between demand and supply does not prevail under monopoly. For a general view of the economic system as a whole it is, however, more convenient to use the first definition, so that equilibrium between demand and supply can exist under monopoly as well as under competition.

§ 3. When equilibrium between demand and supply in the above sense is said to prevail in respect of any particular thing, the reference is sometimes to absolute

---

[1] Throughout this volume η is defined in the Marshallian manner, as a positive, not a negative quantity.

quantities demanded and supplied at a moment *in a market*. Apart from Government interference with prices and from cases in which the supply is so large that, in order for it to be all absorbed, the price would have to be negative, market equilibrium *must* exist at every moment ; for it will pay all concerned to adjust the price so as to make it exist.[1] It is not, however, in absolute quantities demanded and supplied at a moment that economists are chiefly interested. It is rather in *rates* of demand and *rates* of supply per unit of time. Equilibrium as regards these rates we may call, to distinguish it from market equilibrium, flow equilibrium. While, with the exceptions noted above, market equilibrium must always prevail, for flow equilibrium there is no such necessity. Thus, if the taste for tea suddenly expands, the price will go up and market equilibrium will thereby be maintained. But the producers of tea will find that, in selling all the tea now accessible to them at this high price, they are making an abnormal gain. They will, therefore, increase the area of their plantations and go on enlarging their output until further extensions no longer offer abnormal gains. All through this process on every day there will be market equilibrium. But the quantities sold, and probably the price also, per unit of time (of sufficient length) will be continually changing. There will be no flow equilibrium. In like manner, if the technique of

---

[1] If the Government fixes by law an (effective) maximum price for tea, the quantity of tea which at that price sellers wish to sell will be sold. But it may well happen that the quantity which buyers at that price wish to buy is not available. Some would-be buyers will have to go short ; the particular persons who do so being chosen, perhaps in the scramble of the queue, perhaps by a system of rationing. In like manner, if the Government fixes a minimum price below which sales are not permitted, the quantity of tea that buyers want to buy will all be bought. But it may well happen that the quantity which sellers would like to sell at that price is larger than the quantity which buyers will take. There will have to be either a sort of queue among sellers, or, more probably, quotas allocated among them by some official body.

gas production — tea is a less convenient example here
— is suddenly improved, buyers, while always buying
what at the time they desire to buy at the ruling price
in their existing situation, are stimulated to bring about
changes in their situation, *e.g.* by installing gas cooking
stoves, gas heaters, and so on ; and, until they have
accomplished this, the quantity sold per unit of time,
and probably the price also, keeps continually changing.[1]
There is again no flow equilibrium. It is only if and
when buyers and sellers become content with their
situation that flow equilibrium, as well as market equilibrium, is established. Flow equilibrium entails a constant rate of purchase and sale, or of hiring and letting.

§ 4. For the economic system as a whole to be in
flow equilibrium obviously means that *all* the rates of
demand and corresponding rates of supply embodied in
it are in this type of equilibrium. Plainly this condition
cannot be satisfied except in the classical stationary
state. The existence of such a state implies, of course,
unchanging tastes and technique. It implies, too, a
definite relation in every industry between selling
price and marginal cost. Where competition reigns,
the relation is one of equality ; where monopoly reigns,
marginal cost must be less than selling price in a
degree which is greater or less according as demand is
less or more elastic.[2] Strict flow equilibrium implies,
moreover, a stationary population and a fixed stock of
capital equipment. This last implies again that no net
investment or disinvestment is taking place.

§ 5. Besides flow equilibrium in the strict sense, we
may conceive a sort of pseudo or hypothetical flow
equilibrium, which I shall call short-period flow equilibrium, and to which, in some circumstances, actuality
may approximate. This differs from strict (long-period)

---

[1] Cf. Marshall, *Industry and Trade*, pp. 185-6.   [2] Cf. *ante*, § 2.

flow equilibrium in that it does not require, either in individual industries or in the sum of all industries, a nil rate of investment, but allows of a positive rate, provided that this is constant. It is not, of course, flow equilibrium in an exact literal sense. For, if any (net) investment is taking place, the economic situation cannot be the same in successive periods. More especially, if investment takes the form of additions to fixed capital, the rate of output of consumable goods, to the production of which some at least of this equipment is sure to contribute, must be progressively changing. Since, however, the total stock of capital is large relatively to any increment that can normally take place in a short time, and since, moreover, some interval must elapse between a decision to create additional capital equipment and the completion of it ready for service, any reactions on the rate of output of consumable goods due to the occurrence of investment must, from the point of view of a sufficiently short period, be negligibly small. Thus short-period flow equilibrium, while it can never actually exist unless there is also the long-period flow equilibrium of a stationary state, is a condition to which close approximation can be made. In using the concept, what we do in effect is to postulate all the conditions implicit in long-period flow equilibrium, save only that, instead of taking the rate of investment to be nil, we take it to be positive and constant ; and we then ignore the reactions which the existence of this positive rate of investment evokes in the other parts of the economic system — reactions which are in fact trifling in respect of periods that are very short, and which can, of course, be ignored, if we so choose, in respect of periods of any length. This sort of equilibrium is the subject matter of Keynes' *General Theory* ; for this is concerned, as he expressly states,

with " *the equilibrium level* [my italics] of employment,
i.e. the level at which there is no inducement to employers as a whole either to expand or to contract
employment ".[1]

§ 6. What has just been said is the obvious straightforward way of setting out the relation between the
long-period flow equilibrium of a stationary state and
short-period flow equilibrium. There is, however, an
alternative way of setting out this relation. Defining
short-period flow equilibrium in the manner of the last
section, we may regard long-period flow equilibrium as
a special case of short-period flow equilibrium. In the
general case the demand for, and supply of, saving (or
investment) are equal to one another at *some*, no matter
what, (positive) value ; in the special case of long-period
equilibrium they are equal to one another at the particular value, nil. This way of approach enables us to
arrange our material in a convenient and orderly way.
I propose, therefore, to adopt it.

§ 7. It is clear that, with the definitions here employed, while, as between two equilibrium positions with
different rates of flow of consumption plus investment
goods, the stocks of working capital and liquid capital[2]
will be different, it is not possible in any equilibrium
position for either of the stocks to be *undergoing change.*
The flow of net investment consists exclusively of additions to fixed capital. These requirements entail — the
point is an important one — that in states of short-
period flow equilibrium intended investment and actual
investment must always be equal, so that there can be
no question, for example, of shopkeepers being forced

---

[1] *Loc. cit.* p. 27. Thus again on p. 245 he explains that, for the purposes
of his analysis, he " takes as given the existing skill and quantity of available
labour, the existing quality and quantity of available equipment, the existing
technique, the degree of competition, the tastes and habits of the consumer "
— and so on.   [2] Cf. *ante*, Part I, Chapter IV, § 1.

to make unintended investment through inability to sell their stocks. Moreover, so long as any given state of short-period flow equilibrium is being maintained, employment, output and investment must themselves stand at a constant level per month or year ; which implies — unless we suppose an impracticable degree of plasticity in the money rate of wages—that money income and, along with it, the rate of money discount from the banks stands at a constant level. Further, though money rates on short loans and on long loans are not necessarily equal, they must stand one another in a constant relation,[1] so that *the* rate of interest can be represented indifferently by either. Yet again, over any period for which short-period flow equilibrium exists expected prices of consumption goods and money rates of wages must be equal to current prices and money rates of wages. Otherwise a new variable is introduced and a much more complicated problem posited. Equality between expected and current prices and money wage-rates implies identity between rates of interest expressed in money and expressed in terms of any single commodity or composite commodity or of labour.[2]

---

[1] In actual life the relation between short-term and long-term rates of interest varies widely from time to time ; though before the first World War the two sorts of rate in this country seem to have been much the same on the average of good times and bad.

[2] In a non-equilibrium situation the rates at which loans will be undertaken in terms of different commodities will be different according to what changes are expected in the relative values of the several commodities. In this sense the " real " rate of interest ruling now for a loan of given duration differs from the money rate in such measure that the same advantage is expected whether the bargain is struck in money or in " real " terms. If expectations were mistaken, it may turn out that a bargain made at 10 per cent in money yields an actual return of x per cent in goods, whereas one of y per cent was expected. Sometimes the *ex-post* x per cent is called the " real " rate of interest and the *ex-ante* y per cent the commodity rate. In both cases, of course, if the loan is not *in perpetuam*, an element is included that represents appreciation or depreciation of the principal. For the present purpose money rate, commodity rate and real rate for loans of given duration all coincide.

§ 8. Further, it is only when the economic system is *in passage* from one state of flow equilibrium towards another or is, on some other account, in flow disequilibrium that money income per month or year can be in process of change.   From this a consequence of some importance follows.   Though it is legitimate to say that in equilibrium situation A there is a larger amount of money *standing* in hoards than in equilibrium situation B, it is not legitimate to say that more hoarding is taking place ; for in fact no hoarding or dishoarding can be taking place in either equilibrium situation. This is true both of hoarding and of dishoarding of money out of and into the income expenditure circuit in the usual sense and also of hoarding and dishoarding in Prof. Robertson's special sense.[1]   It is necessary to stress this point because the terms hoarding and dishoarding are capable of ambiguous use.   In equilibrium situations the *processes* of hoarding and dishoarding are *ex hypothesi* excluded.   The same thing is true of forced levies.   For these can only result from the process of expanding the stock of money, and in any situation of short-period flow equilibrium this stock is by definition fixed.   For these concepts, then, there is no place in either Part II or Part III of this book.

§ 9. To simplify the argument, it will be assumed throughout our main analysis that no system of unemployment benefit (or anything that takes its place) exists.   This assumption, so far as Part II is concerned, is quite innocuous.   In Part III it is significant ; and the consequences of removing it will be considered later in Chapter XI of that Part.

[1] Cf. *ante*, Part I, Chapter IV, § 11, footnote.

NOTE TO CHAPTER I

THE term " dynamic equilibrium " is sometimes applied to a
system all the parts of which are expanding or contracting at
equal proportionate rates, while technique and so on remain
unchanged. Since one of the fundamental factors of production, namely land, is incapable of physical expansion, an
economic system in strict dynamic equilibrium cannot, where
there is no surplus land, exist except in its limiting form,
namely, a stationary state, for which the rate of change is nil.
Where there is a good deal of surplus land available it can exist.
It should be noted, however, that, if equilibrium is taken to
imply, not only that all the factors of production expand or
contract in equal proportions, but also that the proportions
between different sorts of output remain constant, it can only
be maintained subject to a special condition ; namely, that expansion or contraction proceeds at a constant geometrical rate.
For it is only so that employment in industries making consumable goods and employment in those making capital goods
can maintain a constant relation to each other. For, capital
goods being supposed to last for ever, let the quantity of
capital goods at time t be $f(t)$. The rate of increase of capital
stock, and so of employment in making consumable goods with
its help, at time t is then $f'(t)$ and the rate of increase of investment, and so of employment, in making capital goods is $f''(t)$.
The condition for $\dfrac{f''}{f'}$ to be equal for all values of t to $\dfrac{f'}{f}$ is that
$\dfrac{d}{dt}\left\{\dfrac{f'}{f}\right\} = 0$ for all values ; *i.e.* that expansion or contraction is
proceeding at a constant geometric rate. It is easy to show
that the same condition is necessary if capital goods wear out
after any specified length of time.[1]

[1] Cf. my *Theory of Unemployment*, Part III, chap. viii.

CHAPTER II

THE RELEVANT QUANTITIES AND FUNCTIONS

§ 1. WE have now to distinguish and characterise the quantities and functions with which subsequent discussion will have to do. There are six fundamental quantities : (i) the quantity, to be called x, of labour employed in a representative consumption industry ; (ii) the quantity, to be called y, of labour employed in a representative investment industry ; (iii) the annual rate of interest, to be called r ; [1] (iv) the rate of money wages, to be called w ; (v) the stock of money, to be called M ; and (vi) the income velocity of money, to be called V ; these two last, when multiplied together, constituting money income, I. We shall also have occasion to bring into account S, the stock of capital instruments in existence. For an exhaustive treatment it would be proper to introduce two further elements, h_1 and h_2, the periods of production of consumption goods and investment goods respectively, expressed as fractions of a year. For our purposes, however, these elements can be ignored. The nature of the error resulting from this, which is bound to be small, will be examined in Part III, Chapter XII.

§ 2. There are also seven functional relations, respectively connecting: (i) the quantity of employment

---

[1] It has been objected that r in this system must be regarded, not as a variable, but as a constant, because it has to be equal in equilibrium to the real return on the existing stock of capital, which is a constant. But what in fact r has to be equal to is the expected real return from *new* investment.

in consumption industries with the output of consumption goods; (ii) the quantity of employment in investment industries with the output of investment goods; (iii) a small proportionate rise in the real price, in terms of consumption goods in general, with the associated proportionate fall in the quantity demanded of the representative consumption good from any one of the firms, all assumed to be similar,[1] engaged in producing it; *i.e.* the elasticity of real demand for that good from any one of the firms engaged in producing it, to be called η_1; (iv) a small proportionate rise in real price, in terms of investment goods in general, with the associated proportionate fall in the quantity demanded of the representative investment good from any one of the firms, all assumed to be similar, engaged in producing it; *i.e.* the elasticity of real demand for that good from any one of the firms engaged in producing it, to be called η_2; (v) the quantity of labour demanded for investment with the rate of interest and, it may be, the quantity of employment in consumption industries; (vi) the quantity of labour supplied for investment with the rate of interest and the income of consumption goods; and (vii) the quantity of money income with the rate of interest and, it may be, the aggregate quantity of employment. We have to describe the principal characteristics of these functional relations.

§ 3. Consider first the functional relation between the quantity of employment and the quantity of output per annum in (i) consumption industries and (ii) investment industries. At first sight it might seem that single functional relations can only exist provided that only one sort of consumption good and one sort of investment good are being produced, whereas we are allowing that there may be many sorts. But, since throughout this

---

[1] Cf. *ante*, Preliminary, § 5.

discussion it is postulated that the different sorts of
consumption goods always have the same relative
values and are produced in the same proportions, there
is always an unambiguous quantity of " consumption
goods in general ", consisting of so many composite
units made up of physical units of all of them combined
in these proportions ; and, since a similar postulate is
made about investment goods, the same thing holds
good for investment goods. Thus, even where there are
many kinds of each type of good, we may properly
represent output of consumption goods as a straightforward function of x, say $F(x)$, and output of investment goods in like manner as $\psi(y)$.

§ 4. In real life there is an awkwardness here. For
part of the output of the investment goods industries
does not add to the stock of equipment, but replaces
equipment which is being worn out, partly in the investment goods industries themselves and partly in the
consumption goods industries. For the part used for
replacement in the investment industries allowance can
be made by simply making our function $\psi(y)$ signify
net, as distinguished from gross, output of labour in those
industries. But the part of newly produced equipment
which offsets depreciation in the consumption industries
cannot be brought into account in this way. The labour
that makes it must be regarded as being, in effect, engaged in the consumption industries ; so that net output
of those industries is not a function of their own labour
only, but of their own labour plus some of the labour
in the investment industries. To make this kind of
adjustment, though not difficult in principle, would considerably complicate our exposition without affecting
the substance of the analysis. It is in order to avoid
that, that I have adopted, for this discussion, the highly
unrealistic assumption that equipment, once made,

never wears out or otherwise depreciates.[1]   When this assumption is made, the awkwardness described above is, of course, thought away.

§ 5. With this understanding, what are the characteristics of the two functions $F(x)$ and $\psi(y)$?   It will be remembered that, for short-period flow equilibrium, the total stock of equipment is sensibly constant, in spite of the fact that additions are being made to it.[2]   Hence equipment must be taken as given.   It follows that, the more employment there is in either of our two classes of industry, the more output there will be.   That is to say, F' and ψ' are both always positive.   What of the *rates* at which the rates of increase of output alter as employment grows ?   It may perhaps be suggested that, with equipment given, as employment grows, these rates must always fall, *i.e.* that F'' and ψ'' must be negative for all values of x and y.   But this is clearly wrong.   While F'' and ψ'' must be negative for *some* quantities of employment — with equipment fixed, employment cannot be increased indefinitely without diminishing returns to labour setting in — it is not *physically* impossible, even apart from external economies, that for *some* quantities increasing returns to labour may prevail, *i.e.* F'' and ψ'' may be positive.[3]   Again, for some quantities constant returns may undoubtedly prevail, *i.e.* F'' and ψ'' may be nil.   Thus, when an industry is in a state of moderate depression,

---

[1] Cf. *ante*, Preliminary, § 3.

[2] Cf. *ante*, Part II, Chapter I, § 5.

[3] Mr. Colin Clark in a table and chart printed in his *National Income and Outlay* (pp. 258-9) purports to show that for " industry ", as distinct from other occupations, in this country, over the seven years preceding 1936 both average and marginal cost have been lower for larger than for smaller outputs. The data from which this table is built are not very clearly indicated.   On the assumption that the facts are as stated, they do not, of course, prove that increasing returns prevail in actual conditions.   For capital equipment has been increasing and technique improving.

with a fair amount of idle equipment, marginal prime cost may well be approximately constant over a considerable range. Obviously this will not be so when the industry is working at or near full capacity. Then marginal cost *must* be rising.[1] Still, the fact remains that for conditions of moderate activity, alike in consumption industries and in investment industries, constant marginal prime cost, which is equivalent here to constant marginal productivity of labour, may plausibly be predicated.

§ 6. Turn to the elasticities of real demand as they were defined above, namely, η_1 and η_2. We are given that the conditions affecting the supply and demand of the several sorts of consumption goods are such that the real price of any one of them in terms of the other consumption goods is the same in whatever quantity they are being produced ; and similarly for investment goods. At first sight we might be inclined to infer that *therefore* our elasticities of demand η_1 and η_2 must always be infinite. But this is not so. First, the elasticity of demand for a particular consumption good in the aggregate is for our purposes the elasticity of demand for it when the output of all other such goods is given and its output alone changes. Elasticity in this sense obviously cannot be infinite. Secondly, our elasticity is the elasticity of demand, not for any one consumption good in the aggregate, but for its output from one firm. If an industry contains only a single firm, this elasticity is obviously the same thing as the elasticity of the real demand for the product of the industry as a whole.

---

[1] In the conditions of actual life, where labour is not homogeneous, as it is assumed to be here, but where, as industry expands, inferior men have to be taken on at the current wage — even under piece-wages inferior men are more expensive to employers than better men because they occupy machines longer on a given job — or overtime rates have to be paid to key workers, the likelihood that F'' and ψ'' will be negative at an early stage is *pro tanto* greater.

But when an industry is carried on by a number of firms — it will be remembered that we are assuming all the firms to be similar — the situation is different. If there is perfect competition among the firms our elasticity does not depend at all on the elasticity of demand for the output of the whole industry, but is necessarily infinite ; for, if one firm raises its price ever so little, the other firms will absorb the whole of its market. With imperfect competition this elasticity — since all the firms are similar, it will be the same for all of them — is finite. Its magnitude depends partly on the elasticity of demand for the product of the industry as a whole and partly on the degree of imperfection ruling in the market, that is to say on the extent to which a fall in the price asked for by one firm will enable it to capture demand from others.[1] The greater the degree of imperfection in the market, the more nearly our elasticity approaches to what it would be under single-firm monopoly. It is easy to see that everything that has been said about η_1 in respect of output $F(x)$ of consumption goods also holds good of η_2 in respect of output $\psi(y)$ of investment goods. Thus η_1 and η_2 are functions of $F(x)$ and $\psi(y)$, being liable to vary as these respectively vary.

§ 7. The phrases, quantity of labour demanded for investment and quantity of labour supplied for investment, may perhaps strike a jarring note. For labour for investment is not directly demanded or supplied in the manner conceived here. The immediate object demanded or supplied is money to invest, in the sense of

[1] Thus write p for the price charged by the firm, $\phi(p)$ for a man's purchases at that price and $\psi'(p)$ for the rate at which he will shift his purchases to other firms if his firm's price rises but the prices of other firms do not. Then the elasticity of his demand at price p directed to his firm is $-\dfrac{p(\phi'+\psi')}{\phi}$. If ψ' is (numerically) large, this quantity will be large even though $\phi'=0$. Of course, the ϕ and ψ of this note have quite a different significance from what they have throughout the bulk of this book.

buying, or covering the cost of, new investment goods.
Moreover, of course, when this money is expended, only
a portion of it goes to labour, the remainder being paid
to the owners of capital instruments which co-operate
with labour. Yet again, the amount of money which
has to be expended to secure a given quantity of labour
for investment varies with the rate of money wages.
Thus, obviously, the demand for and supply of labour
for investment are not simply synonyms for the demand
for and supply of investment itself, or, if we prefer it,
of funds for investment. It might seem the more proper
course to make central in our analysis the demand and
supply functions of these funds. But, in truth, that
course is neither more nor less proper than the one here
adopted. To demand or supply, say, y units of labour
for investment *implies* demanding or supplying $p_2\psi(y)$
units of money for investment, where p_2 is the money
price per unit of investment goods. This, as we shall
see presently,[1] is equal to $\dfrac{\psi(y)}{\left(1 - \dfrac{1}{\eta_2}\right)\psi'(y)}$. w units of money,
w being the money rate of wages. That is to say, the
money rate of wages, the productivity function of labour
in investment industries and the value of η_2 being given,
a given quantity of labour for investment implies a
given quantity of money for investment, and vice versa.

§ 8. Turn then more particularly to the demand
function for labour for investment on the assumption,
which is proper here, that the technical conditions, *i.e.*
the forms ψ and F, are given. Clearly the money wage-
rate offered to the marginal man of any assigned number
engaged on investment goods depends upon — under
perfect competition is equal to — all future money yields
expected from his output of investment goods discounted

[1] Cf. *post*, Part II, Chapter III, § 7.

at the rate of interest at which money can be borrowed. It follows immediately that the quantity of labour demanded for investment is a function of the rate of interest r. But is it a function of this variable alone, or is it affected also by the quantity of labour, x, currently engaged in the consumption industries ?

§ 9. There is some risk of confusion here. The rate of interest, depending, as it does, on the expected future yields of the marginal unit of resources invested now, must plainly be larger, for any given amount of current annual investment, the larger is the amount of labour that people expect will be employed to assist the stock of equipment over the average of the future. This expectation itself does, indeed, depend in part on how much labour is *available for employment* now. But it does not depend to any significant extent on how much labour is *actually employed* now. In any event the quantity of labour currently employed, so far as it enters into the determination of the demand for current investment, does this by affecting the value of r, not by affecting current investment otherwise than through r. As against this, it is sometimes claimed that the quantity of labour actually employed should be brought in, on the ground that, the larger the quantity of labour engaged in the consumption industries, the larger is the stock of machines required there. It is true that *in certain circumstances*, if the quantity of labour in consumption industries undergoes an increase, an addition will need to be made to the stock of machines, and that short-period flow equilibrium cannot be re-established until this and, maybe, other things also have been done. But these reactions belong to states of disequilibrium.[1] When the system is in short-period flow equilibrium, with a steady rate

[1] Cf. *post*, Part IV, Chapter VI, §§ 4-8.

E

of employment alike in the investment and in the consumption industries, there is no place for them. I conclude, therefore, though, in view of Mr. Kaldor's dissent,[1] with some hesitation, that the demand function for labour for investment, when expectations and technical factors are given, is a function of one variable only, namely, the rate of interest. We may call it $\phi(r)$.

§ 10. What, then, are the characteristics of this function ? Let us begin by supposing that the sole purpose of investment goods is to serve as instruments for helping labour to make consumption goods in the future, and that the new instruments will all be constructed similarly to those already existing. It is fundamental to our analysis that the stock of capital goods in existence is very large relatively to any addition that can be made to it in the type of period that we are investigating. Therefore the marginal physical product of investment goods looked for is the same irrespective of the size of the addition that is made to the stock of them in any, say, year. It follows that, if the cost in labour per unit of machines made in any year were the same irrespective of the number of machines so made, the return looked for over any period per unit of labour engaged for investment, and so the rate of interest in terms of consumption goods which people would offer for the hire or loan of it, would be the same, the volume of employment being given, whatever the quantity of labour engaged for investment was. It is, however, as we have already seen, impossible for labour devoted to machine-making to yield constant returns beyond a certain point. The reason is that, for the purposes of short-period flow equilibrium, the stock of instruments available to co-operate with it is fixed. Hence the form of the demand function for labour for investment in

[1] Cf. *Economic Journal*, December 1941, and my reply September 1942.

instruments for making consumption goods must be such that, after a point, more labour devoted to investment yields diminishing returns ; and, therefore, after a point, more will be demanded at a lower than at a higher rate of interest in terms of consumption goods.

§ 11. Moreover, we have so far tacitly assumed that all new instruments are situated similarly to those already existing. A picture much more representative of the actual world is given if we imagine the new instruments progressively to be placed in less favoured situations, where more serious natural obstacles have to be overcome or distance from a market imposes a handicap. This corresponds to the fact that in the real world investment is confronted with a number of openings of higher and lower grades of promise. When we look at the matter in this way, it becomes clear that at lower rates of interest in terms of consumption goods larger quantities of labour for investment in instruments will be demanded even though the larger quantities do not produce fewer instruments per unit than the smaller quantities. This fortifies the argument of the last paragraph. That argument is fortified further when we remember that in fact it is not the sole purpose of investment goods to co-operate in producing consumption goods, but that many of them yield direct services to consumers. In general, therefore, I conclude that, in any given state of business psychology and confidence, more labour for investment is likely to be demanded, the lower is the rate of interest in terms of consumption goods, not merely after a point, but over the whole of the range in which we are interested. It must be granted that a part of this reasoning trespasses beyond the rigid bounds of our formal assumptions ; but, after all, models are made for man, not man for models.

§ 12. There is, however, still a difficulty. For the

rate of interest, r, which directly presents itself to us, is a rate in terms, not of consumption goods, but of money. If people expect, or, more strictly, act as though they expected, the price of consumption goods to be higher in the future than now, *i.e.* if a £ is expected to buy fewer consumption goods, the rate of interest offered for money in money must be higher than the rate offered for consumption goods in consumption goods; and conversely. But, if the future prices of consumption goods are expected to be the same as present prices, the rate of interest in consumption goods and the rate in money must be the same. As was indicated in § 7 of the last chapter, for the purposes of the analysis, expected future prices and present prices are taken to be the same. This disposes of our difficulty. We conclude that, equally whether we are thinking of the rate of interest as expressed in money or as expressed in consumption goods, $\phi'(r)$ is likely to be negative for all relevant values of r.

§ 13. Pass to the supply function of labour for investment. When the attitude of lenders towards the future is given, including, in the manner indicated in the last paragraph, their expectations about the future prices of consumption goods, the quantity of labour supplied for investment depends partly on the money rate of interest and partly on the community's current, say, annual, income of consumption goods. It is thus, and nobody, I think, would doubt this, a function, not of one, but of two variables. Let us write for it $f\{r, \text{F}(x)\}$.[1] What is to be said about the nature of this

---

[1] Since by far the predominant part of investment is performed by non-wage-earners, some might prefer to write $f\{r, [\text{F}(x) - x\text{F}'(x)]\}$ instead of $f\{r, \text{F}(x)\}$. There is no point at present in doing this in view of the fact that $x\text{F}'(x)$, is obviously a function of $\text{F}(x)$. But, when we come to consider the consequences of introducing a system of unemployment benefit and assistance, something further will have to be said on this matter.

function ? It is generally agreed that, at a given rate of interest, the quantity of labour supplied for investment will be greater, the greater is the amount of consumption income. It is no answer to say that, when this income is larger on account of extra employment, the additional employees will probably be too poor to make any appreciable contribution towards hiring labour for investment. For, of course, when employment is larger, this entails that the consumption income of non-wage-earners, who are presumably better off, as well as of wage-earners, is larger. Of the fact that, in respect of any given rate of interest, the supply of labour for investment will be larger, the larger is consumption income, we need, therefore, have no doubt. As to whether, when employment is given, more investment will be supplied at a higher than at a lower rate of interest, there is not unanimity. This matter will be discussed in Chapter V, § 2 of this Part.

§ 14. One further comment as regards the supply function is needed. It will be noticed that we have made the supply of labour for investment a partial function, not of total real income, but of real income of consumption goods. The reason for this is that total real income is an ambiguous concept, the precise significance of which depends on a more or less arbitrary decision about the relative weights to be assigned to consumption and investment goods respectively ; whereas, since throughout our analysis it is postulated that, while, indeed, there are many kinds of consumption goods, their relative quantities and values are always the same, the concept, income of consumption goods, is wholly free from ambiguity. This reason of convenience would not, of course, justify my procedure if it led to incorrect analysis. But in the following discussion we are concerned with systems in which the quantity of employment in consumption industries and investment industries severally, together with their respective outputs, are connected by interlocking sets of equations in a determinate manner. Hence no harm is done by the above simplifying device.

§ 15. Finally, we come to the money income function. The quantity of money income accruing in any period is equal to the income velocity of the total stock of money, which it is usual to name V, in respect of the period in question multiplied by this total stock itself, which is usually named M. Let us consider these two elements in order.

§ 16. In accordance with familiar doctrine, V is the reciprocal of the proportion of real income, measured, say, by the consumption income that would emerge if all the labour at work were engaged in making consumption goods—per this period that people choose to hold, on the average, in the form of money. Given the schedule of returns in convenience, security and so on that are yielded by successive units of real resources held by the representative man in the form of money, such an amount of resources must be so held that their marginal yield exactly balances the rate of interest paid for the marginal unit of resources engaged in investment. Plainly in given conditions this marginal yield of convenience and so on will be larger, the less resources are held in money form. But, the larger r is, the less will be so held, and so the larger V will be. Thus, given the schedule of convenience, etc., V is partly a function of the rate of interest, in such wise that $\dfrac{\partial V}{\partial r}$ is positive.

§ 17. But V does not depend only on the rate of interest. The convenience function and general business habits, which, of course, for our purpose, are taken as constant, being given, it depends also in part on the distribution of income between people whose incomes are paid respectively at long and short intervals. The distributional element may be roughly represented by the proportion of total income accruing to wage-earners. The income velocity of money will be larger, the larger this proportion is, because wage-earners presumably turn over their incomes more quickly — hold on the average a smaller proportion of it as a balance — than people whose income receipts come in monthly or quarterly. Thus, if we write P for the proportion of income accruing to wage-earners, V is also partly a function of P, so that $V = \chi\{r, P\}$; and $\frac{\partial V}{\partial P}$, as well as $\frac{\partial V}{\partial r}$, is positive. Now, as will be shown in Part III, Chapter III, there is reason to believe that the proportion P is likely to be very stable in the face of varying conditions. On the strength of this, coupled with our general common-sense knowledge that a small change in P could not in any case evoke more than a very small change in V, we may probably without serious error leave the element P out of account.[1]

§ 18. But this is not all. As real income becomes larger, there is, *prima facie*, reason for thinking that, just as, up to a point, people like to invest a larger proportion of their real income, so also they like to hold real balances in the form of money equivalent to a larger proportion of it. On the other hand, as Prof. Robertson has pointed out to me, the richer people are, the cleverer they are likely to become in finding a way to *economise* in real balances. On the whole, then, we may, I think, safely disregard this consideration also, and write, for

---

[1] It will be understood that the equality $V = \chi(r)$ holds good only of equilibrium conditions. If the amounts of desired and of actual saving are different, V is also a function of the gap between them.

a close approximation, $V = \chi(r)$ where χ' is positive. This function is, of course, liable to be transformed into something different if, as *e.g.* in a panic, people's attitude towards holding resources in the form of money is altered.[1]

§ 19. Turn to the element M. We are postulating, it will be remembered, a closed economic system, so that, even if our community's money is based on gold, there can be no question of foreign drains upon currency or of an influx of currency from abroad. Even so, there are to be distinguished several types of banking and monetary policy. First, the Central Bank may so act as to allow M to rise or fall as the rate of interest rises or falls. This I shall call normal banking policy. Secondly, the Central Bank may try to keep money income constant. Thirdly, it may try to keep the price level of consumption goods constant. Finally, it may adopt a policy directed to keep the rate of interest constant. There are, of course, a large number of other possible banking policies, but our discussion will be confined to those that have been named.[2] Obviously, according as the policy adopted is a normal policy, a constant-income policy, a constant-price of consumption goods policy, or a constant-interest policy, M will be regulated in quite different ways. Each of these policies is, it will be understood, defined by its principle, not by reference to any particular detailed application. Thus, when we say that the banking policy in vogue is that of keeping the price of consumption goods constant,

---

[1] Thus V, that is the function $\chi(r)$, will be changed if people's desire schedule for liquidity changes. This desire schedule is not, so far as I can see, likely to be changed merely because the function ϕ is changed—if it is changed. But for a different view cf. D. H. Robertson, *Essays in Monetary Theory*, p. 26.

[2] I do not bring under review the policy of keeping the *general* price level constant, partly because this concept is ambiguous. Nor do I discuss the policy of keeping money income divided by the rate of money wages constant, since that policy has never been either adopted or advocated.

this must not be understood in a sense that precludes a change from the decision to keep this price constant at one level to a decision to keep it constant at another. The policy is that of keeping the price level of consumption goods constant at whatever level is decided upon at the time. The other policies must, of course, be interpreted in a like sense.

§ 20. It may be well to add a word of caution here. In distinguishing four several types of banking policy, we must not be understood to imply that the aims of these policies can always be successfully achieved by bank action alone. The banks can, indeed, by discount and open-market policy, control the size of M. But M and V are not independent, and it is not always in the power of the banks, when they operate on M, to avoid countervailing reactions on the part of V large enough to defeat their purpose. Thus, suppose that they desire to keep money income constant, and that this income is threatening to fall. New money created to prevent this may be used to pay off bank debts, in which case it is destroyed as soon as created, or it may be held idle in savings deposits, in such wise that V contracts in a proportion inverse to that in which M has expanded. If we prefer a different language, we may say that, though money in the aggregate is increased, active money is left unchanged, because the whole of the new money is held inactive. It is not suggested that these things *must* happen, nor is it forgotten that alterations in the Central Bank's rate of discount may sometimes operate on V directly in the sense desired ; *e.g.* a rise in the rate may be regarded by the business community as a warning, and in that way make V contract. Undoubtedly, however, these things *may* happen. Moreover, there is a further awkward possibility. Psychological reactions may be set up, when the Central Bank takes action to

prevent money income from expanding or from contracting, of a sort that make it impossible for the Bank
exactly to reach its mark. A necessary condition for its
reaching it at all may be that it shall overshoot it. Thus,
in the upper stages of a boom, if the banks call in loans
from business men with a view to offsetting such and
such an expansion of V, their action may, by a psychological reflex, *more than* offset this. In that event, while
endeavouring to cancel expansion, the banks have induced contraction. Again, if at the very beginning of a
down-swing, when a boom is breaking, the banks
attempt, by emitting new loans, to offset a contraction
of V that has now begun, they may, by a psychological
reflex, more than offset this, so that the result is, not
stability, but a reanimated boom.[1] It is not necessary
to pursue this matter further. It is not directly relevant
to our present enquiry — though it is highly relevant to
practice — to decide whether bank policies directed
towards the several ends we have distinguished can in
fact always attain them. We are concerned here with
what will happen if they *do* attain them.

§ 21. On this basis we are able to represent money
income, namely I or MV, as a function of the rate of
interest. We have already seen that V is a function of
that rate, growing as the rate grows. With a normal
banking policy M also is such a function. Thus I may
be written $g(r)$, where g' is positive. With a banking
policy directed to keep money income constant, the
same form may be used, g' in this case being nil. When
the rate of interest is to be kept constant, we may also
use this form, g' being now infinite. Finally with a

[1] In so far as the Central Bank operates on a basis of gold, or of notes the
quantity of which is limited by law, its freedom of action, even in respect of
M, is restricted. For it dare not increase indefinitely its obligations to meet
valid cheques on itself with legal tender money, unless it is assured that a
sufficient supply of such money will always be available to it.

banking policy directed to keep the price of consumption goods constant, we are still free, if we wish, to write $I = g(r)$: but this is subject to a superimposed condition, to be described presently, which determines the function g in a special way.

CHAPTER III

THE ECONOMIC SYSTEM IN SHORT-PERIOD FLOW EQUILIBRIUM

§ 1. HAVING presented the principal elements relevant to our problem, I have now to indicate the manner in which, in order that short-period flow equilibrium may exist, they must be inter-related. In the main discussion the fact that in real life unemployment benefit or something analogous to it often exists will be ignored ; what I have to say on that matter being reserved for Part III, Chapter XI.

§ 2. First, the demand for and supply of labour for investment must exactly balance. Thus we have a first equation

$$\phi(r) = f\{r,\ \mathrm{F}(x)\}. \qquad . \qquad . \quad \text{(I)}$$

§ 3. Secondly, y being written for labour supplied for investment, we have also the equation

$$y = f\{r,\ \mathrm{F}(x)\}. \qquad . \qquad . \quad \text{(II)}\,[1]$$

§ 4. Thirdly, there is in equilibrium a set of relations between quantity of employment and real wage-rates in the consumption and investment industries respectively.

Write W_1 for the real wage-rate in terms of con-

---

[1] This equation can be expressed otherwise, on the assumptions to be set out in the footnote on p. 113, as $y = \eta_{\mathrm{F}(x)} . \mathrm{F}(x) . \dfrac{r + v_{\mathrm{F}(x)} - q_{\mathrm{F}(x)}}{r}$ on the lines of equation (IV) in that footnote ; q being the rate at which the representative man discounts future satisfaction.

sumption goods in general in the consumption industries ; W_2 for the real wage-rate in terms of investment
goods in general in the investment industries. We have
already agreed to write x and y for the quantities of
labour, $F(x)$ and $\psi(y)$ for the quantities of output in
representative consumption and investment industries
respectively, and η_1 and η_2 for the elasticities of demand,
as defined in § 6 of the last chapter, for the representative commodities produced by representative firms in
the two groups. We then know that in conditions of
perfect competition the real wage-rate in each sort of
industry must, for equilibrium, be equal to the discounted real value of its future marginal products.[1] If h_1
and h_2 be the periods of production, in the sense of
interval between the payment of wage to a representative
workman and the final sale of his output in consumption
and investment industries respectively, this implies

$$\frac{W_1}{1 - rh_1} = F'(x)$$

and

$$\frac{W_2}{1 - rh_2} = \psi'(y).$$

We agreed, however, in § 1 of the last chapter to ignore
rh_1 and rh_2, which are small, and the inclusion of which
would complicate the form, without essentially modi-
fying the substance, of our analysis. Hence, instead of
the above equations, we write

$$W_1 = F'(x),$$
$$W_2 = \psi'(y).$$

Under the more general conditions which allow of
monopolistic action, these equations are replaced, in

---

[1] The rate of earnings for fixed capital instruments is, of course, in like
manner, equal to the discounted real value of their future marginal products.
The balance that is left over when labour and fixed capital instruments are
paid on this plan constitutes the earnings of working and liquid capital.

accordance with a familiar proposition in the theory of monopoly, by

$$W_1 = \left(1 - \frac{1}{\eta_1}\right)F'(x)$$

and

$$W_2 = \left(1 - \frac{1}{\eta_2}\right)\psi'(y),$$

where η_1 and η_2 (defined positively) are functions respectively of $F(x)$ and $\psi(y)$ and are both >1. In the present Part attention is confined to this general case.

§ 5. Fourthly, in equilibrium we have a relation, that of equality, between money income and the aggregate selling price of consumption goods plus investment goods.[1] Write p_1 and p_2 for the respective selling prices of these two kinds of goods, and I for aggregate money income. Then we have

$$p_1 F(x) + p_2 \psi(y) = I.$$

§ 6. Fifthly, if we write w for the money rate of wage and take cognisance of the fact that this rate must, for equilibrium, be the same in both sorts of industry, we have

$$\frac{w}{p_1} = W_1,$$

$$\frac{w}{p_2} = W_2.$$

§ 7. The results of the three preceding sections being brought together, the p's and the W's are eliminated, and we have the following single equation :

$$\left\{\frac{F(x)}{\left(1 - \frac{1}{\eta_1}\right)F'(x)} + \frac{\psi(y)}{\left(1 - \frac{1}{\eta_2}\right)\psi'(y)}\right\} . w = I.$$

---

[1] A verbal adjustment must be made in so far as investment or, indeed, consumption, goods are not sold for a price in the market, but are sold, so to speak, by their producers to themselves.

§ 8. What has been said, accurately represents the facts for conditions of equilibrium, because in these conditions, since entrepreneurs' receipts every week are the same, it is immaterial that their receipts this week are in respect of goods the wages bill for which they paid some time ago. But in conditions of disequilibrium this fact, as will be found in Part IV, may be very important.[1]

9. With a banking policy that is normal or of the constant-income type or of the constant-interest type, $I = g(r)$. Therefore the above equation becomes

$$\left\{ \frac{F(x)}{\left(1 - \dfrac{1}{\eta_1}\right)F'(x)} + \frac{\psi(y)}{\left(1 - \dfrac{1}{\eta_2}\right)\psi'(y)} \right\} \cdot w = g(r).$$

For brevity we may write

$$\frac{F(x)}{\left(1 - \dfrac{1}{\eta_1}\right)F'(x)} = K_1(x),$$

since all the elements in the former expression are functions of x;[2] and, similarly,

$$\frac{\psi(y)}{\left(1 - \dfrac{1}{\eta_2}\right)\psi'(y)} = K_2(y).$$

The above, namely our third main equation, then becomes

$$(K_1 + K_2) \cdot w = g(r). \qquad \qquad \text{(III)}$$

§ 10. With a banking policy directed to keep the price level of consumption goods constant, the above third equation yields place to a different one. This has to represent the fact that the price of the representative consumption good — our p_1 — is held constant. From §§ 5 and 6 it is readily seen that

---

[1] Cf. *post*, Part IV, Chapter VI, §§ 9-11.

[2] But cf. *post*, Part III, Chapter II, § 3.

$$p_1 = \left\{ \frac{1}{\left(1 - \dfrac{1}{\eta_1}\right)F'} \right\} \cdot w = \frac{K_1}{F} \cdot w.$$

Hence we have in this case the different third equation

$$\frac{K_1}{F} \cdot w = C \text{ (constant)}. \qquad . \qquad \text{(III) } (b)$$

§ 11. For our present purpose the essential matter is, not what precise form our third equation assumes in different circumstances, but the fact that in it one unknown appears in addition to those already present in the other two equations. This unknown is, of course, the money rate of wage, which we have agreed to call w. Thus we have, no matter which form of the third equation is used, four unknowns, x, y, r and w, in conjunction with three equations. Obviously this is not a determinate system. We are one equation short. In order to make it a determinate system — apart from the special case referred to in the next footnote — it is necessary and sufficient to add one more independent condition or equation. In the abstract, of course, an infinite number of alternative conditions or equations are available to us. If, however, we wish to keep contact with reality, two only are of interest : (i) the condition that aggregate employment is equal to the quantity of available labour, so that we may write $(x + y) = Q$ (constant) ; (ii) the condition that money rates of wages are fixed by authority or collective bargaining, so that we may write $w = T$ (constant). When either of these conditions is added to our first two equations and to whatever form of the third equation we choose to select, we have, except in one special case,[1] a determinate interlocking system.

---

[1] When the third equation is $(K_1 + K_2) . w = g(r)$, the system is, in truth, always determinate. It is also always determinate if the third equation is

$$\frac{K_1}{F} \cdot w = C,$$

§ 12. When our fourth equation has the form $(x + y)$ = Q, this equation, together with the first two, determines x, y and r, regardless of w. Then, x, y and r being known, w is determined by the third equation, no matter which of the two alternative forms described in §§ 9-10 it assumes. Thus there is a certain priority in the relations of x, y and r to one another over the relation of any one of them to w. The values x, y and r determine one another and, thereafter, jointly determine w. But, when the fourth equation has the form $w = $ T, there is no corresponding priority. No one and no two of the other equations, whichever form the third assumes, in combination with the fourth, by themselves determine any of x, y and r. It is thus no more correct to say that w determines $(x + y)$ *through* r than it is to say that w determines r *through* $(x + y)$. In fact neither of these statements is correct ; unless we mean merely that, w and all the relevant functions being given, $(x + y)$ could not have the value that it has unless r had the value that it has ; or vice versa. We have, as it were, to borrow Marshall's illustration, a number of balls lying together at the bottom of a bowl. The positions of all mutually determine one another ; or, more strictly, the whole surrounding environment jointly determines the positions of all.

§ 13. The last paragraph was concerned with a secondary matter. The essential fact is that, apart from the exception noted in the footnote to p. 70, when, to the system of three equations as described in §§ 2-10, no matter which of the alternative forms the third assumes, there is added a fourth equation either of the

---

and the fourth equation is $(x+y) =$ Q. But, with the third equation as above and the fourth equation $w = $ T, there is one possible condition in which the system will not be determinate. This condition is that the same real rate of wage in the representative consumption industry is compatible with any quantity of employment.

form $(x + y) = Q$ or of the form $w = T$, the system is
determinate. This implies that no further independent
conditions can be introduced so long as all those already
given are maintained. More particularly, when the
system is constituted with a fourth equation of the form
$(x + y) = Q$, the alternative fourth equation of the form
$w = T$ cannot also hold good. For in that event the
system would be over-determined ; that is to say, we
should be postulating the joint existence of conditions
that are incompatible with one another. It is important
to understand what precisely it is that is thus rendered
impossible. It is *not* impossible for the State to decree
that a money wage-rate of some defined amount shall
be paid everywhere and also that a defined number of
workpeople shall be employed. There might well,
indeed, be great practical difficulty in enforcing two
such decrees together, but it is not impossible *in principle* to enforce them. Nor can we legitimately infer
from our analysis that this must prove impossible *in
practice*. What, then, *is* implied ? It is implied, quite
simply, that one of the other equations in the system
cannot be satisfied ; more precisely that *either*, at the
established rate of interest, the quantity of investment
demanded is not equal to the quantity which people
wish to supply, *or* that, at the established rate of wages,
the quantity of labour demanded and the quantity on
offer are not equal. That is to say, the conditions
necessary to short-period flow equilibrium as described
in Part II, Chapter I, are not all satisfied.

CHAPTER IV

STABILITY CONDITIONS

§ 1. IT is obvious that, of the variables comprised in our model, x, y, r, w, W_1 and W_2 must all be positive, and in equilibrium must have such values that the functions F, F', ψ, ψ', K_1, K_2 and g are all positive. Moreover, since in equilibrium

$$\left(1 - \frac{1}{\eta_1}\right)F' = W_1 \quad \text{and} \quad \left(1 - \frac{1}{\eta_2}\right)\psi' = W_2, \; \eta_1 \text{ and } \eta_2,$$

which, it will be remembered, are defined in a positive sense, must each be > 1. Further, in Chapter I of this Part we found that over the relevant range ϕ' must be regarded as negative and $\frac{\partial f}{\partial F}$ and, consequently, $\frac{\partial f}{\partial F} \cdot F'$, as positive, while, with what I have called a normal monetary and banking policy, g' is by definition positive. There are, however, certain other signs, the determination of which is very important for our analysis, and which in my first edition I held could be determined unequivocally from what we may conveniently call stability considerations. From these considerations I believed myself entitled to assert that $\left(\frac{\partial f}{\partial r} - \phi'\right)$ must be positive (or nil), that K'_1 must be positive, $\left(\frac{K'_1}{K_1} - \frac{F'}{F}\right)$ positive or nil and K'_2 positive in

73

all circumstances. In truth, however, my reasoning was faulty. In this Chapter, therefore, I propose to review again the general question what inferences stability considerations allow us to draw about the signs of the above expressions.

§ 2. The way of approach is as follows. Since the purpose of our investigation is to obtain an insight into what happens in the actual world, we may properly exclude from discussion equilibrium situations of a sort that, while theoretically possible, could not be found in practice. Three sorts of equilibrium may be distinguished ; stable equilibrium, typified by a boat upright on its keel, under which, when a small accidental disturbance occurs, forces come into play to restore the original situation ; unstable equilibrium, typified by an egg balanced on its end, under which, on such a small accidental disturbance occurring, forces come into play to drive the system further and further away from the original situation ; and neutral equilibrium, typified by an egg lying on its side, under which small accidental disturbances are simply accepted, calling into play neither of these two types of force. In view of the fact that in the actual world small accidental disturbances are continually occurring, there is nothing to be gained by studying unstable equilibrium. Therefore for our models we may properly postulate that conditions entailing this sort of equilibrium are excluded. We have to examine the implications of this postulate.

§ 3. There are two sorts of unstable equilibrium which may be thus excluded, first unstable equilibrium as regards employment and (or) investment in the aggregate, secondly unstable equilibrium as between the outputs of the several firms engaged in particular industries, i.e. where firms are so poised that, if one of them secures a small accidental increase in output, instead of losing thereby and being driven to contract again, it is driven to expand still further and oust its rivals from the market. The existence of either sort of instability is evidently incompatible with the system's maintaining itself for more than a moment. Let us consider first what is implied by excluding the former more general kind of instability.

§ 4. In my first edition I took the view that, if a small disturbance in any element in the system, quantity of labour engaged in any firm in the consumption industries or anything else, taken by itself alone, would call into play forces accentuating the disturbance, the equilibrium must be regarded as unstable, and, therefore, the conditions that allow of it as inadmissible. It has been pointed out, however, by Mr. Tsiang that a disturbance in one element may lead to movements in other elements, the stabilising tendency of which outweighs the destabilising tendency of the original movement. In such cases, though the equilibrium may perhaps properly be called imperfectly stable, it is, nevertheless, effectively stable. The conditions that allow of it cannot, therefore, be ruled out on the ground that it is impossible for them to maintain themselves in real life. The only conditions that *can* be ruled out are those that entail instability in the face of small accidental changes, when direct as well as indirect reactions are taken into account.

§ 5. We start with the general equation :

$$\phi(r) = f\{r, \, \mathrm{F}(x)\}. \qquad . \qquad . \qquad \text{(I)}$$

In my first edition I derived from this, as the condition necessary to exclude unstable equilibrium,

$$\left\{\frac{\partial f}{\partial r} - \phi'\right\} => 0 \; ;$$

for it is plain that, if the curve relating rate of interest and labour supplied for investment out of a given income is inclined negatively, it can only be backward-rising, not forward-falling. But this derivation ignores the possibility that, when r changes, reactions may be set up in x which prevent the system from being unstable, though it would be so in the absence of reactions on x. Some different approach is, therefore, required that will allow of these reactions being taken into account.

§ 6.[1] With a banking and monetary policy of what I have called the normal type, as also with one directed to keep money income constant, there stands, along with equation (I) above, a second equation—w being taken as constant and equal to unity—

$$g(r) = K_1(x) + K_2\{\phi(r)\} ; \qquad . \qquad . \text{ (II)}$$

for we have already $y = \phi(r)$.

In order to exclude instability when indirect as well as direct reactions are taken into account, we require the condition

$$\frac{d}{dx}\Big\{f - \phi\Big\} = > 0, \; subject \; to \; g(r) = K_1(x) + K_2\{\phi(r)\}. \quad \text{(A)}$$

This condition is alternative to, *i.e.* comes to the same thing as, and has the same implications as the symmetrical condition

$$\frac{d}{dx}\Big\{K_1(x) + K_2\{\phi(r)\} - g(r)\Big\} = > 0, \; subject \; to \; f = \phi. \; . \quad \text{(B)}$$

The condition required to exclude instability can then be worked out and is found to be

---

[1] I owe the mathematical analysis comprising this section to Mr. Champernowne.

$$\frac{\partial f}{\partial F} \cdot F' = > \frac{\left(\dfrac{\partial f}{\partial r} - \phi'\right)}{\phi' \cdot K_2' - g'} \cdot K_1', \qquad . \qquad . \quad (C)$$

where K_2' signifies $\dfrac{dK_2}{d\{\phi(r)\}}$.

This condition obviously does not imply anything about the signs of $\left(\dfrac{\partial f}{\partial r} - \phi'\right)$ or of either K_1' or K_2', even though we know from outside that $\dfrac{\partial f}{\partial F} F'$ is positive, ϕ' negative and g' positive (or nil).

§ 7. With a monetary and banking policy directed to keep the price level of consumption goods constant, the second general equation (II) distinguished above, w as before being taken as constant and equal to unity, gives place to $\dfrac{K_1}{F} = C$ (constant).

In order to exclude unstable equilibria we must thus have $\dfrac{d}{dx}\left(\dfrac{K_1}{F}\right) = >0$. This implies

$$\frac{K_1'}{K_1} - \frac{F'}{F} = >0. \qquad . \qquad . \qquad . \quad (D)$$

This implies further that K_1' is positive : but nothing can be inferred about the signs of $\left(\dfrac{\partial f}{\partial r} - \phi'\right)$ or of K_2'.

§ 8. Turn to the other type of instability distinguished in § 3. Does the need for excluding that type of instability tell us anything of interest about signs ?

In my first edition I invoked stability considerations in regard to the equilibrium conditions $\left(1 - \dfrac{1}{\eta_1}\right)F' = W_1$, and $\left(1 - \dfrac{1}{\eta_2}\right)\psi' = W_2$, maintaining that, in order to exclude instability, we must postulate that

$$\frac{d}{dx}\left\{\left(1 - \frac{1}{\eta_1}\right)F'\right\} \quad \text{and} \quad \frac{d}{dy}\left\{\left(1 - \frac{1}{\eta_2}\right)\psi'\right\}$$

are both $< = 0$, which obviously implies that K_1' and K_2' are both > 0.

This, however, is not right. It is necessary to distinguish between the case of perfect competition, when $\frac{1}{\eta_1}$ and $\frac{1}{\eta_2} = 0$ and the case of imperfect competition.

§ 9. We have agreed that, for short-period equilibrium analysis, external economies should be left out of account. That being so, under perfect competition any, say, nth firm, for which F_n'' is positive, must be in unstable equilibrium. It is legitimate to generalise from this and infer that under perfect competition, in order to exclude unstable equilibrium, F'', and similarly ψ'', must be $< = 0$. This, it is easy to see, implies that K_1' and K_2' must be positive.

§ 10. It might seem at first sight, and this is what I myself believed when I wrote my first edition, that under imperfect competition positive values for

$$\frac{d}{dx}\left\{\left(1 - \frac{1}{\eta_1}\right)F'\right\} \quad \text{and} \quad \frac{d}{dy}\left\{\left(1 - \frac{1}{\eta_2}\right)\psi'\right\}$$

could also be excluded. But this is not so. Write p_n for the price per unit of a particular consumption good produced by a particular firm in terms of units of the composite consumption good. In order to exclude instability (w being constant) we must then have

$$\frac{d}{dx_n}\left\{\left(1 - \frac{1}{\eta_1}\right)F_n' \cdot p_n\right\} < = 0.$$

In my first edition I treated p_n as a constant on the ground that my model required the relative prices of all consumption goods to be the same in all equilibrium situations.   Hence I inferred immediately

$$\frac{d}{dx_n}\left\{\left(1 - \frac{1}{\eta_1}\right)F_n{}'\right\} < = 0.$$

Mr. Tsiang has shown,[1] however, that to regard p_n as constant for the analysis of the stability of individual firms implies asserting that the individual entrepreneur "expects *ante facto* the price of his own product to remain always the same relative to other prices"; which is incompatible with the conditions of imperfect competition that we are assuming to prevail.   If, however, p_n is not regarded as a constant, $\frac{dp_n}{dx_n}$ must clearly be negative.

Consequently $\frac{d}{dx_n}\left\{\left(1 - \frac{1}{\eta_1}\right)F_n{}'.\ p_n\right\} < = 0$ does *not* imply $\frac{d}{dx_n}\left\{\left(1 - \frac{1}{\eta_1}\right)F_n{}'\right\} \gtrless = 0$.   Hence with imperfect competition we cannot, as we can with perfect competition, derive from stability considerations relevant to particular firms the general conditions that $\frac{d}{dx}\left\{\left(1 - \frac{1}{\eta_1}\right)F'\right\}$ and $\frac{d}{dy}\left\{\left(1 - \frac{1}{\eta_2}\right)\psi'\right\} < = 0$, or, what is implied in them, that $K_1{}'$ and $K_2{}'$ must be positive.

§ 11. The above results may be summarised thus. The requirement that both of the two sorts of instability distinguished in § 2 shall be excluded does not enable us in any circumstances to infer the sign of $\left\{\frac{\partial f}{\partial r} - \phi'\right\}$.   In conditions of perfect competition this requirement enables us, no matter what type of monetary and banking system prevails, to infer that $K_1{}'$ and $K_2{}'$ must be positive.   In conditions of imperfect competition, nothing can be inferred about the signs of $K_1{}'$ and $K_2{}'$ with

---

[1] *Economic Journal*, December 1944.

a normal banking and monetary system or with one directed to keep money income constant. But, with one directed to keep the price level of consumption goods in general constant, it can be inferred that $\dfrac{K_1'}{K_1} - \dfrac{F'}{F} = > 0$, and that K'_1 is positive.[1]

[1] If there were only a single sort of consumption good — investment goods being ignored — imperfect competition, even the absorption of all production into a single firm, would leave $\dfrac{1}{\eta_1} = 0$ just as under perfect competition. Since it is impossible to force up the price of a commodity in terms of itself, nobody would be induced to restrict output in order to raise prices. Thus, while perfect competition would imply infinite demand elasticity in terms of the composite consumption good, infinite elasticity would not imply perfect competition. If then there is only one sort of consumption good, $\dfrac{d}{dx}\left\{\left(1 - \dfrac{1}{\eta_1}\right)F'\right\}$ reduces to F'', just as it does under perfect competition. But in this case for F'' to be negative does not entail unstable equilibrium and is not, therefore, excluded, as it is under perfect competition. The case, however, is of no practical interest.

CHAPTER V

THE DETERMINATION OF CERTAIN SIGNS OTHERWISE THAN FROM STABILITY CONSIDERATIONS

§ 1. The fact that the amount of help for determining the signs of $\left(\dfrac{\partial f}{\partial r} - \phi' \right)$, K_1' and K_2' that stability considerations provide is, as was seen in the last chapter, very slight, naturally impels us to enquire whether knowledge about these signs can be obtained in any other way. That is the subject matter of this brief chapter.

§ 2. The relation between the amount that people with given real incomes are likely to save and the rate of interest has been a good deal discussed among economists. It has been argued that for some people in some situations a higher rate of interest will call out a lower rate of saving, that is to say $\dfrac{\partial f}{\partial r}$ will be negative.

Our concern, however, is with the people of a modern community taken as a whole, or, to put the same thing otherwise, with a representative man. This matter is well summed up by Marshall in these words: " Though the rate of saving of many people is but little affected by the rate of interest, while a few, who have determined to secure an income of a certain fixed amount for themselves or their family, will save less with a high rate than with a low rate of interest ; yet a strong balance of evidence seems to rest with the opinion that a rise in the rate of interest, or demand price for saving, tends to increase the volume of saving ".[1] That is to say, a strong balance seems to rest with the opinion that $\frac{\partial f}{\partial r}$ is positive. I do not think that anything has happened since Marshall's time to reverse this judgment; though there may be reason for adding to it the rider that the positive value of $\frac{\partial f}{\partial r}$ is probably small. But, of course, if $\frac{\partial f}{\partial r}$ is positive, *a fortiori* $\left(\frac{\partial f}{\partial r} - \phi' \right)$ is positive, since we know that ϕ' is negative. Granted that, on the evidence, $\frac{\partial f}{\partial r}$ is probably positive, it follows that $\left(\frac{\partial f}{\partial r} - \phi' \right)$ is probably positive with a higher degree of probability. What I claimed in my first edition to be necessary is in fact probable.

§ 3. We have seen that $\frac{d}{dx}\left\{ \left(1 - \frac{1}{\eta_1} \right) F' \right\} < \, = 0$ implies $K_1' > 0$ and similarly that $\frac{d}{dy}\left\{ \left(1 - \frac{1}{\eta_2} \right) \psi' \right\} < \, = 0$ implies $K_2' > 0$. I can, however, find no good reason, independently of stability considerations, for holding that $\frac{d}{dx}\left\{ \left(1 - \frac{1}{\eta_1} \right) F' \right\}$ and $\frac{d}{dy}\left\{ \left(1 - \frac{1}{\eta_2} \right) \psi' \right\}$ are more likely to be negative than positive. There is nothing to prevent F'' or ψ'' from being positive, and there is, perhaps, more ground for thinking that increasing output will entail increasing elasticity in people's demands for the purchases of a representative commodity from a representative firm engaged in making it than for thinking

---

[1] *Principles*, 5th edition, p. 534.

the opposite.[1] This, however, is not conclusive. For while, in conditions where positive values for

$$\frac{d}{dx}\left\{\left(1 - \frac{1}{\eta_1}\right)F'\right\} \quad \text{and} \quad \frac{d}{dy}\left\{\left(1 - \frac{1}{\eta_2}\right)\psi'\right\}$$

are excluded, K_1' and K_2' *must* be positive, they *may* also be positive though positive values for these other expressions are not excluded. Are they likely in fact to be positive ? Write P_1 and P_2 for the proportionate shares of the outputs of the consumption and investment industries respectively accruing to labour in these industries. Then $K_1 = \frac{x}{P_1}$ and $K_2 = \frac{y}{P_2}$. It will be shown in Chapter III of Part III that in the actual world P_1 and P_2 jointly, and we may fairly presume severally also, manifest a high degree of stability. If they were absolutely stable and, *a fortiori*, if they decreased as x and y increased, it would follow at once that K_1' and K_2' must be positive. But K_1' and K_2' will also be positive if P_1 and P_2 increase as x and y increase, pro-

---

[1] In his book on *The Trade Cycle*, Mr. Harrod argues that in conditions of imperfect competition increased aggregate output is likely to be associated with diminished elasticity of representative demands because, as people become better off and able to buy more consumption goods in general, it becomes less worth their while to shift their purchases from one shop or firm to another for the sake of a small gain (*loc. cit.* p. 21). There is, however, an important consideration on the other side. The elasticity of demand for the output of a particular firm in imperfect competition depends also on the character of the consumption goods that people buy. As they become able to buy more consumption goods in general, they devote a larger proportion of their expenditure on those goods to satisfying less urgent wants, in respect of which the demand is notoriously more elastic than it is in respect of necessaries. Thus Prof. Allen and Dr. Bowley, who have made a statistical study of Family Expenditure within certain income ranges, write : " It is to be expected that substitution becomes more easy for most goods as aggregate consumption rises ; the larger expenditure is spread over a wider range of items and the possibility of substituting other items for a given item are thereby increased. It follows that the elasticity of demand for any item with respect to changes in its price is likely to increase with aggregate consumption. Demands tend to become more elastic as aggregate consumption level rises " (*loc. cit.* p. 125). I have substituted for "income" in this passage "aggregate consumption" throughout.

vided that they do not increase in a proportion larger than that in which x and y increase.   For

$$K_1' = \frac{d}{dx}\left(\frac{x}{P_1}\right) = \frac{1}{P_1}\left\{1 - \frac{x}{dx} \cdot \frac{dP_1}{P_1}\right\};$$

and K_2' is related in a similar way to P_2 and y.   In view of the statistical evidence there is a reasonable presumption that this proviso will be satisfied.   I conclude, therefore, that K_1' and K_2' are probably positive.

CHAPTER VI

THE CLASSICAL VIEW

§ 1. WE may now take up again the argument of Chapter III. *A priori* there is no reason why our fourth equation should not have either the form $(x + y) = Q$ or the form $w = T$; *i.e.* should not stipulate either for full employment or for some specified arbitrarily fixed money rate of wage. If we were completely unregardful of the actual world, these two possibilities would be on a level, and we should be equally interested in both. In fact, however, we are not completely unregardful of the actual world; and therefore, for us, it is important to decide how far these alternative possibilities are related to the facts. This leads up to a discussion of what has sometimes been called the " classical view ", and of which Marshall and myself are supposed to be modern representatives.

§ 2. According to Keynes, the classical view consists in asserting that in the model world described in our Preliminary Chapter the fourth equation is in all circumstances of the form $(x + y) = Q$ (constant). Put otherwise, and referred to the actual world, this means that " full employment " always exists; full employment being interpreted broadly as the employment of all would-be wage-earners minus such as are estopped from employment through defects of mobility or other like friction. This view of the classical economists, their critics proceed to point out, logically implies that changes in the demand and supply attitude towards investment always and necessarily leave aggregate employment unaffected. The fact that, in discussing industrial fluctuations, no economist, classical or other ever does assert this, is a tribute to common sense paid in despite of logic. *Logically* the " classical school " are bound to reject Government attempts to alleviate a slump by means of Public Works and to welcome economy campaigns in times of depression. These latter help to replenish depleted stocks of capital, while, since, on the classical view, employment is always and necessarily full — in spite of statistics to the contrary ! — they cannot harm that. This, of course, is a travesty. The classical view is not one which either asserts or implies that full employment always exists, *i.e.* that our fourth equation always has the form $(x + y) = Q$.

§ 3. What, then, *is* the classical view ? It is, in its most rigorous form, that full employment does, indeed, not always exist, but always *tends* to be established. In terms of the construction with which we are here working, this means that, if the economic system were not subject to disturbances, our fourth equation would always have the form $(x + y) = Q$. Since, in fact, there are disturbances and since money wages are in some degree sticky, this equation, as regards any short interval, is likely to have the alternative form $w = T$. But there is always a strong force making for the establishment of the equation $(x + y) = Q$. This force operates on the various values of T, which rule at different times, in such a way that, on the average of good and bad times together, the equation $(x + y) = Q$ is, so to speak, dominant behind the scenes. This does not, of course, imply that *on the average* full employment, in the sense defined above, exists. Since we know that employment is sometimes less than full, while it can obviously never be more than full, that would be nonsense. It means that, whereas, if the system were not subject to disturbances full employment would always exist, in actual fact employment on the average falls short of full employment by a certain quantity attributable to the disturbances. For, of course, the system is subject to disturbances, friction is not absent and labour is not completely mobile. The percentage which, on the average of good and bad times, employment constitutes of the available labour force, is not a hundred per cent, but some smaller percentage, approximating more closely to a hundred per cent the more nearly the ideal of a stable, frictionless and completely mobile system is approached. As I put it in my *Theory of Unemployment* : " With perfectly free competition among workpeople and labour perfectly mobile . . . there will always be at work a strong tendency for wage-rates to be so related to demand that everybody is employed. Hence, in stable conditions everyone will actually be employed. The implication is that such unemployment as exists at any time is due wholly to the fact that changes in demand conditions are continually taking place and that frictional resistances prevent the appropriate wage adjustment from being made instantaneously." [1] This, it should be observed, does not imply that the percentage of unemployment among would-be wage-earners over the average of good and bad times is necessarily the same. It will only be the same so long as the economic setting as regards friction, mobility and so on is the same.

§ 4. The above account is perhaps a little pedantic. We need not restrict the term " classical view " to the thesis that under perfectly free competition among

------

[1] *Loc. cit.* p. 252.

workpeople the norm to which employment tends will be nil unemployment, or full employment in the literal sense. We should, I think, include under it a recognition of the fact that in actual life, in place of perfectly free competition among workpeople, there may stand " wage policy " directed to a different norm. This wage policy is exercised sometimes through collective bargaining on the part of trade unions, sometimes through State action establishing minimum rates of pay. It is not *necessary*, merely because these agencies are employed, that the goal of the policy should be a system of rates higher than those which perfectly free competition among wage-earners tends to bring about. There is reason to believe, however, that the goal at which wage policy aims is sometimes, in some centres of production at all events, a wage-rate substantially higher than the rate which, if adopted everywhere, would yield nil unemployment. Several considerations point towards this conclusion.

First, in industries that are sheltered from foreign competition, particularly in fundamental industries such as the transport industry, where a stoppage of work would inflict great injury on the general public, wage-earners are in a very strong bargaining position. Even though the demand for labour has an elasticity greater than unity, so that the aggregate earnings in the industry are less with a higher wage-rate than with a lower one, the men may, nevertheless, press — and press successfully — for the higher rate. For adverse reactions on unemployment will not leap to the eye ; and, even if they did, the leaders in charge of the bargaining might well prefer smaller aggregate earnings that give good incomes to a comparatively small number of men to larger aggregate earnings made up of a great number of poor incomes. Policy on this matter will depend to an important extent on the nature of the provision that is made for unemployed workpeople. If the unemployed members of a trade union have to be cared for exclusively by that union, so that heavy unemployment means a heavy drain on union funds, this fact will act as a check upon claims for higher wages. If, however, unemployed members are cared for, in the main, at the expense of other people, the union's contribution being no larger when there are many unemployed than when there are few, this check does not operate. There can be little doubt that the system of State-aided unemployment insurance with substantial rates of benefit, which has been widely extended in this country since the early 1920s, has enabled wage-earners to maintain rates of wages at a higher level than they would otherwise have been able to do.

Secondly, an important influence is exercised by what may almost be described as a technical accident. Under time-wage systems it is impracticable for collective bargains to take full account of small differences of capacity between individuals in any general class. Special arrangements may, indeed, be made for men suffering from some obvious physical defect or for abnormally slow workers, but these are necessarily very rough and imperfect. Consequently, the wage per unit of capacity will often be fixed somewhat higher for less able than for more able men. If, in these conditions, the rate per unit of capacity were set low enough to allow all would-be wage-earners in the class in question to be employed, the abler men would be receiving substantially less than their marginal worth. Naturally this would be resented. In wage bargains made subject to the condition of a common standard it is, therefore, likely that a compromise rate will be fixed somewhere intermediate between the marginal worth of the abler and the less able workers. If this is done the less able workers are bound to be allotted more than the wage proper to full employment.

Thirdly, public opinion in a modern civilised State builds up for itself a rough estimate of what constitutes a reasonable living wage. This is derived half-consciously from a knowledge of the actual standards enjoyed by more or less " average " workers. Hence it is to be expected that the lowest class of workers, who congregate in occupations needing very little skill or strength, will have a marginal worth, if all of them are employed, less than what public opinion regards as a reasonable minimum payment for *any* worker to receive. Public opinion then enforces its view, failing success through social pressure, by the machinery of Trade Board legislation. In these circumstances, unless the receipt of payment in excess of their worth quickly lifts inefficient workpeople's quality to the level of their pay, or, by quickly stimulating employers to improved methods, achieves equilibrium by an indirect route, their actual wage will stand above the level to which free competition tends and at which there is no unemployment.[1]

§ 5. We are now ready for our main problem. If the classical view, whether in its more or its less rigorous form, correctly represents the facts, there must clearly exist some mechanism by which it may be supposed that, in a given environment, the trend of employment is tied, as it were by an elastic string, to the trend of the number comprised in the available labour force. Unless we are able to make for ourselves a picture of such a mechanism and to show reason for believing that it will work, the case for the classical view is weak. On

---

[1] The above section is taken in the main from my *Theory of Unemployment*, pp. 253-6.

the other hand, if we can do this, that case is *pro tanto* strong.

§ 6. Advocates of the classical view would, I think, describe the mechanism which they believe to be at work more or less as follows : When the percentage of unemployment is heavy, competition among wage-earners for work, hampered and delayed as it is by frictions and elements of monopolistic policy, leads presently to the acceptance of lower money wages, whereas, on the other hand, when the percentage of unemployment is small, competition among employers for scarce labour tends to push money wages up. When, however, money wages are reduced, this in general makes it profitable to employers to engage more men ; and conversely. Thus, when the proportion of the available labour force in employment falls below the norm, a process is brought into play which tends to raise it ; and, again, conversely. With no friction and no immobility, whether the norm was full employment in the literal sense or something less than full employment, these correcting adjustments would continue to maintain the norm. In active life, when friction and immobility exist, they would constitute it the constant centre round which employment oscillated.

§ 7. It is not, however, enough to describe this supposed mechanism in general terms. We have to enquire what conditions must be satisfied if it is to work, and whether these conditions are likely to be satisfied in actual life. The conditions required are easily set down. They are two in number. First, money wage-rates are not rigidly fixed, but tend in the long run to move down under the pressure of falling money demand. Secondly, with all practically probable monetary and banking policies reductions in the money rate of wages make it to the interest of employers, other things being

equal, to engage more workpeople ; so that the volume
of employment tends to be larger than before.   If both
these conditions are satisfied our mechanism will work.
But, if either of them fails, it will not.   Until recently
both of them were generally believed among economists
to hold good ; but in recent years doubts have been
suggested about each of them.

§ 8. The first need not detain us long.   It is obviously impossible to decide, in general and in the abstract,
whether money wage-rates are held rigid against falls.
This is a question that can only be answered on the basis
of actual experience for conditions to which that experience may fairly be supposed relevant.   The claim that
money wage-rates are rigid is not supported by the
evidence available for this country.   Dr. Bowley's index
of money wages, corrected for the fact that the proportion of men engaged in the better-paid occupations
has tended to grow, shows, between 1880 and 1914,
decreases in 1885, 1886, 1901, 1902, 1903, 1904 and
1909.[1]   Thus on a number of occasions the general
average of rates has fallen ; and that not merely as a
reaction from violent upward movements such as oc-
curred in the immediate post-war boom of 1919–20.   If
the average rate has fallen, *a fortiori* particular rates
must have fallen, and, since the maintenance of a
general average rate as such seems very unlikely to be
made an object of policy, the fact that particular rates
have fallen is direct proof that money wage-rates have
not been rigid.   It is sometimes suggested, indeed, that,
though what has been said is true of the past, in the
present for a variety of reasons money wage-rates have
become rigid.   The facts do not support this contention.
It is true, no doubt, that wage-earners in some degree
look upon money wages as " things-in-themselves ", and

_____
[1] *Wages and Income since 1860*, p. 6.

resist reductions even when prices are falling. But the suggestion that they disregard altogether changes in the price level, particularly in the cost of living, is untenable. The mere fact that, in the period of rapid price changes that followed the 1914–18 war, a cost-of-living sliding-scale for wages was adopted over a wide range of industry in Great Britain is sufficient evidence of that. But there is also more recent evidence. Between 1924 and 1934 in this country there was a general reduction in weekly full-time rates of money wages for workpeople of corresponding grades of 6 per cent. Nor is this all : " This general average conceals wide variations in different groups of industries. In mining and quarrying and in the textile industry the reduction averaged about 15 per cent; in the building and contracting and certain materials group about 9 or 10 per cent ; in transport, 5 or 6 per cent ; in the chemical, engineering and metals, clothing, food and drink, paper and printing and electricity, gas and local authorities groups only about 1 or 2 per cent ; and the figures for agriculture show an increase averaging about 6 or 7 per cent." [1] Nobody, of course, doubts that money wage-rates in this country have always been sticky, in the sense that downward movements are resisted and are not brought about so rapidly as they would be in the absence of collective bargaining, wage boards and so on. Many would agree further that in the post-1918 period, during which unemployment insurance and assistance have greatly strengthened the hands of trade unions, this stickiness is more marked than it used to be. None the less, the evidence is conclusive that in this country they neither are now nor ever have been *rigid*. Now trade unions are certainly not less powerful in England than elsewhere. It is reasonable to infer, therefore, that in current

---

[1] *Statistical Journal*, 1935, Part IV, pp. 653-4.

conditions in the modern world as a whole money wage-rates are not rigid. This does not, of course, exclude the possibility of situations developing presently in which they *will be* rigid. For ordinary working purposes, however, we need not trouble about that. The first of our two conditions *is* satisfied.

§ 9. Turn to the second condition. There is a preliminary complication. If a fall in wages induces an expectation that they will shortly fall still further, some potential hirers of labour may hold up their demand, just as potential buyers of boots might do if an actual cheapening of boots were accompanied by an expectation that they would soon be cheaper still. It must be remembered, however, that labour is not, like boots, a durable commodity. If people do not hire to-day's labour to-day, they cannot hire it at all. Thus this consideration is probably less important than it seems to be at first sight. Moreover, when the impulse driving wage-rates down comes from the pressure of unemployment, everybody will know that, once a *sufficient* cut is made, the pressure will cease and, therefore, the downward tendency will stop. Hence, we may concentrate attention on cuts in money wage-rates not associated with expectations of further cuts, or, more strictly, on differences between money wage-rates as between two positions of short-period equilibrium in respect of which all the relevant functions are given. We have to show that lower levels of money wage-rates will in fact stimulate employers to engage more labour.

§ 10. In Chapters IV and V we found that with any monetary and banking policy likely to prevail in practice we might properly expect that $\left(\dfrac{\partial f}{\partial r} - \phi'\right), \dfrac{\partial f}{\partial F}.F', K_1'$ and K_2' would be positive; and, with a monetary and banking system directed successfully to keep the price level of

consumption goods in general constant, that $\left\{ \dfrac{K_1{}'}{K_1} - \dfrac{F'}{F} \right\}$
would be positive. Granted these signs, the formulae
obtained in the mathematical Appendix describing the
consequences of cuts in money wage-rates in the sense
defined above show that, alike under perfect and imperfect competition, cuts will stimulate employment.
The argument to this effect cannot be developed verbally
in a summary way. It will, however, be developed in
the course of the following Part, the results of the
analysis being brought together in the mathematical
Appendix.

§ 11. Both the conditions required to enable the
mechanism described in § 7 to work having been satisfied, the classical view may be said to have stood up
successfully against attack in the arena of theory. Let
us ask, then, how it fares when confronted with the facts,
or rather with that sample of them which is furnished
by the available British statistics. From 1853 down to
the outbreak of the 1914 war the evidence, for what
it is worth, goes to show that in this country employment, on the average of good and bad times together,
stood at an approximately constant percentage of the
available labour force. The percentage of men out of
work, as recorded by the trade unions, moved in a
succession of waves with fairly clear-cut maxima and
minima. During the course of each wave the percentage
varied widely. But, if we take the average annual percentages in the successive waves, whether we measure
the waves from one maximum to the year before the
next maximum, or from one minimum to the year before
the next, we find that the averages for all the waves
only differ slightly. The percentages for successive
waves measured in each of these two ways are given
in the following tables :

AVERAGE UNEMPLOYMENT FROM ONE MINIMUM YEAR TO
YEAR BEFORE NEXT MINIMUM YEAR

1853–59	.	.	5·2	1882–89 . . . 5·9
1860–64	.	.	4·8	1890–98 . . . 4·6
1865–71	.	.	4·7	1899–1905 . . 3·9
1872–81	.	.	4·2	1906–13 . . . 4·5

AVERAGE UNEMPLOYMENT FROM ONE MAXIMUM YEAR TO
YEAR BEFORE NEXT MAXIMUM YEAR

1852–57	.	.	4·4	1879–85 . . . 6·1
1858–61	.	.	5·7	1886–92 . . . 5·2
1862–67	.	.	5·0	1893–1903 . . 4·2
1868–78	.	.	3·8	1904–08 . . . 4·6

Thus according to these statistics the average percentage
of workpeople seeking employment, who were actually
employed, was never less than 94 per cent and never
more than 96 per cent over the whole series of waves
from 1853 to 1908, so that the average amount of employment and the available labour force must have
stood throughout in very nearly the same proportion to
one another. Meanwhile, the size of the available labour
force itself increased enormously. The Census figures
for the " gainfully occupied " population (males) for
Great Britain were in 1881 (the first year of record)
8·85 millions and in 1911, 12·93 millions. The growth
of the available labour force was, therefore, we may
presume, in the neighbourhood of 45 per cent. It is
a commonplace, of course, that the trade union figures,
based as they are on very limited data, do not provide
an exact measure of movements in the percentage of
employment. Even so, nobody can seriously doubt
that, during the period covered, very large percentage
changes in the available labour force were associated
with approximately equal percentage changes in the
quantity of labour normally employed. Broadly speaking, the volume of employment over the average of good

and bad times was a constant proportion of the available labour force.

§ 12. The period between 1919 and the outbreak of the second war hardly lasted long enough to enable us to compare the average levels of employment over a series of cycles. We cannot, therefore, say whether the percentage trend during this later period was or was not approximately horizontal. There can, however, be no doubt that, when full allowance has been made for changes in methods of record, the percentage of unemployment stood, in a general way, much higher than before. Whereas the average percentage over the pre-1914 period was about 4·5 and the maximum 11·9, between 1920 and 1938 the average was 13·3 and the maximum 21·9. What light does this summary of facts throw upon the conclusion to which theoretical analysis has led us ?

§ 13. The large excess in the average unemployment percentage in the inter-war period is readily explained by the great difference between the post-1918 and the pre-1914 economic setting — the peculiar circumstances of the distressed areas, the decay of the export trades, difficulties about transference of labour and the increased bargaining strength of trade unions consequent upon the development of unemployment insurance. It does not, therefore, in any way witness against the conclusion which theoretical analysis suggests. On the other hand, there is nothing in the post-1918 figures positively to support that conclusion.

§ 14. With the pre-1914 figures, however, the case is quite different. The great stability of the average percentage of employment through a long succession of cycles is strong evidence — since obviously employment cannot determine the size of the available labour force — that the size of this force was the dominant determinant of the average volume of employment. Either the economic setting, in the matter of friction, mobility and so on, varied very little, or, if it varied seriously, the influence of its variation was almost completely masked and overwhelmed. For this period, then, there is strong statistical support for the classical view. The history of fifty years in a single country can never, of course, *prove* any proposition of a general kind ; and theoretical analysis, in a field where so many things are possible and relevant considerations are so easily overlooked, must always be to some extent provisional. Still, in this examination the classical view as it really is — to be carefully distinguished from current caricatures of it — has not, I suggest, done badly.

CHAPTER VII

MARSHALL ON THE RATE OF INTEREST

§ 1. IT is not the purpose of this book to criticise other writers. The argument of the preceding chapter has, however, a close connection with Keynes' attack on Marshall's treatment in his *Principles* of the rate of interest. Some discussion of the matter is not, therefore, out of place.

§ 2. Marshall wrote : " Interest, being the price paid for the use of capital in any market, tends towards an equilibrium level, such that the aggregate demand for capital in that market at that rate of interest is equal to the aggregate stock forthcoming at that rate ".[1] That is to say, the rate of interest and the amount of real income devoted to investment tend to be so adjusted that the quantity of real income demanded for investment at that rate of interest is equal to the quantity offered at that rate ; in such wise that there are no demands unsatisfied and no offers declined.

[1] *Principles*, p. 534. From the context it is clear that " stock " is here used (somewhat unfortunately) as a synonym for flow. At first sight there might seem to be an ambiguity in the above statement, because Marshall does not say whether he conceives interest as measured in terms of money or in terms of some specifiable composite commodity, *i.e.* whether he is speaking of money interest or of real interest. The *Principles* are, however, worked out upon the explicit assumption that values are " expressed in terms of money of a fixed purchasing power " (p. 534), so that the money rate of interest and the real rate of interest must be identical. In view of this, there seems to be no ground for " the perplexity " which Keynes said he felt at " the incursion of the concept interest [by which he means money interest], which belongs to a monetary economy, into a treatise which takes no account of money ". (*General Theory*, p. 189.)

§ 3. For any period, then, the quantity demanded and the quantity supplied may each be expressed as a function of the rate of interest alone. If s is written for the quantity of real investment, and r for the rate of interest, s and r are determined by a demand equation $s = \phi(r)$ together with a supply equation $s = f(r)$. This conception has been attacked in strong terms by Keynes on the ground that the supply of investment is in fact a function of *two* variables, the volume of employment as well as the rate of interest.

§ 4. It will be well to clear out of the way a preliminary matter, about which there is no dispute. In Marshall's account there is, as the reader will have noticed, no explicit reference to productive capacity as an element affecting the supply of real investment. *Prima facie*, therefore, this supply appears to be regarded as independent of productive capacity. But, of course, Marshall did not in fact so regard it. *Per contra*, he states expressly that saving — which here means the same thing as supply of real investment — depends, not merely on the will, but also on the power to save.[1] Thus — and nobody seriously denies this — his supply function is what it is because the community's productive power is what it is. The quantity of real investment supplied at any time depends, in his view, both on the rate of interest offered and on the community's productive power. But this productive power, while, of course, a consequence of economic happenings in the past, and so gradually altering as more and more productive power in the shape of capital equipment is accumulated, is, from the standpoint of any *present* time, a constant. It does not and should not appear as a variable. Account is taken of it in the *form* of the function.

[1] *Principles*, Book IV, chap. vii, § 10.

§ 5. So much is clear and evidently legitimate. Keynes, however, points out that the quantity of resources for investment offered at a given rate of interest is dependent, not merely on the community's productive power, but also on the extent to which that power is employed. Clearly, if only half of it were employed, real income would be so far reduced that the quantity, and, indeed, the proportion, of income, whether expressed in real or in money terms, offered for investment would very likely be quite different from what it would be with productive resources fully employed. Hence, unless it is premised that the quantity of resources, or, for simplicity, of labour employed, is determined, so to speak, from outside, in such wise that, in considering investment and interest, we are entitled to regard it as a constant, Marshall's analysis breaks down. He is, in effect, either representing the supply function of resources for investment as a function of one variable, whereas it is in fact a function of two, or, alternatively, if he realises that it is a function of two variables, he is imagining that a system containing two equations and three unknowns is determinate ; which is, of course, ridiculous. Keynes believes that Marshall has committed one or other of these gross blunders ; and this is the essence of his attack on what he calls the classical school.

§ 6. The answer to this charge is perfectly clear. Marshall in his *Principles* was studying long-run tendencies. Industrial fluctuations were to have been the subject of a later volume, which, to our great misfortune, was never written.[1] For the investigation of long-run tendencies he *does* premise that the quantity

---

[1] Critics of Marshall at the present day do not always remember, what is obvious to his pupils, that the *Principles* was conceived as an introductory volume.

of labour employed is determined, so to speak, from outside, in such a way that, in discussions of investment and interest, it may be taken as given. He regards it as determined by the quantity of people available for work in the sense explained in the first chapter of Part I. Had he not regarded it so, he would have been guilty of the formal fallacy with which Keynes charges him. As things are, his structure is quite untouched by this criticism. The critic has simply failed to understand him.

CHAPTER VIII

THE SIZES OF AVAILABLE REAL INCOMES AND THE PROPORTIONS SAVED

§ 1. THE subject matter of this chapter lies off the route of our main argument. But the method of analysis developed in it opens the way to the problem to be tackled in the chapter which follows — a chapter which forms, so to speak, the terminus of that route. In view of this, and also because the present subject matter is, I think, of interest for its own sake, I have included the chapter here in spite of the fact that large parts of it are really logical excrescences. It will, of course, be plain to the reader that the symbols x, ϕ and η, as used in this chapter, have meanings different from their meanings in other parts of the volume.

§ 2. In any given situation everybody has a certain income, out of which he makes a certain amount of saving, in the sense of income minus expenditure on consumption ; which may be positive, nil or negative. Thus, in respect of any income period, there is necessarily some arithmetical relation between every man's income and his saving.

§ 3. In modern States, for many persons, a substantial part of accruing income is not available to them, in the sense that they are in a position to control its use. Thus the undistributed profits of companies are strictly a part of the incomes of the shareholders, belonging to them in proportion to their several holdings : though

H

it is not, of course, customary to reckon them as such. Again, the Government absorbs in taxation, if indirect taxes are taken into account, some proportion of nearly all incomes ; for very large incomes the proportion in England approached (under the war budgets) towards 97½ per cent. Now the proportion which is saved from any total income is affected by what is done with those non-available parts of it, over whose disposition the income receivers have no control.[1] Clearly, therefore, we cannot hope to find a general rule for the way in which saving varies with income in respect of *total* income. We can only consider *available* incomes in relation to the saving made out of them. My problem is concerned with the comparative proportions in which individuals with available incomes of different sizes may be expected to make savings.

§ 4. At first sight it might seem that this problem is eminently one for the statistician. We should study the facts for the country and period in which we are interested. Since the proportion of available income that a man saves obviously depends on a great variety of other factors besides his present income, we certainly should not find that all men with the same income save the same proportion. But we could find for incomes of all sizes the average proportions that were saved — the proportions that the average or representative man at each income level saves. The data could be set out in such a way as to show whether there was in fact, in the country and at the period under review, any tendency

---

[1] It is sometimes a condition of employment that a certain part of the employee's income shall be contributed to a pension or insurance fund. This part is, in a sense, not available. But for my purpose it is, I think, best regarded as available. For often the saving made in this way is *alternative* to other saving that the employees would have made had there been no contribution rule ; and, whether this is so or not, what they do with the remainder of their income is, in general, affected by the fact that they are saving this part. It would thus, I think, be more misleading to exclude than to include it.

for the proportion of available income saved to rise, remain unchanged or fall as available income rose ; whether the tendency was different in direction or in force over different ranges of available income ; and so on. This information, if we could obtain it, would be valuable. It would not, indeed, completely satisfy our curiosity. We should still need to *explain* how it came about that the facts were what they were. But it would constitute at least a secure platform and jumping-off place. Unfortunately, statistics of the kind required are not in any country adequate for a full-dress statistical investigation. I propose, therefore, in the main part of this chapter, to attack ˙my problem theoretically. In a final section I shall refer briefly to two statistical studies carried out in the United States for 1935–36.

§ 5. At the outset it should be emphasised that our problem differs in a fundamental respect from that of determining the proportions of incomes of various sizes that will be saved by any community or country as a whole. For the community a complex of interacting influences determines alike the total amount of income in the community, the total amount of saving and the rate of interest. For an individual, however, the amount that he decides to save does not appreciably affect either the size (at the time) of his income or the rate of interest. Moreover, while for the community there may, in certain states of disequilibrium, be a difference between what, in a sense, the public wish to save and what they do save, for the reason that A's saving may affect B's income, for a comparison among individuals there is no such distinction. What they wish to save and what they do save are the same thing.

§ 6. This being understood, it is further clear that our theoretical analysis can only proceed on an " other

things being equal " basis. In actual life different men
have different natures, so that even in the same situation their actions will diverge. We must, to get over
this, confine ourselves to the question; What differences
in saving will be entailed by differences in available
incomes for men who are essentially similar in general
make-up ? Again, different men have very different
responsibilities as regards size of family and so on. We
must suppose our similar men to have similar responsibilities. Yet again, different men may have very
different expectations. One expects to be superannu-
ated and to be much poorer twenty years hence than he
is now ; another to inherit property and to be much
richer. Again, one looks forward to having presently
a family to feed and educate, and, later on, as his children grow up, expects that they will be able to support
themselves ; another reckons upon being a permanent
Benedict. Obviously, of men with equal incomes now,
those who look forward to a future of greater needs and
smaller incomes will save more than those whose expectations are of an opposite sort. Hence for our
present purpose we ought, at least in the first instance,[1] to compare men whose expectations are similar.
The simplest way to do this is to assume that each of
our men expects henceforward to enjoy, apart from the
fruit of saving, a real income equal to what he is enjoying
now, and also to be subject to the same responsibilities,
as regards dependants and so on, as he is subject to now.
In like manner and for similar reasons, we assume that
each of our men expects the rate of money interest and
the general price level to be substantially the same in
the future as they are now, or, more exactly, that he
acts as though he expected this. The argument can be
further simplified without any difference being made to

[1] Cf. *post*, § 20.

its essence by adding the somewhat extravagant further assumption that each of our men expects to live for ever.

§ 7. There is a further complication. Consider two men who are similar in general make-up, both of whom have hitherto been accustomed to incomes of, say, £600 and have saved, say, £50 a year. One of them finds his income increased to £2000. It is certain that the proportion of the new income that he saves while he is still habituated to the £600 income level will be much larger than it will be later on when he has become habituated to the £2000 level. More generally, the proportions of various incomes that any man of given character and responsibilities might be expected to save depend largely on what the income level is to which he is accustomed. It is essential to avoid ambiguity about this. To that end the present discussion will be restricted to men each of whom is habituated to that scale of available income that he is actually receiving. Fundamental similarity in their character, as postulated above, implies, not that, having different incomes, they have the same standard of life, which, of course, would be very unlikely, but merely that, if A, who is accustomed to a £600 income, had been accustomed to a £2000 one, he would have acted in the way that B, who is in fact accustomed to that income, does act ; and vice versa.[1]

§ 8. In these conditions the factors *prima facie* relevant to the proportion of income saved may be set out as follows. The first factor is the amount of a man's *real* income. Plainly it makes no difference to the proportion whether money income is large and prices high

---

[1] Had we been considering the effect of *changes* in the amount of an individual's income on the amount of his saving, we should have had to note further that this effect is likely to be different if A's income alone is, say, halved or doubled, from what it would be if he and his friends and neighbours were all in the same boat. But for comparisons between different men, all with established incomes, this class of consideration does not arise.

or money income small and prices correspondingly low. The significant thing is not money income but real income. Since, however, we are concerned with the comparative saving policy of different people in the same environment, the price level will be the same for all of them, and may be taken as a given fact. Thus, since for our problem the relation of money income to real income is fixed, differences among the real incomes of individuals can be *represented* by differences in their money incomes ; so that we may speak indifferently in terms of either. This, of course, would not be so if we were making a comparison between people at different periods in which price levels were different. The second factor is the rate of interest — on our assumption that prices are not expected to change there can be no difference between real rate and money rate — which is ruling in the market for loans of given maturity and given degree of risk. The complex of rates ruling for loans of different maturities and different degrees of risk may be *represented* for our purpose by the rate yielded by money spent on Consols. This is to be regarded, for the purposes of our problem, as fixed by the conditions governing the general equilibrium, and is independent of the comparative saving policy of particular individuals. The third factor is the rate at which our man, or rather all the men we are comparing, discount, in respect of each several income level, future satisfactions, and so, in the conditions of stability here assumed, future incomes. This rate is sometimes more compendiously called the rate of time preference. For any man, in respect of a given income, it might, of course, be different for periods of different lengths, *e.g.* 5 per cent per annum for a one-year postponement and 6 per cent per annum for, say, a two-year postponement, and so on. Any type of irregularity whose nature is known could be dealt with by a sufficiently elaborate algebraic analysis. For simplicity, however, it will be assumed that our men's rate of time preference per annum, when they have a given income, is the same for periods of all lengths. This rate *may* be different for similar men, according as they are in receipt of large or small incomes. Whether it is in fact different will be considered presently. The fourth factor is the schedule of marginal utilities that would be derived by our typically constituted man from different quantities of income, *to which he has become accustomed*, devoted to consumption — which we may call, if we will, his consumption marginal utility curve, or, for brevity and euphony, his consumption utility curve. A fifth factor is the present value of the direct amenity utility, in the form of power, sense of security and so on, if any, which a typically constituted man expects to derive from *having* his marginal unit of present saving, as distinct from the utility which he expects the future incomes due to that unit to yield. These factors together determine, for each several level of available income, for what amount of saving the marginal satisfactions from income consumed and from income saved will be equal, and, therefore, what amount, and so proportion, of income will be saved.

§ 9. The above factors determine this, however, only if we make some definite assumption about our man's future intentions. Thus, if a man intends to keep his saving invested for *n* years, consuming its yield every year, and to withdraw the principal and consume that after *n* years, the proportion of income he will wish to save this year will be different according as *n* has a small, a large or an infinite value. *In what follows I shall postulate that such saving as is made is intended to be permanent.* Even so, a number of alternative assumptions are possible. Most of the implications of a general kind concerning the relation between size of income and amount of saving will be similar on any plausible assumption. Plainly, however, the precise formula expressing this relation will, except in the special case of nil saving,[1] be different with different assumptions ; so that for a clear-cut treatment we must concentrate on some definite one. An assumption especially easy to handle would be that our men reckon (i) never to withdraw the principal of their saving for consumption and (ii) to consume in the future the whole of their income. It is, however, unlikely that anyone, who expects, as we are supposing everyone to do, that he will receive, apart from the fruits of saving, the same income in the future as he is receiving now, will reckon to save something from his present, but not from his future incomes. A more satisfactory assumption, therefore, is that a man saves in this year, or other short period, so much income, designing to tuck away permanently as principal what he saves now, and then to save next year the same proportion of his then income as he saves this year from his present income. This assumption, which Mr. Champernowne proposed to me, I shall adopt.[2] When it is merely a question of determining the conditions in which a man will save nothing, the same result follows from this assumption as from the one distinguished above. But in the general case this is not so.

§ 10. It will help to clarify the discussion that follows if we begin by setting out the conditions in which it will

---

[1] Cf. *post*, last paragraph of note to § 11.

[2] In an unpublished paper Mr. Champernowne has shown that this assumption is not an arbitrary one, but is in ordinary cases consequential on a man, who expects his income from work henceforward to be constant, planning his consumption so as to maximise his future satisfaction discounted at his rate of time preference.

be to a man's interest to make no saving and no dis-saving (negative saving). What will these conditions be ? First, let us ignore what I have called the amenity value of *having* some saving as distinct from deriving income from it, *i.e.* let us regard this amenity value as nil. In this case — subject, of course, to the provisos set out in § 6 — our man will save nothing and dissave nothing if his rate of time preference is exactly equal to the rate of interest. This is a well-known proposi-tion. Anyone to whom it is not apparent is referred to Frank Ramsey's article on " The Mathematical Theory of Saving ", in the *Economic Journal* of December 1928. Secondly, let us reckon with the fact that to *have* some saving probably does yield to our man some amenity utility. Plainly the prospect of this will afford him some inducement to save. Consequently, if his rate of time preference is equal to the rate of interest, he will save something. In order that he may save nothing, his rate of time preference must exceed the rate of interest by an amount sufficient to compensate for the amenity value of his marginal unit of saving. We may express this by saying that our man will neither save nor dis-save, provided that his rate of time preference minus a specifiable correcting factor is equal to the rate of interest. But this is not the only condition in which a man will save and dissave nothing. He will also do this if the relevant part of his consumption utility curve is absolutely, or very nearly absolutely, inelastic ; which implies that he is very poor indeed. There are thus two conditions, such that, if *either* of them is satisfied, our man will not save anything. If we write r for the rate of interest, q_x for the rate of time preference of a man with income x, v_x for the correcting factor for such a man, and η_x for the elasticity (defined as positive) of his con-sumption utility curve for consumption x, he will save nothing provided that *either* $(r + v_x - q_x) = 0$ *or*, to a close approximation, $\eta_x = 0$.[1]

§ 11. Let us now pass to conditions in which η_x is sensibly positive, and in which $(r + v_x - q_x)$ is not nil.

Let us write a for the amount, and $\dfrac{a}{x}$ for the proportion of his income that our man saves. Can we construct a formula that will tell us the relation between the proportion $\dfrac{a}{x}$, on the one hand, and the elements, rate of interest, rate of time preference, correcting factor and elasticity of consumption utility curve, all in respect of consumption $(x - a)$, on the other ? It is, I am afraid, impossible to arrive at such a formula by unaided common sense. From what was said in the last paragraph we might guess at an equation, into one side of which $(r + v_{x-a} - q_{x-a})$ enters, while the other side is *relevant to* our man's saving. But, as to whether the other side should be a or $\dfrac{a}{x}$ or some more complex expression involving a, common sense can proffer no hint. Mathematical analysis, as shown in the footnote,[2] yields,

---

[1] The reason for the qualification " to a close approximation " is that the formula given at the end of the section that follows, as is apparent from the accompanying footnote, is obtained by ignoring second differentials. If these were not ignored, $\dfrac{a}{x}$ would appear as a multiple, not of η_x, but of η_x plus or minus some small quantity.

[2] We have x for income, a for saving, q_{x-a} for our man's rate of time preference when he has income x and consumption $(x - a)$, $\phi(x - a)$ for the marginal utility of consumption $(x - a)$, η_{x-a} for the elasticity of the consumption utility function in respect of consumption $(x - a)$, r for the rate of interest, which, from the standpoint of an individual, is given, and $U_{S, (x-a)}$ for the amenity utility derived from *holding* the marginal unit of income x for a year instead of consuming it now. In this last expression S represents our man's holding of accumulated capital, and the form $U_{S, (x-a)}$ has been chosen to indicate that its value depends partly on S and partly on $(x - a)$.

On the assumption set out in § 9 of the text, equilibrium requires that, when the element $U_{S, (x-a)}$ is nil, the utility of the last £ spent this year shall be equal to what the utility of this £ would be if it were invested and so were

however, on the assumption set out at the end of § 9, and provided that a is small relatively to x, the following approximate formula :

$$\frac{a}{x} = \frac{\eta_{x-a}}{r} \cdot \left\{ r + v_{x-a} - q_{x-a} \right\}.$$

§ 12. From the above formula it appears that $\dfrac{a}{x}$

to become £$(1+r)$ to be consumed next year, discounted at our man's rate of time preference. That is to say, it is equal to $(1+r)$ times the discounted value of the marginal £ spent next year. When the element $U_{8,\,(x-a)}$ is not nil it is equal to the above value plus $\dfrac{U_{8,\,(x-a)}}{1+q_{x-a}}$. Hence we have the equation

$$\phi(x-a) = \phi\left\{ (x+ra)\left(1-\frac{a}{x}\right)\right\}\frac{1+r}{1+q_{x-a}} + \frac{U_{8,\,(x-a)}}{1+q_{x-a}}, \qquad \text{(I)}$$

i.e. $$\phi(x-a) = \phi\left\{ (x-a)\left(1+\frac{ra}{x}\right)\right\}\frac{1+r}{1+q_{x-a}} + \frac{U_{8,\,(x-a)}}{1+q_{x-a}}. \qquad \text{(II)}$$

Provided the a is sufficiently small relatively to x to allow second and higher powers of a to be ignored, this equation yields

$$\frac{a}{x} = \frac{\eta_{x-a}}{r(1+r)} \cdot \left\{ r - q_{x-a} + \frac{U_{8,\,(x-a)}}{\phi(x-a)} \right\}, \qquad \text{(III)}$$

where η_x means, as in Marshall's usage, $-\dfrac{\phi}{x\phi'}$, not $\dfrac{\phi}{x\phi'}$. If we write v_{x-a} for $\dfrac{U_{8,\,(x-a)}}{\phi(x-a)}$, this equation becomes

$$\frac{a}{x} = \frac{\eta_{(x-a)}}{r(1+r)} \cdot \left\{ r + v_{x-a} - q_{x-a} \right\}.$$

When periods are taken so short that r is very small indeed relatively to unity, this equation approximates to that given in the text, namely

$$\frac{a}{x} = \frac{\eta_{x-a}}{r} \cdot \left\{ r + v_{x-a} - q_{x-a} \right\}. \qquad \text{(IV)}$$

From equation IV it follows that $a = 0$ provided that $r + v_{x-a} - q_{x-a} = 0$, which, when $v_{x-a} = 0$, is equivalent to the condition, $r - q_{x-a} = 0$. It is easy to see that this condition is the same as would have been obtained with the alternative assumption suggested, but not developed, in § 9, namely that our man expects to invest the same absolute amount in future years, which is, in this case, nothing, that he is investing now. The marginal utility of income consumed must then be equal to the discounted value of the marginal utilities of all future yields from the marginal £ of investment now plus the discounted value of all future marginal utilities derived from *holding* that £ invested. That is to say, $\phi(x) = \dfrac{r}{q_x} \cdot \phi(x) + \dfrac{U_{8,\,x}}{q_x}$; which, of course, can be transposed into

$$r - q_x + \frac{U_{8,\,x}}{\phi(x)} = 0, \text{ or } r + v_x - q_x = 0.$$

may be either positive or negative. Clearly η_{x-a}, where η is defined in Marshall's manner, cannot be negative. Therefore $\dfrac{a}{x}$ is positive or negative according as $\{r + v_{x-a} - q_{x-a}\}$ is positive or negative. *In order not to confuse the argument, I shall confine attention, in the analytical portion of what follows, to the cases in which $\{r + v_{x-a} - q_{x-a}\}$ is positive, and, therefore, saving only, not dissaving, can occur.* Since, for the purposes of our problem, r is given, it follows that, provided neither of the two conditions for nil saving (or dissaving) is satisfied, $\dfrac{a}{x}$ is larger, the larger is η_{x-a} and the larger is $\{v_{x-a} - q_{x-a}\}$. It follows that, over any range in respect of which both η_{x-a} and $\{v_{x-a} - q_{x-a}\}$ increase with x, the proportion of income saved is larger for larger than for smaller incomes ; and conversely. Over ranges in respect of which η_{x-a} and $\{v_{x-a} - q_{x-a}\}$ move in opposite senses as x increases, it is not possible to say how the proportion of income saved is related to size of income, unless the magnitudes, throughout the relevant range, of the elements η, v and q are known. Plainly, the next stage is to ascertain what, if anything, can be known about the relation of these magnitudes to the size of incomes.

§ 13. Consider first the elasticity of different parts of the consumption utility curve, or, more generally, the form of that curve. If our schedule, curve or function referred to a man accustomed to one single level of income, there would be no doubt at all that for him the marginal utility of consumption would be smaller for larger than for smaller incomes. For our actual problem, when each man is supposed to be accustomed to his actual income, this is not quite so clear. Marginal utility will not fall so rapidly with increases of consumption in this case. Still, over a considerable range, the curve seems sure to be a falling one. Can we say anything beyond this about its form ? Relying only upon judgment and vague experience, we observe that there are certain urgent needs, which are presumably very similar whether a man is accustomed to a large consumption or to a small one. This suggests that the earlier — left-hand — parts of our curve are likely to be specially inelastic, and that, over the region of very small and small consumptions, they will become progressively more elastic. That is to say, for values of $(x - a)$ below a certain moderate maximum, elasticity *probably* increases as consumption grows. Thereafter it probably becomes approximately constant at a high level.[1]

§ 14. *Prima facie* it seems impossible for anything further to be known on this matter. We must not, however, rest content with *prima facie* impressions. There are in existence a number of different people with very various real incomes, to which they have respectively become accustomed. A substantial body of data about these real incomes being thus available, it would be rash to rule out *a priori* the possibility of educing from them something further and more exact. There is, indeed, a difficulty. What our analysis requires is information about the form of the *consumption* utility curve, while the available data are about incomes. But it is easy to see that when, as is in general the case, the proportion of income saved is small (*i.e.* where a is small relatively to x), the elasticity of the consumption utility curve in respect of consumption $(x - a)$ will only differ very slightly from the elasticity of the income

---

[1] Consumptions below the *strict* minimum of subsistence may, of course, be ruled out of account ; for, by definition, people with such incomes cannot live.

utility curve in respect of income x.[1] Within this region, therefore, if it can be shown that the elasticity of the income utility curve increases rapidly as income increases, we are entitled to infer that the elasticity of the consumption utility curve will increase rapidly as consumption increases.

§ 15. Now Prof. Ragnar Frisch has devised a method for measuring the elasticity of the income utility curve in respect of small incomes by manipulating the material yielded by investigations into family budgets. For the range of material studied by him, the elasticity of the income utility curve does, in fact, increase rapidly as real income increases. Broadly speaking, as between the lowest family income and an income three times as large, he found that it multiplied itself three times.[2] We infer, then, for incomes on this level, that the elasticity of the consumption utility curve also increases rapidly as consumption increases. Higher ranges of income are not covered by Prof. Frisch's data, and extrapolation here is dangerous. Still, in the absence of other evidence, Prof. Frisch's work creates, I think, some presumption — a *little* extrapolation seems legitimate — that, at all events until incomes of a moderate size, say, for this country, from £500 to a £1000 per year, are reached, the elasticity of the consumption utility curve will in fact be larger, the larger is x. For higher incomes it may no longer increase as x increases. There is nothing to suggest that it will

----

[1] For, writing η_1 for the elasticity of the income utility curve in respect of income x, and η_2 for that of the consumption utility curve of consumption $(x - a)$, where a is the amount saved from income x, we obtain

$$\eta_2 = \eta_1 \cdot \frac{d(x - a)}{(x - a)} \cdot \frac{x}{dx}.$$

[2] More exactly, while income rose 2·7 times, elasticity rose 2·3 times — from -0.16 to -0.38. (*New Methods of Measuring Marginal Utility*, p. 64.)

decrease, but neither have we any assurance that it will not do so.

§ 16. Turn next to the element q_{x-a}, *i.e.* the rate of time preference of a man accustomed to consumption $(x - a)$. We may take it, I think, that q_{x-a} can in no circumstances be negative. I can see no reason to believe that a man enjoying and accustomed to a consumption of any given size will have a *higher* rate of time preference than a man of similar nature enjoying and accustomed to a smaller one. As between two men with different consumptions, both of which are very large, I can equally see no reason to believe that the man with the larger consumption will have a *lower* rate of time preference than the other. But with consumptions on a low scale things are different. With a very small consumption the pressure of present needs is so urgent that it tends to blind us to the future. This is evident in other fields. Thus a man with a slight toothache will weigh up more or less rationally the benefit of immediate extraction against the disadvantages of subsequent false teeth. But a man with a violent toothache will have his attention so focused on the pain of the moment that he will vote for immediate extraction without thinking about future consequences at all. This class of consideration, I think, makes it certain that q_{x-a} will be larger for very small consumptions than for moderate ones ; but after consumptions — and incomes — have passed a certain moderate size, q_{x-a} may stand at a practically constant level.

§ 17. There remains the element v_{x-a}, which I have called the correcting factor. In the footnote to § 11, v_{x-a} was defined as equal to $\dfrac{U_{s,(x-a)}}{\phi(x - a)}$, where $\phi(x - a)$ is the marginal utility of consumption $(x - a)$. Now the magnitude of $U_{s,(x-a)}$ depends, as is indicated in that footnote, upon two things, (i) the level of a man's consumption $(x - a)$, and (ii) the size of his stock of already accumulated capital, S.   It is certain that to a man with a small income a much larger amenity, in the form of sense of security, is yielded by the possession of a pound in store than to a man with a large one ; and we may fairly suppose, in the absence of knowledge, that a larger amount of amenity in general is yielded to him.   Again, it is certain that a £ of new saving yields more amenity when added to a small store than when added to a large one ; and there is a general presumption that, other things being equal, the larger a man's scale of income, the larger (partly as cause and partly as effect) the stock of capital that he is likely to have.   It follows, in a rough general way, that $U_{s, (x-a)}$ is likely to be largest for men with small consumptions, and to grow progressively smaller, with a rate of progression presumably falling, as consumptions increase.   As we have seen, however, v_{x-a}, the correcting factor, is equal, not to $U_{s, (x-a)}$, but to $\dfrac{U_{s, (x-a)}}{\phi(x - a)}$; and, as x increases, it is almost certain that the denominator $\phi(x - a)$ falls.   Hence it need not happen that v_{x-a} is smaller for large than for small values of $(x - a)$.   We have, indeed, no means of knowing in what sense the magnitude of v_{x-a} varies for given variations in $(x - a)$.

§ 18. We are now in a position to summarise the practical consequences of our abstract analysis in conjunction with the judgments about fact to which we were led in the preceding sections.   Let us begin by considering the problem on the assumption that the correcting factor is nil or negligible throughout.   We then have the following results.   First, for very small available incomes the proportion saved will be nil, or, all events, extremely small.   This follows from the fact that the income utility curve for very small incomes is highly inelastic. Secondly, as incomes move up from the low level at which there is no saving to a comparatively high level, we have found that (i) a more elastic part of the consumption utility curve is likely to be reached, and (ii) the rate of time preference is likely to fall. Each of these alterations taken separately implies, other things equal, that the proportion of income saved will be larger for larger than for smaller incomes. Since an increase in income carries with it both of them, it follows that, over this range of incomes, the proportionate amount saved is almost sure to be larger for larger than for smaller incomes. In the range of high and very high incomes the situation is less clear. The rate of time preference will very likely remain constant as incomes rise, while the elasticity of the relevant part of the consumption utility curve may, for all we know, decrease. It may happen, therefore, that the proportion of income saved will fall off. On the face of things, however, it seems very unlikely that the absolute amount saved will do other than continue to grow.

§ 19. How are these conclusions modified when account is taken of the fact that the correcting factor is not likely to be nil or negligible throughout? In view of what was said in § 17, the correct answer, as it seems to me, is that these conclusions are not overthrown, but are rendered insecure. On the data accessible to us they remain *probable* conclusions. But, since we are aware of other data, incapable of evaluation, which *may* reverse them, we can only regard them as provisional. Plainly the proposition that the *absolute amount* of income saved will be larger for larger than for smaller incomes is less insecure than the corresponding proposition about the proportion of income saved.

I

§ 20. One further point may be added. The whole of the foregoing analysis has been based on the assumption that the men we are comparing expect to have, apart from the fruits of saving, the same incomes in the future as they have now. What we have been studying is, therefore, the comparative saving policy that different persons, all subjected to this condition, are likely to pursue. Of course, in fact, few persons expect to have the same incomes (or responsibilities) in the future as they have now. Nevertheless, our results can be extended with a reasonable degree of probability to real life, provided that our comparisons are confined to two or more classes of persons, in each of which the members may be expected *on the average* to violate this postulate either in the same sort of way, or, if they violate it in different ways, in ways whose divergence is of a kind favourable to our results. Thus, if, as a general rule, poor people expected to have smaller incomes in the future and rich people larger, our analysis would *not* allow any confident inference about the comparative savings policy likely to be pursued by rich and poor persons in real life. In fact, however, there is ground for believing that poor people are more likely than rich people to expect growing incomes, particularly if we extend our view beyond a single life and bring into account the long-term effects of heavy progressive death duties. This consideration suggests that the case for expecting rich people to save proportionately more than poor people is stronger, not weaker, in the conditions of real life than it is in the simplified conditions assumed in our analysis.

§ 21. Let us turn in conclusion to the American statistical studies, both based on data for 1935–36, which were referred to in § 4. The analytical basis is as follows. With x written for income and a for saving, the problem is to determine the value of $\frac{d}{dx}\left(\frac{a}{x}\right)$ for various income levels. Write E for what is usually called the elasticity of saving in relation to income, namely $\left(\frac{da}{a} \div \frac{dx}{x}\right)$. It is easily shown that $\frac{d}{dx}\left(\frac{a}{x}\right) = \frac{a}{x^2}(E - 1)$. Therefore $\frac{d}{dx}\left(\frac{a}{x}\right)$ is positive or negative according as E is greater or less than unity, and is larger (if positive), the larger is E.

In the *Quarterly Journal of Economics* for November 1938, Mrs. Gilboy investigated the values of E for a number of groups in the United States.[1] The broad result of her study is to show that the relation of income to saving differs, as we should expect, " according to level of incomes, place, occupation and degree of urbanisation ".[2] But, over the main body of the data covered, it is found that E varies from 3 to 9 for incomes below 2000 or 2500 dollars in five regions that have been studied ; that for larger incomes up to about 10,000 dollars — the limit for which there are adequate data — it is less, dropping to approximately 2 for all five regions.[3] This implies that up to 10,000 dollars the proportion of income saved increases as income increases ; but the rate at which the proportion grows is, in general, smaller for larger than for smaller incomes.

In an article in the *American Economic Review* of September 1939 on " The Relationship between Income and Savings of American Metropolitan Families ", Mr. Mendershausen has obtained results for incomes under

---

[1] Unfortunately Mrs. Gilboy cast her article into the form of a criticism of Keynes, who, she asserted, had maintained, as a general psychological law, the proposition that $\frac{d}{dx}\left(\frac{a}{x}\right)$ is always positive. In fact, Keynes' proposition is that $\frac{d}{dx}(a)$ is always positive.

[2] *Loc. cit.* p. 138.   [3] *Ibid.* p. 137.

10,000 dollars, which confirm the above conclusions. But he also makes a further point, which Mrs. Gilboy, who, as I have done, intentionally left aside negative saving,[1] did not bring out. He shows that at very low income levels average families not merely save nothing, but incur deficits : and that the " break-even point ", at which there are neither savings nor deficits, varies in the different cities studied from 2290 dollar incomes in New York to 1310 dollar incomes in Columbus (Ohio).[2]

For incomes of over 10,000 dollars the statistics available to these two writers are not adequate to allow of any clear-cut conclusions. But the general tendency for E to fall as income grows over the ranges of income that they have studied suggests that for very large incomes it might well fall to 1 or less than 1. That is to say, the proportion of incomes saved might no longer grow as income grows, but, *per contra*, as the reasoning of § 18 suggested, might even contract. It may be well, however, to repeat that for the proportion of income saved to contract as income grows does not imply that the absolute amount of income saved contracts.[3]

---

[1] *Quarterly Journal of Economics*, Nov. 1938, p. 135.

[2] *Loc. cit.* p. 526.

[3] For, in order that $\frac{d}{dx}(a)$ may be negative, $\left\{ \frac{d}{dx}\left(\frac{a}{x}\right) + \frac{a}{x^2} \right\}$, not merely $\frac{d}{dx}\left(\frac{a}{x}\right)$, must be negative.

CHAPTER IX

THE SPECIAL CASE OF LONG-PERIOD FLOW EQUILIBRIUM

§ 1. WE now return to the main argument. For an economic system to be in long-period flow equilibrium is the same thing as for it to be in a stationary state. The introduction of new inventions, varied techniques and shifts in people's attitude towards the future are, of course, precluded. All the conditions requisite to short-period flow equilibrium must be satisfied, and *also* the quantity of labour for investment that is supplied, besides being equal to the quantity demanded, must be equal to 0. It might be thought at first sight that to introduce this new condition must, since a system in short-period flow equilibrium is already determinate, involve over-determination. But that is not so. In the formulae of Part II, Chapter III, we were able to write $\phi(r)$ for the demand function for labour for investment, and $F(x)$ for the output of consumption goods due to x units of labour. But that was because we were referring to specified times, at which the stock of accumulated capital equipment in existence was given. From a more general point of view, when this stock cannot be taken as given, these functions give place to the functions $\phi(r, S)$ and $F(x, S)$, where S is the amount of the stock. From our present standpoint S is an additional unknown, which allows of there being an additional equation. Thus we have, for long-period flow equilibrium, a first set of three equations

$$\phi(r, S) = f\{r, F(x, S)\},$$
$$y = f\{r, F(x, S)\},$$
$$y = 0,$$

in place of the first set of two equations,

$$\phi(r) = f\{r, F(x)\},$$
$$y = f\{r, F(x)\},$$

which we found appropriate for short-period flow equilibrium. When any further pair of two equations is added, we have five equations and five unknowns; and the system is, in general, determinate. If a stationary state — long-period flow equilibrium — is to exist at all, it must necessarily conform to these conditions.

§ 2. Moreover, the money rate of wage must be such as to satisfy whatever form of the fourth equation (corresponding to the third equation of Part II, Chapter III) is appropriate to the policy which the banks elect to follow. If we accept the " classical view " as expounded in Chapter VI, in a stationary state, since no disturbances occur there, " full " employment must prevail; which implies that the fifth and last equation must be of the form $(x + y) = Q$ (constant). This means, of course, that, given the quantity of labour available for work, should stationary conditions be attained, only one quantity of aggregate employment, namely, the quantity equal to this, or, with more realistic conditions contemplated in Chapter VI, § 4, falling short of this in a fixed measure — but, nevertheless, to be called here " full " — is possible.

§ 3. It does not follow that, when conditions of productivity, *i.e.* the form of the function F, are taken as given — which for our present purpose can properly be done — only one kind of full employment stationary state is possible. The relevant equations, it is easy to see, are reduced to two, namely :

$$(1) \quad \phi(r, S) = f(r),$$
$$(2) \quad \quad f(r) = 0.$$

These are sufficient to determine the two unknowns r and S. Apart, therefore, from imposed restrictions (*e.g.* the restriction that r cannot be negative) there must be some combination of values of r and S in respect of which a stationary state with full employment will be established. But there need not be only one such combination — one pair of values of r and S. *A priori*, if we knew nothing about the forms of ϕ and f, there might, of course, be an indefinitely large number of solutions.

As a matter of fact, there is reason to believe that $\dfrac{\partial \phi}{\partial S}$ and $\dfrac{\partial \phi}{\partial r}$ are negative, while $\dfrac{\partial f}{\partial r}$ is probably positive. This suggests that there are *two* solutions ; one in which S is small and r large, the other in which S is large and r small. Thus (i) when S, and so the real income of the representative man, is sufficiently small, he will save (or invest) nothing, even though the rate of interest obtainable if he did invest were very high ; and (ii) when the rate of interest obtainable for investment is sufficiently low — in consequence of a large accumulation of capital — he will save (or invest) nothing in spite of his real income being very large. In the former case we have a low-level, in the latter a high-level stationary state, both of these being states of full employment.

§ 4. If the variables r and S were free to assume any values whatever, whether positive or negative, there would be nothing further to say. In fact, however, external conditions restrict the range of possibility. Thus, obviously, in a closed economy — which cannot have capital debts to outside bodies — it is impossible for S to be negative. In like manner, as will be shown immediately, there is a lower limit below which r cannot fall. It is clearly possible that these restrictions may prove incompatible with the validity of the two equations set out above, or, while leaving them valid for some roots, may rule out other roots which would be capable of satisfying the equations. *Prima facie*, therefore, it is not *necessary*, on the data adduced so far, that *any* full employment stationary state shall be attainable even in principle.

§ 5. Considerations, however, of the kind set out in the last chapter make it plain that, if the representative man's real income, on account of S for him being very small, is less than some definable positive amount, he will not save anything, no matter what rate of interest may be on offer.[1] That is to say, a low-level full employment stationary state *must* be possible. We are, therefore, in doubt only about a high-level full employment stationary state. The common view until recently has been that in a closed economy, in which no new inventions or technical improvements are being made and in which the size of the population is fixed, such a high-level full employment stationary state is not only possible, but is the *inevitable* goal towards which the whole (economic) creation moves. As, year after year, more capital is accumulated, openings for profitable investment are progressively filled up till the marginal efficiency of capital, and so the rate of interest, falls to a level at which it no longer offers the representative

---

[1] Our assumption about the indestructibility, etc., of capital goods makes negative saving by the representative man impossible.

man [1] any inducement to save, and long-period flow equilibrium is necessarily attained. This, as has already been indicated, is true, provided that there is no internally imposed limit below which the rate of interest offered by demanders cannot fall. But, if this rate has a lower limit, the issue is less clear ; and in fact it is easily proved that the rate *has* a lower limit.

§ 6. The first stage of this proof may be set out as follows. In conditions of movement, when the relative values of various things are expected to be different in the future from what they are now, rates of interest offered for loans of no matter what maturity, will be different, according to what the commodity is in terms of which they are expressed. If the net rate of interest in terms of chairs is 5 per cent, if £100 buy 100 chairs now and are expected to buy 85 a year hence, the net annual rate of interest in terms of money must be approximately 23 per cent. But in any state of short-period flow equilibrium [2] and, *a fortiori*, in a stationary state relative values are not expected to alter. Consequently, rates of interest offered for loans of any assigned maturity must be the same, no matter in terms of what commodity they are expressed. It follows that, if there is a minimum below which the rate of interest in terms of any one thing cannot fall, this minimum must also hold good for all other things.

§ 7. So much being understood, we proceed to the second stage. It may well be that the state of industrial technique being given, after capital accumulation has been carried sufficiently far, no further opportunity for

----

[1] The representative man is defined as a man so constituted that, if all members of the community were representative men, it would act as it in fact does act. Of course, when he is saving nothing, this does not imply that everybody is saving nothing. Thus *some* men may be saving, *e.g.* for their old age ; but, if this is so, others, *e.g.* those who have attained old age, must be dissaving an equivalent amount.

[2] Cf. *ante*, Part II, Chapter I, § 7.

investment exists that would yield other than a high negative return. But this does not imply that in actual fact capital accumulation can be carried so far that the marginal efficiency of capital, and so the rate of interest offered, becomes a large negative quantity. The reason is that in this kind of situation demanders of resources for investment would concentrate their demand on money, and would not devote it to hiring men to make goods at a loss. Why should they do that ? They can hold money — modern money — for themselves at practically no cost. This implies that at slightly less than a nil rate of interest they will stop investing, in the sense of making additions to physical capital. It will pay them better to hold any resources that are offered to them for investment in the form of unspent money. Hence the marginal efficiency of capital and the rate of interest offered by demanders cannot in any equilibrium situation stand appreciably below nothing.

§ 8. It is sometimes suggested that this is an understatement ; and that the minimum level at which, in equilibrium, the rate of interest can stand is substantially greater than nothing. Thus Keynes writes : " The costs of bringing borrowers and lenders together and uncertainty as to the future of the rate of interest set a lower limit, which, in present circumstances, may perhaps be as high as 2 per cent or $2\frac{1}{2}$ per cent on long term ".[1] In my opinion these figures, as regards a stationary state — different from " present circumstances " — are much too high. The situation contemplated is not one in which the prospects for investment are standing at a low level and are expected very shortly to improve. There is no expectation of improvement, and, therefore, no inducement to hold resources liquid

[1] *General Theory*, p. 219.

against a brighter future.   Nor is there any uncertainty about what the rate of interest in the future is going to be.   Moreover, Keynes, I think, failed to notice that what is relevant is not the average, but the marginal, cost of bringing borrowers and lenders together, and that many people invest in their own businesses, where these costs are nil.   I do not think that, for my problem, the rate at which interest will be held up from falling further in consequence of capital accumulation can be put appreciably higher than nothing.

§ 9. In these circumstances, if we suppose ourselves in a situation in which the low-level full employment stationary state has been left behind, and some investment is taking place, the economic system will move forward smoothly towards a high-level full employment stationary state, provided that, whatever the stock of accumulated capital may be, there is some positive rate of interest at which no new investment will be supplied. For, if that is so, as capital goes on being accumulated, the rate at which no new investment is demanded must presently coincide with the rate at which none is supplied.   If, however, the rate at which no new investment will be supplied is liable, when capital accumulation has been carried a certain distance, to be negative, there may be no amount of capital accumulation in respect of which the demand price for new investment falls to the level of the supply price.   In these conditions the equilibrium of a high-level full employment stationary state will never be reached.

§ 10. Now, if people saved only for the sake of the incomes that their saving would presently yield, investment supplied would be nil, not only in respect of a low-level full employment stationary state, where poverty prevents any saving from being made, no matter what the rate of interest, but also when, in any given state of

capital accumulation, the rate of interest, at which they
are prepared to supply exactly a nil flow of new investment, would be equal to the representative man's rate
of time preference,[1] *i.e.* in the language of the last
chapter, to q. But, as we saw in that chapter, no matter
how rich a man may be, he is sure to discount the future
to *some* extent ; he is bound always to value a future
satisfaction — as distinguished from event — less than
an equal present one. Thus the representative man's
rate of time preference, q, is positive in all circumstances.
It follows that, apart from outside disturbing influences,
the equilibrium of a full employment stationary state
must ultimately emerge.[2]

§ 11. In actual life, however, people desire additions
to accumulated wealth, not merely for the income they
will presently yield, but also for the amenity, in sense
of power, sense of security and so on, which the *possession* of them carries. In these conditions the rate of
interest at which they would be prepared to supply
exactly a nil flow of new investment would be equal,
not to the representative man's rate of time preference
proper, but to this rate corrected by subtracting something to allow for that amenity ; that is to say, in the
language of the last chapter, to $(q - v)$, where v is positive.   If, then, v is sufficiently large, it may happen, for

---

[1] The rate of time preference proper is the rate at which future *satisfactions*
are discounted. But, since in a stationary state the representative man's
income, whether expressed in terms of commodities or of money, is expected
to be the same in the future as it is now, the rate of time preference proper,
the rate expressed in terms of commodities — any composite commodity —
and the rate expressed in terms of money, must all be equal, so that there is
no need to distinguish among them.

[2] During the *process towards* this stage, since, with accumulating capital
equipment, output will have been expanding, unless money income has been
expanding parallel with output, prices will have been falling and the fall will
have been expected. Consequently, while both the money and the real rate
of interest will have been falling, the former will throughout have stood lower
than the latter.

all possible amounts of capital accumulation, that the
rate of interest at which exactly nil new investment will
be supplied is negative.   That is to say, it may happen
that there is no level of capital accumulation for which
the demand price for one unit of new investment stands
as low as the supply price, *i.e.* at which the equilibrium
of a high-level full employment stationary state can
establish itself.

§ 12. The only way, then, to prove that the equilibrium of a high-level full employment stationary state
is always possible would be to show that in the last
resort forces will be brought into play which prevent
$(q - v)$ from being negative.   Can this be shown ?   To
answer that question, let us suppose that a stage has
been reached where the rate of interest has fallen to nil,
no new investment is being demanded, but, since $(q - v)$
is negative, the representative man still desires to save.
He will try to satisfy this desire by making purchases
of already existing durable things.   Those persons who
possess such things, since the quantity of them cannot
be increased, will continually ask, and those who do not
possess them will continually offer, higher and higher
prices in terms of consumable goods.   Thus the value
of land and similar property and, above all, the value
of money, which is an especially convenient store of
value, will continually rise.   The process by which this
comes about can be described in various sets of words,
about which dispute sometimes takes place.   One way
of putting the matter is to say that people, being unwilling to expend the whole of their money income on
consumption, and unable to find anybody who would
expend the balance in investment, are forced continuously to transfer money away from that part of the
total stock which is, into that part which is not,
" active " and relevant to income, *i.e.* to hoard money

out of the active part of the stock.[1]   This entails, unless
it is stopped by a deliberate State policy of compen-
satory public loans, a continuous reduction in the
aggregate volume of money income, or, if we prefer it,
of aggregate money demand.   So far nothing has
emerged to prevent $(q - v)$ from being negative.   Provided, however, that full employment is still maintained, in accordance with the " classical view ",
through an appropriate succession of adjustments in
money wage-rates, something will emerge.   With the
notation of the last chapter, v is a short expression for
$\frac{U_{s,x}}{\phi(x)}$, where $U_{s,x}$ is the amenity utility of *having* a
marginal unit of investment and $\phi(x)$ the utility of the
marginal unit of real income consumed.   Now, since
money income is continuously contracting, and prices,
therefore, falling, the existing stock of money—as also
the stock of land and of some other sorts of property,
such as Old Masters, which are especially suitable as
embodiments of, or receptacles for, saving—is continually becoming more and more valuable in terms of consumption goods.   Hence, in accordance with what was
said in Chapter VIII, § 17, the amenity utility of a marginal unit of investment, namely $U_{s,x}$, grows continually
smaller.   But, since investment in capital instruments
is no longer going on, the representative man's real
income is no longer growing.   Hence the utility of the
marginal unit of real income consumed, namely $\phi(x)$, is
unchanged.   It follows that the element $\frac{U_{s,x}}{\phi(x)}$ progressively contracts, approaching nearer and nearer to
nothing, as money income falls.   Consequently, since

[1] Writers who deny that it is possible to hoard money so long as the stock
of it is fixed, on the ground that all money must always be somewhere (*i.e.*
in some hoard), are, of course, using the term hoarding in a different sense
from this.

our element q is always positive, $\left\{ q - \dfrac{U_{s,\,x}}{\phi(x)} \right\}$, namely
$(q - v)$, must, when money income has contracted suffi-
ciently, not merely become positive, but approach to q.
The conditions which prevented a high-level stationary
state from being established are thus destroyed.[1]
Money income, after the critical point has been reached,
falls, perhaps substantially, and prices with it ; but
presently a new high-level full employment stationary
state may, nevertheless, establish itself.[2] This is always
a possibility.

§ 13. There is, however, an alternative possibility.
Though, as was argued in Chapter VI, the classical view
is probably valid for ordinary conditions, it may well
break down in the extraordinary conditions contemplated above. Money wage-rates may refuse to go on

[1] It has been argued that, since a large part of the existing stock of money
(including bank money) is offset by Government debt, the net increase in the
value, in terms of income goods, of the stock of capital wealth consequent upon
an appreciation in the value of money is much smaller than it might seem
to be at first sight. This argument, as Prof. Robertson has pointed out
to me, is open to the reply that what chiefly affects the attitude of the
public towards saving is the real value of the capital wealth held by the
public, not that of the capital wealth held by the public and the Government
together.

[2] A possible objection should be noted. As was pointed out in my
Economics of Stationary States, p. 14, the fact that an equilibrium position
exists, such that, if it is attained, there is no reason for departure from it,
does not in all circumstances imply that that position will be, or even tends
to be, eventually attained. In the physical world frictional resistances
compel a pendulum, which has been lifted away from the equilibrium position,
presently to return to that position, and not for ever to oscillate round it.
But in the economic world we cannot know, *a priori*, that entrepreneurs who
have over-produced in one year will not be led by their losses to under-produce
to an equal or even greater extent in the next, and so on. Is it possible that
the equilibrium situation of a high-level stationary state should constitute in
this way a centre, not of rest, but of oscillation ? I do not think we can
prove that this is impossible. It is surely, however, *probable* that people
eventually will learn by experience, and will not continue always making
decisions that lead to the same type of loss. If this be so, the oscillations
must eventually fade away, so that, in the absence of new factors of
disturbance, the economic system will presently come to rest in the high-
level stationary state.

falling parallel with money income and the money wages
bill, so maintaining full employment, down to the point
at which the downward movement is arrested in the
way just described. This downward movement may
be brought to a stop before that by an outburst of
public resentment, by the slow growth of a resistance
movement, or, may be, by the Government decreeing
minimum rates of money wages. Should any of these
things happen, any further downward movement in
money income must carry with it a contraction in employment ; and the fall in money income is eventually
arrested, with employment much below what is popu-
larly called full and with people's desire to save brought
into balance with their desire to invest through the
representative man — representative, of course, of
employed and unemployed together — having become
so poor that he no longer desires to save any of
his income.[1] When, at the expense of an enormous
standing volume of unemployment, real income has
fallen to that level, there is no tendency towards
further contraction either in money income or in employment. A low-level stationary state containing
much less than full employment has been attained ;
the system has come to an equilibrium of a truly
deplorable kind. Clearly this *may* happen. Whether,
in the conditions postulated in our model world, it is
likely to happen, is a matter on which opinions may
well differ.

[1] Cf. *General Theory*, pp. 217-18.

NOTE TO CHAPTER IX

KEYNES' THEORY

IN his *General Theory* Keynes claims, not merely that his vision of the Day of Judgment, as I have become accustomed to call it, represents what *may* happen in certain hypothetical conditions, but what, in the absence of heavy, continuous Government investment in public works and so on, is *likely* to happen in the actual world. If sensible policies are adopted, capital equipment, he suggests — of course he was writing before the outbreak of the last war — will accumulate so rapidly that, within perhaps one generation, no openings will be left for investments that yield any positive net return (*i.e.* gross return minus an allowance for the costs of bringing borrowers and lenders together) ; so that *quite soon* the monetary processes leading to his Day of Judgment will be set in motion. If the argument of the preceding chapter is correct, unless the inducement to save offered by the amenity of *holding* savings exceeds a certain magnitude, these monetary processes will never be set in motion, but, before they can come into play, a high-level full employment stationary state will be attained. Further, if they do come into play, they may lead up, not to the Day of Judgment, but to a high-level stationary state associated with reduced money, but unreduced real, income. That, however, is not all. The continuing contraction in openings for investment as accumulating capital fills up old openings, upon which Keynes' argument depends, is only certain to take place on the assumption that new inventions and improvements are not made. In actual life, of course, they will be made and so will provide new openings for investment, which may well offset, or more than offset, those which are closed. An era which has witnessed the development of electrical apparatus, motor cars, aircraft, gramophones and wireless, to say nothing of tanks and other engines of war, and of the innumerable small improvements continually appearing in many types of machinery,[1] is not one in which we can reasonably forecast a total disappearance of profitable openings for new investment. Moreover, if the situation should become such that the *average* of new capital assets yielded nothing, it is still probable that *some* capital assets would yield something, and many would be expected to do so. In view of these considerations, even though we were agreed that, in a world without inventions and improvements, the Day of Judgment was likely, or even certain, ultimately to arrive, in the actual world we would not need to feel serious alarm.[2]

[1] The great importance and frequency of minor changes in technique are well illustrated in Chapter III of the third volume of Clapham's *Economic History of England*.

[2] In some current discussions the authors appear to suppose that the sort of low-level equilibrium conceived by Keynes had somehow actually established itself — or half established itself — in this country in the inter-war period, thus accounting for the high unemployment percentage which then prevailed. But Keynes himself, as I understand him, never maintained this. For him the low-level equilibrium was a possibility — a danger threatening in the future if we did not guard against it by keeping the demand for investment high — by no means a current fact.

PART III

DIFFERENCES AMONG POSITIONS OF SHORT-PERIOD FLOW EQUILIBRIUM

CHAPTER I

INTRODUCTORY

§ 1. In Part II we were concerned with the conditions which must be satisfied by systems in short-period flow equilibrium. In all these systems the first two equations were the same, while for the third a number of alternative forms were displayed. Given any form of the third equation, it was shown that, in order for the system to be determinate, there had to be a fourth equation also. Abstractly, of course, any number of such equations can be imagined. But for us, it was pointed out, the only two interesting equations are equations that determine respectively the aggregate quantity of employment and the money rate of wages. When *either* of these is fixed, so to speak, from the outside, the whole system is, in general, determined. This implies that, so long as the other equations given in the system hold good, *both* cannot be fixed from outside ; for that would mean that the system is overdetermined, embodying in itself conditions that are mutually inconsistent. In the present Part we are concerned with another class of problem. When, as between two systems, one or more of the conditions imposed are different, the values of the unknowns will, in general, be different. This is so, equally whether in the two systems the fourth equation specifies the aggregate quantity of employment or the money rate of wage. We might, if we wished, investigate the implications of

differences between two systems of the former kind.
Thus we might ask how, when either the aggregate
quantity of employment or any of the functions ϕ, f,
F or ψ differed in the two systems in given ways, the
money rate of wage would differ ; or we might ask the
same question about the rate of interest, or about the
quantity of employment in the consumption industries
alone, or about the quantity in the investment industries alone.   To answer these questions fully we should
have to develop for each of these *quaesita* — rate of
money wage, rate of interest and so on — an analysis
of like general character to, though differing, of course,
in detailed content from, the analysis that is, in fact,
developed in the chapters that follow.   In this volume,
however, our dominant interest is, not in the money
rate of wage, or in the rate of interest, or even in the
quantity of employment in the consumption industries
separately or in the investment industries separately,
but in the *aggregate quantity of employment*.   When this
quantity is given already from outside, further probing
is beyond our scope.   Systems, therefore, in which the
fourth equation states the quantity of aggregate employment will not be studied.   Attention will be confined to those in which that equation states the money
rate of wage.   We posit two systems of this type, and
we ask in what way, when they differ in certain respects,
the aggregate quantities of employment embodied in the
two are related to one another.   It is, of course, assumed
that there are, so to speak, enough unemployed workers
to go round, so that the establishment of the appropriate equilibrium is not estopped in either system by
a shortage of men.[1]

[1] If in either system it *were* so estopped, adjustment would presumably
be made through a breach in the condition that the money wage-rate is given.
Competition among employers would inevitably force up this wage-rate.   It is
important to remember in this connection the general assumption we are

§ 2. This statement is, however, too general. It implies an investigation impracticably wide. Our objective must, perforce, be limited, and, to this end, there must be further particularisation. Our two systems contain, besides the money rate of wage, w, the seven functions that have so far been designated g, ϕ, f, F, ψ, η_1 and η_2, and the two compound functions,

$$K_1, \textit{i.e.} \quad \frac{F}{\left(1 - \dfrac{1}{\eta_1}\right)F'} \quad \text{and} \quad K_2, \textit{i.e.} \quad \frac{\psi}{\left(1 - \dfrac{1}{\eta_2}\right)\psi'}.$$

We conceive η_1 and η_2 as functions of $F(x)$ and $\psi(y)$. These functions may, of course, be different as between two systems. The implications of such differences will be studied briefly in the last chapter of this Part. Until then I shall leave them out of account. On this understanding, we recognise that two economic systems may differ in respect of several of the other functions at the same time. Indeed this is not merely possible, but, in actual life, is highly probable. It may come about either (i) because the states of two or more functions are the joint effects of some underlying cause, or (ii) because the state of one itself directly or indirectly causes that of another, or (iii) by mere accident. One important example of the first type of non-accidental correlation is associated with differences in business optimism and business pessimism. These act both on

---

making, that labour is homogeneous and perfectly mobile (compare *ante*, Preliminary Chapter, § 3). This assumption, which excludes bottlenecks and shortages of particular kinds of labour, enables us to evade difficulties that, in a more realistic study, would have to be faced. Thus, to take an extreme case, suppose that there is a falling-off in the demand for coal-miners at a time when workpeople in all other industries are fully employed. Then, if coal-miners are completely immobile — unable to move into any other occupation — unless the slump in coal-mining itself is directly countered, whether by a stimulation of demand or by a cut in the money wage-rates of coal-miners, there is no way in which the aggregate volume of employment can be prevented from contracting.

the demand function for real investment by way of
people's expectations of returns from given quantities
of labour devoted to investment, and also, by affecting
people's comparative desires to invest resources and to
hold them liquid, upon the money income function.
Thus optimism stimulates employment in a double way,
both by expanding the demand function for labour for
investment and by raising the money income function ;
and pessimism depresses employment in a like double
way. The most important and obvious example of the
second type of correlation relates to reactions from the
level of employment on the money rate of wages. A
higher demand function for labour for investment, which
is maintained, is fairly sure to be associated, other things
being equal, with a higher money rate of wages, which
will partly, wholly, or conceivably more than wholly,
offset the tendency for aggregate employment to be
larger : the amount of employment devoted to investment will, of course, in any case be larger. When two
systems differ in respect of several functions, not merely
of one, the net result on aggregate employment can be
obtained by simply adding together the results of each
difference singly. In what follows attention will be confined to the implications of single differences, the task
of addition being left to the reader.

§ 3. Now the money rate of wage, being a single
figure, can only differ in one system from what it is in
another by being higher or lower. But each of the
functions g, ϕ, F and ψ, being functions of one variable,
may differ, not merely in this way, but also in the shapes
of the curves they represent. The function f, being of
two variables, has even wider opportunities. It is thus
out of the question to examine exhaustively the implications of all possible types of difference even in respect
of a single function. I shall, therefore, limit my enquiry

to the implications of equi-proportional differences in the functions g, ϕ, f, F and ψ. Thus I suppose that systems A and B differ in such wise that, for *any* rate of interest, the quantity of labour demanded for investment in B exceeds the quantity demanded in A in one (the same) proportion ; or that, for any combination of interest rate and income of consumption goods the quantity of labour supplied for investment in B exceeds that in A in one (the same) proportion. That is to say, the demand function for labour for investment being represented by $m\phi(r)$, m is equal to unity in system A and to some other quantity in system B ; and so for all the other functions.

§ 4. Further, in order to get a clear-cut and quantitatively precise result, I have to use the method of differentiation. Consequently, I can treat directly only very small differences in the money rate of wage and in each of the functions. Our formulae are thus in like case with those obtained for the consequences of an *ad valorem* (or, equally, a specific) tax on the price of an isolated commodity, which, for extremely small taxes, are always exact, but for substantial taxes are only exact provided that the relevant demand and supply functions are linear. The more widely the functions depart from linearity, the less reliable these formulae are — the less satisfactory approximations they yield. The same thing is true of the analysis worked out here.

CHAPTER II

THE FORMAL TECHNIQUE

§ 1. It might seem that, for normal, constant-income and constant-interest banking policies, the plan indicated in the last chapter can be carried through by writing, in the equations set out in Part II, Chapter III, §§ 2, 3, 7, 9 and 10, new variables m_1, m_2 and so on in front of each of w, g, ϕ, ψ, f and F; so that we should read m_1w, m_2g, $m_3\phi$, $m_4\psi$, m_5f and m_6F in place of these expressions. For all the expressions other than ϕ this is true. But $\phi(r)$, it will be remembered, represents the quantity of labour demanded for investment when technical conditions of production, namely, the forms of the functions ψ and F, are given. When, as between two systems, these forms differ, it seems *prima facie* that the quantities of labour for investment demanded in them must also differ, even though m_3 is the same in both systems. As regards the function ψ, reflection confirms this. It is not difficult to see that a larger productivity of labour in the investment industries, *which is special to those industries*, has an effect on the quantity of labour demanded for investment the same as, and capable, therefore, of being expressed in the form of, a proportionately smaller rate of interest. Hence inside the bracket, instead of r, we must write $\dfrac{r}{m_4}$. It might perhaps be thought that m_6 stands in the same position as m_4, because a large m_6 implies a large

144

return to labour devoted to investment. But, since a large m_6 also implies a correspondingly large rate of real wage paid to labour for investment, this is not so.[1] Hence the expression to put in place of $\phi(r)$ in the first equation of Part II, Chapter III, § 2, is simply $m_3\phi\left(\dfrac{r}{m_4}\right)$. For normal, constant-income and constant-interest banking policies, therefore, the appropriate set-up of equations is :

$$m_3\phi\left(\frac{r}{m_4}\right) = m_5 f\{r,\, m_6 \mathrm{F}\}, \qquad . \qquad . \quad \text{(I)}$$

$$y = m_5 f\{r,\, m_6 \mathrm{F}\}, \qquad . \qquad . \quad \text{(II)}$$

$$m_2 g = (\mathrm{K}_1 + \mathrm{K}_2)m_1, \qquad . \qquad .\quad\text{(III)}$$

It may be asked, perhaps, why, in respect of these banking policies, m_6 and m_4 do not appear in the third equation. The answer is that

$$\mathrm{K}_1 = \frac{m_6 \mathrm{F}}{\left(1 - \dfrac{1}{\eta_1}\right)m_6 \mathrm{F}'} \quad \text{and} \quad \mathrm{K}_2 = \frac{m_4 \psi}{\left(1 - \dfrac{1}{\eta_2}\right)m_4 \psi'} \;;$$

in which expressions, of course, the m's cancel out.

§ 2. For a banking policy directed to keep the price of consumption goods constant, the set-up is the same, except that, in place of equation (III) above, we have the equation

$$\frac{d}{dm_n}\left(\frac{\mathrm{K}_1 m_1}{\mathrm{F}m_2 m_6}\right) = 0 \quad . \qquad . \quad \text{[III]} \, (b)$$

This equation is arrived at as follows. The price of consumption goods, p_1, which has to be kept constant

---

[1] Thus, if S be written for the existing stock of capital instruments, the expected future annual return to the marginal unit of consumption goods expended on engaging labour for investment

$$= \frac{m_6\left\{\mathrm{F} - x\left(1 - \dfrac{1}{\eta_1}\right)\mathrm{F}'\right\}}{\mathrm{S}} \cdot \frac{m_4 \psi'}{m_6 \mathrm{F}''},$$

where the m_6's cancel out.

in any given system, is equal, as was shown in Part II, Chapter III, to $\frac{K_1}{F}.w$, *i.e.* to $\dfrac{w}{\left(1 - \dfrac{1}{\eta_1}\right)F}$. Therefore we must insert m_1 and m_6 before w and F, thus obtaining $\left(\dfrac{K_1 m_1}{F m_6}\right) = C$, since w, being a constant, may be written $= 1$. But the condition that the price of consumption goods is kept constant does not mean that it is to have the same value as between two systems in which total money incomes are different ; any more than the condition that money income is to be kept constant precludes us from comparing two systems, each of which has a constant-income banking policy, but which aim at keeping different incomes constant. In other words, it is not p_1, but $\dfrac{p_1}{m_2}$, not $\left(\dfrac{K_1 m_1}{F m_6}\right)$, but $\left(\dfrac{K_1 m_1}{F m_2 m_6}\right)$, which must remain unaltered whatever happens to any m. Thus we reach our equation

$$\frac{d}{dm_n}\left(\frac{K_1 m_1}{F m_2 m_6}\right) = 0.$$

§ 3. So far everything has been fairly simple. But it is now necessary to bring to light a complication, which was not relevant to the analysis of Part II and which, therefore, could up to now be disregarded. We agreed in Part II, Chapter II, § 6, to regard η_1 as a function of $F(x)$ and η_2 as a function of $\psi(y)$. This was well enough so long as the functions F and ψ were not subject to change. Now, however, they *are* subject to change. Hence η_1 is a function of $m_6 F(x)$ and η_2 of $m_4 \psi(y)$: so that, instead of $K_1(x)$, which is appropriate when the technical conditions of production in the consumption industries are given, we have $K_1(x, m_6)$, representing

$$\frac{1}{1 - \dfrac{1}{\eta_1\{m_6\mathrm{F}(x)\}}} \cdot \frac{\mathrm{F}(x)}{\mathrm{F}'(x)}.$$

In like manner, instead of $\mathrm{K}_2(y)$, we have $\mathrm{K}_2(y,\ m_4)$, representing

$$\frac{1}{1 - \dfrac{1}{\eta_2\{m_4\psi(y)\}}} \cdot \frac{\psi(y)}{\psi'(y)}.$$

When we are studying the consequences of variations in any of the m's other than m_6 or m_4 this does not, of course, matter. Nor does it even matter for variations of m_6 or m_4 when conditions are such that η_1 and η_2 either are infinite, that is to say in conditions of perfect competition, or are constant. But, where η_1 and η_2 are neither infinite nor constant, it does matter for these variations. In sum, as will appear in § 3 of the Appendix, the complications we have been describing are not relevant to these variations in Models I (A), I (B) and II, but are relevant to them in Model III.

§ 4. In general, then, we conceive of two systems : system A, in which all the m's are equal to unity, and a number of versions of system B, in each of which one of the m's is slightly greater than unity. There is, then, for a given difference in each m, an associated difference in aggregate employment. It is these associated differences that we are primarily concerned to determine. We are also interested in the employment multipliers, namely the differences in aggregate employment divided by the associated differences in employment in the investment industries, that result from differences in the money rate of wage and in each of the functions distinguished above. Finally we are interested, though in this case less keenly, in the corresponding money multipliers, namely the differences in money income divided by the associated differences in money investment.

§ 5. Our *quaesita* may conveniently be represented by a table of letters. This will shorten exposition. If the reader will trouble to memorise the meaning assigned to the different letters, he will find the task ahead of him considerably lightened. The letter D is used to represent differences in aggregate employment, not absolutely, but divided by the associated difference in the relevant m; [1] the letter M for employment multipliers; the letter N for money multipliers. The suffixes 1, 2, 3 . . . are attached to these letters to distinguish the differences in aggregate employment and in the multipliers that are associated with differences, as between two economic systems, in respect of each of the several functions, or, if we prefer it, balancing factors. We thus obtain the following table :

Causal Factor	Associated Difference in Aggregate Employment multiplied (in each case) by $\dfrac{m_n}{dm_n}$	Associated Employment Multiplier	Associated Money Multiplier
Difference in money wage-rate . . .	D_1	M_1	N_1
Difference in money income function . .	D_2	M_2	N_2
Difference in demand function for labour for investment . .	D_3	M_3	N_3
Difference in productivity function of labour in investment industries .	D_4	M_4	N_4
Difference in supply function of labour for investment . .	D_5	M_5	N_5
Difference in productivity function of labour in consumption industries	D_6	M_6	N_6

[1] Thus $D_n = \dfrac{d}{dm_n}\{x+y\}$: so that the absolute difference in $(x+y)$ $= \{dm_n . D_n\}$, or, since m_n is written $= 1$, $\dfrac{dm_n}{m_n} . D_n$.

The task which lies before us is to investigate the signs and, so far as may be, the values of the quantities which the letters in the preceding table, in various circumstances, represent.

CHAPTER III

THE MODELS

§ 1. In the preceding Part there was no purpose in discussing anything other than the most highly generalised form of my model world. Here, however, it is useful to introduce also simplified forms, about which definite conclusions can be reached in cases where this is not possible with the general model. The models to be studied I shall call Model III (the general model), Model II and Model I, of which last there are two forms, (B) and (A).

§ 2. Model III being constituted in the manner described in Part II, Chapter III, Model II is that special case of Model III in which perfect competition prevails in all industries. This implies that in each industry, whether a consumption industry or an investment industry, the money rate of wage is equal to the value of the marginal product of labour. Model I has two forms, Model I (B) and Model I (A). The essential characteristic of both is that the proportionate share of income accruing to labour is constant in the face of variations in the quantity of employment; *i.e.* wage-earners' income is always the same fraction of total income, this fraction, of course, being less than unity. Moreover, the fraction is assumed to be the same in consumption industries and in investment industries. In Model I (B) monopolistic power, which, as we have seen, implies the existence of a number of industries, is being exercised. The money rate of wage is, therefore, not equal to, but is less than the value of the marginal product of labour. In Model I (A), on the other hand, perfect competition prevails, which implies, as was noted above, that the money rate of wage is equal to the value of the marginal product of labour. Both forms of Model I are, of course, special cases of Model III, but Model I (A) is, whereas Model I (B) is not, also a special case of Model II. For many purposes, as will appear presently, the two forms (B) and (A) of Model I function in the same way, and it is not necessary to distinguish between them. For some purposes, however, this is not so.

§ 3. The fundamental condition imposed on both forms of Model I is arbitrary in character, and there might seem at first sight to be little reason for studying specially either of these forms. In fact, however, there is good ground for doing this. There is considerable statistical evidence to suggest that in real life this condition is not very widely departed from. On the contrary, over long periods, during which the proportionate quantities of labour and equipment have altered substantially, the proportionate shares of income, which these factors have respectively enjoyed, have remained very nearly constant. Thus, for England, Dr. Bowley found that the proportionate share of income going to property was nearly the same in 1880 and 1924, at round about 37 per cent of the whole ; while the proportionate share going to *manual* workers over the whole period 1880 to 1935 was very nearly the same, from 40 to 43 per cent.[1] Of course these percentages relate to pre-tax incomes. Prof. Douglas has obtained fairly constant proportions for other countries. Mr. Kalecki has, moreover, brought together a table,

---

[1] Cf. *Wages and Income since 1860*, pp. xvi and 96.

L

according to which the proportionate share of *gross* home-produced annual income going to labour in Great Britain between 1924 and 1935 inclusive was never less than 40·8 per cent and never more than 43 per cent.[1] These facts suggest that in real life variations in the proportionate share of income enjoyed by capital and labour respectively, though they play some, do not play a very important, rôle.

§ 4. For studying, in respect of the several models, the problems posited in the last chapter, the most attractive method in point of logic would, of course, be to work first with the general Model III and, thereafter, to show how, if at all, the results reached are modified in the more specialised conditions of the other models. This method is, in fact, followed in the mathematics of the Appendix. In the text, however, we are concerned, not merely to set out the consequences for aggregate employment of differences between differently constituted economic systems, but also to elucidate, so far as may be, why these consequences are what they are. This can be done more easily the less complex is the model we are handling. Therefore I shall treat Model I (A) first and most at length, and then, the general principles having been made plain, shall trace out more sketchily the implications of the other models. The whole of the *results* of Chapters IV-X are embodied in the methematical tables of the Appendix. The ex-

---

[1] *Essays in the Theory of Economic Fluctuations*, p. 16. In a nearly comparable table for the U.S.A. Mr. Kalecki finds, for the period 1919–34, a range extending from 34·9 to 39·3 per cent (*loc. cit.* p. 17). In this country the proportionate share of aggregate "private" income, excluding "pay and allowances for the armed forces", accruing (pre-tax) to wages was officially estimated at 36 per cent in 1938 and at 40 per cent in 1947 (Cmd. 7371, Table V). The numerous controls and restrictions affecting especially non-wage incomes may have been partly responsible for this change, if it was a real one. The fact, however, that the Statistics Abstract for 1935-46 (Table 279) gives 37 per cent for 1938 and 38 per cent for 1946 raises doubts.

pressions there given are, of course, reached by algebraic manipulations. The working of these, which, while not difficult in principle, is in some cases very cumbrous, is not printed. Anyone who desires to check for himself this working would probably find it less troublesome to repeat the analysis *ab initio* rather than to verify step by step another person's algebra.[1]

§ 5. Throughout this analysis three sets of facts, already noted in Part II, must be borne in mind. First, it was shown in Chapter II of that Part that ϕ' must in its nature be negative, while g', $F'\dfrac{\partial f}{\partial F}$, η_1 and η_2 cannot be negative. Secondly, it was shown in Part II, Chapter V that $\left(\dfrac{\partial f}{\partial r} - \phi'\right)$, K'_1 and K'_2 are probably positive. These propositions will be found, in the analysis which follows, to enable definite answers about signs to be reached in a number of cases where, apart from them, this would be impossible. Thirdly, it was shown in the note to Part II, Chapter III, § 11, that with a banking policy directed to keep the price of consumption goods constant, systems of the type we are investigating are in certain conditions indeterminate as regards the aggregate quantity of employment. Obviously comparisons, of the type in which we are interested, between two such systems, or, indeed, between one such system and another which is determinate, are impossible. In the chapters that follow the cases in which, for this reason, our analysis breaks down are indicated.

§ 6. For a normal, a constant-income and a constant-price banking policy, the D's will be investigated, for each of the models we have distinguished, in Chapters IV-VII; the M's in Chapter VIII and the N's in

---

[1] For this algebraic working I am indebted, as was stated in the Preface, to Mrs. Glauert.

Chapter IX. There remains a banking policy directed to keep the rate of interest constant. This policy differs from the other three in that, under it, all the D's, all the M's and some of the N's have the same values in all three models. Therefore the discussion of it can be brief. Nothing will be said about it till we come to Chapter X, where it will be treated by itself.

CHAPTER IV

MODEL I (A)

§ 1. In accordance with the programme sketched out above, I proceed to a detailed study of the simplest of our models, namely Model I (A). In this model, as in all the others, when banking policy is either normal or directed (successfully) to keep money income constant, we have three fundamental equations :

$$m_3\phi\left(\frac{r}{m_4}\right) = m_5 f\{r,\ m_6 \mathrm{F}(x)\}, \qquad . \qquad . \qquad \text{(I)}$$

$$y = m_5 f\{r,\ m_6 \mathrm{F}(x)\}, \qquad . \qquad . \qquad \text{(II)}$$

$$m_2 g(r) = \{\mathrm{K}_1(x) + \mathrm{K}_2(y)\}m_1, \qquad . \qquad . \qquad \text{(III)}$$

The third of these equations is, of course, a combination of the same equation with $m_1 w$ written in place of m_1 and of a further equation

w = a constant, which may be written = 1.

The functions K_1 and K_2 are further defined by the simplifying condition

$$\mathrm{K}_1 = \frac{\mathrm{F}}{\mathrm{F}'} = \mathrm{C}_1 x, \qquad . \qquad . \qquad \text{(IV)}$$

$$\mathrm{K}_2 = \frac{\psi}{\psi'} = \mathrm{C}_1 y, \qquad . \qquad . \qquad \text{(V)}$$

where C_1 is a constant greater than unity. That is to say, it is postulated both that (i) the proportionate share of income accruing to labour has the same value, $\frac{1}{\mathrm{C}_1}$, in the consumption industries and in the investment industries, this value being independent of the quantity

155

of labour at work; and (ii) that conditions of perfect competition — this is provided for by the equalities $K_1 = \dfrac{F}{F'}$ and $K_2 = \dfrac{\psi}{\psi'}$ — prevail throughout both types of industry. The third equation thus becomes $m_2 g(r) = C_1(x + y)m_1$. When banking policy is directed to keep the price of consumption goods constant, the place of the third equation is taken by a more complex formula in the way explained in Part III, Chapter II, § 2. The form of it relevant here is $\dfrac{d}{dm_n}\!\left(\dfrac{C_1 x m_1}{F m_2 m_6}\right) = 0$. I shall investigate in this chapter the several D's listed in the table on page 148. The reader will remember that the D's are not absolute differences in $(x + y)$, but absolute differences multiplied in each case by the appropriate value of $\dfrac{m_n}{dm_n}$. It will be recalled that in this model we are never confronted with an indeterminate situation, and, therefore, that the analysis directed to ascertain the signs of the several D's can never break down.

§ 2. Under sub-head I, I shall treat of a normal banking policy; under sub-head II — a very brief discussion is sufficient here — of a banking policy directed (successfully) to keeping money income constant; finally, under sub-head III, of a banking policy directed to keeping the price of consumption goods constant.

Sub-head I: A Normal Banking Policy

D_1. *Difference in aggregate employment associated with a small difference in the money rate of wage*

§ 3. Let us suppose that systems A and B are alike in all respects save that in B the money rate of wage is higher than in A. From the fact that in this model, in accordance with our definition, money income and aggregate money wages stand in a constant proportion it follows that, unless there is more money income, there must be less employment, in system B. But, with a normal banking policy, if there is to be more money income, the rate of interest must be higher. This implies that less labour is demanded, and so less employment exists, in the investment industries. Further, if the rate of interest in system B is higher, the quantity of real income produced, and so of employment, in the consumption industries must be lower ; for otherwise more labour for investment is on offer than is required, and there is no equilibrium. Hence, even if there is more money income in system B, there must be less aggregate employment. Thus in any event D_1 is negative. The extent to which aggregate employment is lower in system B is obviously greater the less responsive money income is to variations in the rate of interest. It is also greater, as is shown in Table X of the Appendix, the more responsive is the supply of labour for investment, and (ii) the more responsive in the opposite sense is the demand for labour for investment, to variations in the rate of interest.

D_2. *Difference in aggregate employment associated with a small difference in the money income function*

§ 4. It is evident that the consequences for aggregate employment of a money income function higher in a given proportion must be the same as those of a money wage-rate lower in a corresponding proportion, no matter whether the money income function is higher because of a lower desire for liquidity or of a larger stock of money. Thus D_2 is positive. Moreover, the circumstances which make the excess of employment in system B, as against system A, numerically larger or smaller when the money income function is higher, are evidently the same as those which make it larger or smaller when the money wage-rate is lower.

D_3. *Difference in aggregate employment associated with a small difference in the demand function for labour for investment*

§ 5. Let us suppose that, all other functions, including the rate of wages, being the same, systems A and B differ in that the quantity of labour for investment demanded in B is larger than in A in one (the same) proportion in respect of every rate of interest. This obviously entails the rate of interest being higher in system B than in system A. But, if the rate of interest is higher in B, under a normal banking policy there must be more money income. Since, then, in this model the share of income going to labour is always the same, and since we are supposing the rate of money wages to be equal in systems B and A, it follows that the volume of employment must be larger in B. Hence, under a normal banking policy, employment in B — the system with the more expanded demand function for labour for investment — must be larger than in the other. D_3 is positive. Further, it is easy to see that the excess will be greater the more responsive money income is to given differences in the rate of interest. It is less easy to see, but the algebraic results set out in Table X of the Appendix show that the excess will be greater, (i) the less markedly an enlarged rate of interest expands the supply of labour for investment, (ii) the less markedly it contracts the demand for labour for investment, and (iii) the less markedly an enlarged holding of consumption income affects the supply of labour for investment.

D₄. *Difference in aggregate employment associated with a small difference in the productivity of labour in the investment industries*

§ 6. We now suppose our two systems to differ in that each quantity of labour devoted to making investment goods in system B is more productive in a given proportion than each quantity in system A. It then follows that the same quantity of labour for investment must be demanded in system B as would have been demanded if this productivity had not been higher, but a correspondingly lower rate of interest had prevailed.[1] The implications for aggregate employment of larger productivity of labour in respect of investment goods are thus, in the main, the same as those of a more expanded demand function for labour for investment. This problem is, therefore, so far as signs go, simply a variant of that treated in the preceding section. D₄ is positive.

D₅. *Difference in aggregate employment associated with a small difference in the supply function of labour for investment*

§ 7. Next let us suppose that, all other things being equal, system B differs from system A in that the quantity of labour for investment supplied, say, per annum, is larger in a given proportion in respect of every combination of interest rate and quantity of consumption income. Evidently the quantity of employment in the investment industries must be larger in

---

[1] This statement is broadly true. To make it exactly true we must assume that over the relevant range ϕ' is constant, *i.e.* that the demand function is linear.

system B. This implies, however, that the rate of interest must be lower. For otherwise the quantity of investment demanded could not be larger to match the larger quantity supplied, and there would be no equilibrium. But under a normal banking policy a lower rate of interest entails a smaller money income. Hence aggregate employment must be *smaller*. Thus a more expanded supply function of labour for investment, while it affects the quantity of employment in the investment industries in the same sense as a more expanded demand function, affects aggregate employment in the opposite sense. The money rate of wages and all other relevant factors being given, aggregate employment — as distinct from employment in the investment industries — is damaged by an increase in thriftiness, or, in Keynes' language, " propensity to save ". D_5 is negative. It is easy to see that aggregate employment will be affected more adversely the more responsive money income is to differences in the rate of interest. Mathematical analysis shows that it is affected more adversely (i) the less markedly an enlarged rate of interest affects the demand for, (ii) the less markedly it affects, in the opposite sense, the supply of labour for investment, and (iii) the less markedly an enlarged holding of consumption income affects the supply of labour for investment.[1]

D_6. *Difference in aggregate employment associated with a small difference in the productivity of labour in the consumption industries*

§ 8. In this problem we suppose that the productivity of labour in respect of consumption goods is higher in system B than in system A in the same proportion for all quantities of labour engaged upon them.

[1] Cf. Appendix, Table X.

It is easy to see that greater productivity of labour in the consumption industries makes people more willing to supply labour for investment, given that the amount they are willing to supply at any *specified* rate of interest and income of consumption goods is not varied. Thus aggregate employment must be affected in the same manner as it is when people are more willing to supply labour for investment at a specified rate of interest and with a specified income of consumption goods, but the productivity of labour in the consumption industries is not varied. Thus the present problem is simply a variant of the preceding one. D_6 is necessarily of the same sign as D_5, *i.e.* negative. The circumstances tending to make it larger or smaller are the same as those tending to make D_5 larger or smaller.

Sub-head II

§ 9. I now pass to a banking policy directed (successfully) to keeping money income constant. First, when system B differs from system A in having a higher rate of money wages, it is obvious that aggregate employment must be lower in B than in A in the proportion in which the money rate of wages is higher. Secondly, when system B differs from system A in having a higher money income function, it is equally obvious that aggregate employment must be higher in B than in A in the proportion in which the money income function is higher. Thus D_1 must be negative and D_2 positive, as they are under a normal banking policy. It appears, however, from Appendix, Table X, that their magnitudes, in contrast to what happens with a normal banking policy, are independent of the extent to which either the demand or the supply of labour for investment is responsive to variations in the rate of interest.

They are both numerically larger the more responsive
is the supply of labour for investment to variations in
the income of consumption goods.   Thirdly, since in
Model I (A) the share of income accruing to workpeople
is a constant proportion of total income, so long as
both money income and the money rate of wages are
fixed, it is impossible for aggregate employment to vary,
no matter what happens to the other balancing factors.
That is to say, all the D's, other than D_1 and D_2, are
equal to 0.

Sub-head III

§ 10.   There remains [1] the case of a banking policy
designed to keep the price of consumption goods constant, subject to one exception, namely that, when the
money income function is different in two systems, the
price of consumption goods is not the same in both, but
varies in proportion to the level of the money income
function.   As already explained, to deny this exception
would be equivalent to excluding the possibility that
the banking system may aim in different systems at
different price levels for consumption goods.   The third
basic equation, $m_2 g(r) = C_1(x + y)m_1$, distinguished in § 1
above, here gives place to the more complex form

$$\frac{d}{dm_n}\left(\frac{K_1 m_1}{F m_2 m_6}\right) = 0.$$

The equality $K_1 = C_1 x$ still holding good, this general
form reduces to

$$\frac{d}{dm_n}\left(\frac{C_1 x m_1}{F m_2 m_6}\right) = 0.$$

---

[1] We may also, if we choose, imagine a banking policy which maintains a
constant proportion between money income and the rate of money wages.
On this plan, if the period of production be regarded as negligible, it is obvious
that all money wage-rates, no matter by how much they differ, will be associated, other things being equal, with the same volume of employment.   But
such a plan has never been advocated.   Cf. *ante*, Part II, Chapter II, § 19, *n*.

The algebraic implications being reserved for the Appendix, I shall, as under sub-heads I and II, discuss the state of the several D's in ordinary language.

D_1

§ 11. In this case the money wage-rate is higher in system B than in system A, but the price of consumption goods is, nevertheless, the same. This implies a higher real rate of wage in system B. Now in Model I (A) the real rate of wage is equal to the marginal productivity of labour in the consumption industries. Hence, since in this case increasing returns are incompatible with stable equilibrium, a higher real wage-rate in system B than in system A carries with it less employment in the consumption industries there. For otherwise the condition, that the proportionate share of income accruing to wage-earners in each sort of industry shall be constant, would not be maintained. But, if there is less employment in the consumption industries, it follows from our analytic scheme that the rate of interest must be higher ; so that less labour is demanded in the investment industries. Hence aggregate employment in system B must be smaller than in system A. D_1 is negative. Since the rate of interest is higher in system B, D_1 is a larger negative quantity, the less responsive the supply of labour for investment is to variations in the rate of interest, the more responsive the demand for labour for investment is to these variations, and the more responsive the supply is to the size of consumption income.

D_2

§ 12. In this case, the price of consumption goods being higher and money wage-rates the same in system

B as in system A, the real rate of wages is lower. It is easily proved algebraically, and is, indeed, obvious to common sense that D_2 is in all circumstances equal in magnitude and opposite in sign to D_1.

D_3

§ 13. In this case, since both the price level of consumption goods and the money rate of wage are the same in system B as in system A, employment in the consumption industries must be the same. But, that being so, it follows from our analytic scheme that, the demand function for labour for investment being more expanded in system B, the rate of interest must be higher. Consequently, according as a higher rate of interest is associated, other things being equal, with a higher, the same or a lower supply of labour for investment, there must be more, the same or less employment in the investment industries there. Hence employment in the aggregate must be larger, the same or smaller. As was observed in Part II, Chapter V, § 2, the general, though not the unanimous, opinion of economists is that a higher rate of interest entails, other things being equal, a larger supply of labour for investment. On the assumption that this is so, D_3 is positive. It is larger the more the supply of labour for investment expands, and the more the demand for it contracts, when the rate of interest is increased.[1]

D_4

§ 14. In this case, instead of the demand function for labour for investment being higher in system B, the productivity of labour in respect of investment goods is higher. The same reasoning as above is obviously

[1] Cf. Appendix. Table XI.

applicable. On the same assumptions as before, D_4 is positive. Larger responsiveness in (i) the supply and (ii) the demand for labour for investment to variations in the rate of interest affect the size of D_4 in the same sense as that in which they affect the size of D_3.

D_5

§ 15. Once more, the real rate of wage being the same in system B as in system A, employment in the consumption industries must be the same. The supply function of labour for investment being more expanded, while the demand function is unchanged, there is more employment in the investment industries in system B. D_5 is positive. This is in contrast to what happens under a normal banking policy. For there, as we have seen, D_5 is negative. Under the type of banking policy now under review D_5 is (numerically) larger, the more responsive is the demand for labour for investment, and the less responsive is the supply, to variations in the rate of interest.

D_6

§ 16. In this case, instead of, as under the heading D_5, the supply function of labour for investment being more expanded in system B, the productivity of labour in the consumption industries is higher. This necessarily entails more employment there, provided that, as with the type of banking policy we have been postulating, the real rate of wage is held fixed. Reasoning analogous to that of the preceding section demonstrates that there is also more employment in the investment industries. Hence D_6 is positive. This again is in contrast to what happens under a normal banking policy. The influences that tend to make D_5 (numerically) large tend also to make D_6 large. The size of consumption income is here also relevant. The more responsive labour supply is to this, the larger is D_6.

CONCLUSION

§ 17. By way of conclusion to this chapter, a word may be added to anticipate a possible objection to what has been said about the differences, D_3, D_4 and D_5. It may be urged that, if the number of wage-earners engaged in the investment industries and taking out their wages in consumption goods is larger in system B than in system A, the number engaged in consumption industries there *must* also be larger, because the extra men at work in the investment industries in system B automatically set men to work in the consumption industries to provide the consumption goods absorbed in their wages. If this were correct, a part of our analysis would be refuted. But it is not correct. The requirement of extra workers in the investment industries for consumption goods can be satisfied without there being any extra production of consumption goods. I do not merely mean that it can be satisfied for the moment by a draft on the stocks of these goods in shops. It can be satisfied continuously by non-wage-earners diminishing their consumption of these goods so as to be able to invest more in engaging labour in investment industries ; and also, in such a country as England — though we are at present ignoring this — out of resources set free from providing for unemployed persons.[1] It must be admitted, indeed, that this way out would be in a measure barred if the amount of saving, and so of labour supplied for investment, were *completely* insensitive to the rate of interest. But,

[1] For a fuller discussion of these matters, cf. my *Theory of Unemployment*, Part III, Chapter IX.

granted, as is almost certainly the case, that the amount of labour for investment supplied is in some degree sensitive to the rate of interest, the way out is free. There is no reason why aggregate employment should not be larger even in conditions when employment in the consumption industries cannot be larger. The objection we have been considering thus breaks down, and the conclusions we have reached remain intact.

M

CHAPTER V

MODEL I (B)

§ 1. MODEL I (B) differs from Model I (A) in that, whereas it is still true that the proportionate share of income accruing to labour, alike in the consumption and the investment industries, is a constant, it is no longer true that this constant is the reciprocal of $\dfrac{F}{xF'} = \dfrac{\psi}{y\psi'}$, *i.e.* that perfect competition prevails. Rather we may write for it, not C_1, but C, where

$$C = \frac{F}{x\left(1 - \dfrac{1}{\eta_1}\right)F'} = \frac{\psi}{y\left(1 - \dfrac{1}{\eta_2}\right)\psi'}$$

and $\dfrac{1}{\eta_1}$ and $\dfrac{1}{\eta_2}$, which are respectively functions of $F(x)$ and $\psi(y)$, are not equal to 0, but are, each of them, positive and less than unity.[1] In what way does the introduction of this complication make it necessary to modify, for Model I (B), the conclusions about the D's that were reached in the last chapter for Model I (A) ?

§ 2. On consulting Table VII of the Appendix, we find that, with a normal banking policy, C enters into the denominator only of all the expressions for

---

[1] When we come to Model III we shall have to treat η_1 as a function of m_6 $F(x)$ and η_2 of m_4 $\psi(y)$. In the present model, however, although it is a special case of Model III, the condition that the proportionate shares accruing to labour shall be constant is incompatible with the η's being dependent on m_6 and m_4. Cf. Appendix, § 3.

the D's. We find further that it enters in such a way
that every D has the same sign as in Model I (A).

§ 3. With a banking policy directed (successfully) to
keeping money income constant, the same thing is true
of D_1 and D_2. All the other D's are equal to 0 in
Model I (B), just as they are in Model I (A); so that,
in respect of these D's, there is no difference between
the models.

§ 4. With a banking policy directed (successfully)
to keeping the price level of consumption goods constant, Table IX of the Appendix, along with the note
attached to it, shows that the sign of every D is again
the same as in Model I (A) so long as we have to do
with determinate situations. But in this model indeterminate situations are not excluded. Conditions *may*
be present in respect of which the analysis breaks down
for all the D's.[1]

[1] Cf. Appendix, § 7.

CHAPTER VI

MODEL II

§ 1. MODEL II differs from Model I (A) in that we do not assume the proportionate share of income accruing to wage-earners to be constant, but do still assume that conditions of perfect competition prevail. For a normal banking policy and for a policy directed to keep money income constant, the first three basic equations, namely

$$m_3\phi\left(\frac{r}{m_4}\right) = m_5 f\{r, \, m_6 F(x)\}, \qquad . \qquad . \quad \text{(I)}$$

$$y = m_5 f\{r, \, m_6 F(x)\}, \qquad . \qquad . \quad \text{(II)}$$

$$m_2 g(r) = (K_1 + K_2) m_1, \qquad . \qquad . \quad \text{(III)}$$

are the same as in Model I (A), but the third equation is qualified, not by the equalities

$$K_1 = \frac{F}{F'} = C_1 x,$$

$$K_2 = \frac{\psi}{\psi'} = C_1 y,$$

but only by the equalities

$$K_1 = \frac{F}{F''},$$

$$K_2 = \frac{\psi}{\psi'}.$$

Thus we may not write $m_2 g(r) = C_1(x + y) m_1$, but only the more general form,

$$m_2 g(r) = \left\{ \frac{F}{F'} + \frac{\psi}{\psi'} \right\} m_1.$$

For a banking policy that keeps the price of consumption goods constant, this third equation is not

$$\frac{d}{dm_n}\left(\frac{C_1 x m_1}{F m_2 m_6} \right) = 0, \quad \text{but} \quad \frac{d}{dm_n}\left(\frac{m_1}{F' m_2 m_6} \right) = 0.$$

On the basis of these facts, which need no further elaboration, I shall investigate the signs of our D's. Obviously, of that special case of Model II which is identical with Model I (A) there is no need to say anything further. Attention will be confined to other cases.

(a) *A normal banking policy*

§ 2. It is not practicable within reasonable limits to analyse our problem in ordinary language, as was done in Chapter IV for Model I (A). We must be content to set down and, so far as may be, elucidate the results of the algebraic analysis of the Appendix. By appropriate manipulation of our equations, we obtain expressions for all the D's. These expressions, of course, have, each of them, a numerator and a denominator. The denominator is found to be the same for all of them, and must be positive. In determining the signs of the D's, we have, therefore, only to consider the numerators. Remembering this, let us enquire directly whether the conclusions which we obtained for Model I (A) are still valid in Model II. Our algebra shows — what is not, indeed, difficult to see by common sense — that, all the other determinants being given, if the money rate of wages is higher in system B than in system A, aggregate employment must be smaller in system B, whereas if the money income function is higher for system B, aggregate employment must be larger. Thus in these two cases Model II necessarily works in the same way as Model I. That is to say, D_1 and D_2 have the same signs in Model II as they respectively have in Model I (A). It is found further that the numerical magnitudes of D_1 and D_2 are affected in Model II by the same influences as in Model I (A).

§ 3. When in system B the demand function for labour for investment, or the productivity function of labour in investment industries is higher than in system A, or the supply function of labour for investment is more expanded, or the productivity function of labour in the consumption industries is higher, our algebra shows that the signs of D_3, D_4 and D_5, *may* be different in Model II from what they are in Model I (A). For in each case there is a term in the numerator of the relevant expression whose sign may be either positive or negative. If this term reduces to nil, Model II works in the same way as Model I (A). But, if it is not nil, one or more of the conclusions reached for Model I (A) *may* be reversed. The term which thus threatens our peace is

$$\left\{ \frac{d}{dx}\left(\frac{F}{F'}\right) - \frac{d}{dy}\left(\frac{\psi}{\psi'}\right) \right\}.$$

§ 4. If this term is negative *and sufficiently large*, the conclusions of Model I (A), for the cases where system B differs from system A in having either (i) a higher demand function for labour for investment, or (ii) a greater productivity of labour in the investment industries, are reversed. Aggregate employment will be smaller instead of, as in Model I (A), larger than it is in system A. That is to say, D_3 and D_4 will be negative instead of positive. At first glance this seems impossible, or at least highly paradoxical. It is not, however, so in fact. For the call for a larger quantity of labour in the investment industries may entail — if the elasticity of marginal productivity there is small — the proportionate share of income accruing to non-wage-earners in those industries being much larger. If this is so, the amount of money income available for expenditure in the consumption industries may, in spite of the fact that aggregate income is larger, be much smaller. This may entail a lowering of employment there which more than offsets the raising of employment in the investment industries. More generally, the greater demand for investment in system B may be accompanied by so much larger a proportionate share of money income going to non-wage-earners in investment and consumption industries together that, in spite of a higher aggregate money income, the absolute amount of money income paid over to labour, and so, since the money rate of wages is supposed fixed, aggregate employment, may be smaller.

§ 5. Again, if the term $\left\{\dfrac{d}{dx}\left(\dfrac{F}{F'}\right) - \dfrac{d}{dy}\left(\dfrac{\psi}{\psi'}\right)\right\}$ is positive *and sufficiently large*, when system B differs from system A in having a more expanded supply function of labour for investment, aggregate employment will be larger instead of, as in Model I (A), smaller than in system A. D_5 will be positive, not negative. The explanation is that, while in this case the rate of interest, and so aggregate money income, must be lower in system B, aggregate money income is cut less than the absolute share of it accruing to non-wage-earners is cut. This means that more money is available for hiring labour, and consequently, the money wage-rate being fixed, there is more employment in system B than in system A. In like manner D_6 will be positive, not negative.

§ 6. It will have been noticed that the possibility of D_3, D_4, D_5 and D_6 having in Model II signs different from what they have in Model I (A) depends on the expression $\left\{ \dfrac{d}{dx}\left(\dfrac{F}{F'}\right) - \dfrac{d}{dy}\left(\dfrac{\psi}{\psi'}\right) \right\}$ being, not merely negative or positive as the case may be, but also upon its being *sufficiently large*. Now we have no general reason for thinking that the conditions of production in consumption and investment industries respectively will differ in one way rather than another, and still less reason for thinking that they will differ *substantially* in any way. In the absence of special knowledge, this ignorance gives colour to the claim — though the ground here is very slippery — that *probably* the relevant expression, whether it be positive or negative, is fairly small ; which implies that *probably* the signs of D_3, D_4, D_5 and D_6 will turn out to be the same in Model II as in Model I (A). This somewhat tenuous probability refers to the general case of Model II. If we restrict our view to the special case where conditions of production in the consumption and investment industries are exactly alike, so that $\dfrac{d}{dx}\left\{ \dfrac{F}{F'} \right\} = \dfrac{d}{dy}\left\{ \dfrac{\psi}{\psi'} \right\}$, the probability becomes a certainty. The same thing is, of course, true of the still more special case where $\dfrac{d}{dx}\left\{ \dfrac{F}{F'} \right\} = \dfrac{d}{dy}\left\{ \dfrac{\psi}{\psi'} \right\} = 1$, *i.e.* the case where constant returns rule over the relevant range in both consumption and investment industries. Constant returns, as we saw, are incompatible with the conditions postulated for Model I (A), but they are admissible under Model II.

(b) *A banking policy that keeps money income constant*

§ 7. So far we have supposed the banking policy to be normal. If, instead, it is one that aims (successfully) at keeping money income constant, D_1 is negative and

D_2 is positive, as with a normal banking policy. In general, the other D's may be either positive or negative, but, when $\dfrac{d}{dx}\left\{\dfrac{F}{F'}\right\} = \dfrac{d}{dy}\left\{\dfrac{\psi}{\psi'}\right\}$, they all reduce to 0. That this is so will be evident on an inspection of Table VI in the Appendix.

(c) *A banking policy that keeps the price level of consumption goods constant*

§ 8. Apart from the case of constant returns in the consumption industries, the analysis is on the same lines as that followed for Model I (A).

A higher level of money wage-rate, the prices of consumption goods being given, obviously implies a lower real wage-rate ; and a higher level of the money income function, the money wage-rate being given, a lower real wage-rate. In conditions of perfect competition we have seen that increasing returns are incompatible with stable equilibrium. Since, therefore, constant returns have been for the moment ruled out, only diminishing returns are left. When they prevail, it is evident that higher real wage-rates must carry with them smaller, and lower real wage-rates larger, employment in the consumption industries. An argument precisely similar to that developed in §§ 11-12 of Chapter IV then shows that D_1 must be negative and D_2 positive, just as they are with a normal banking policy.

For D_3, D_4 and D_5 the central fact is, just as it was for Model I (A), that no difference in the rate of real wage is possible. But under conditions of competition, with constant returns excluded, a fixed rate of real wage implies a fixed quantity of employment in the consumption industries. The real wage-rate determines this quantity absolutely. Hence, as between two systems, aggregate employment, if it differs at all, can only differ to the extent that employment in the investment industries differs. On this basis it can be shown that D_3 and D_4 are positive, nil or negative, according as, other things being equal, the supply of labour for investment is larger, the same or smaller, the higher the rate of interest. D_5 is positive in all circumstances. D_6 is the consequence of a higher productivity function of labour in the consumption industries, which, in the conditions here supposed, must entail more employment there. It readily follows that D_6 is positive. Thus the uncertainties that exist as regards the signs of D_3, D_4, D_5 and D_6, under a normal banking policy, are not now present.

§ 9. In the preceding paragraphs constant physical returns have been ruled out. But, as we have seen, constant physical returns in the consumption industries, while incompatible with the conditions of Model I (A), are admissible under Model II. When they prevail, under a banking policy directed (successfully) to keeping the price of consumption goods constant, systems A and B are both indeterminate. The signs and values of all the D's are, therefore, indeterminate also.[1]

[1] Cf. Appendix, § 7.

CHAPTER VII

MODEL III

§ 1. WHEREAS in Model II action in accordance with the rules of perfect competition was postulated, alike in consumption and in investment industries, Model III is so generalised as to take into account imperfect competition with different degrees, it may be, of imperfection in the two classes of industry. The formulae of Model II are thus simply those for Model III with the generalising symbols removed.

(a) *A normal banking policy*

§ 2. In Model III the money rate of wages need not be, as it must be in Model II, equal to the value of the marginal product of labour in each type of industry. But Model III differs from Model II, not only in this, but also in a second respect. In that model, as we saw in Part II, Chapter IV, § 9, for positions of stable equilibrium the marginal productivity of labour cannot be rising in either consumption or in investment industries. That is to say, neither F'' nor ψ'' can be positive. In Model III this condition is not imposed. It is not necessary for stability that marginal prime costs shall be falling or at least not rising.

§ 3. It appears at first sight that in Model III the denominator of the expressions for the D's — which is, as before, the same for all of them — is no longer, as it

was in Model II, necessarily positive, but *may* be either
positive or negative. This would imply, of course, that
the signs of all the D's are ambiguous ; so that, quite
literally, in Model III, with a normal and with a constant-income banking policy, all things would be possible. But, in accordance with what was said in Part II,
Chapter V, let us take it that $\left(\dfrac{\partial f}{\partial r} - \phi'\right)$, K'_1 and K'_2
are positive. It follows that the denominator, namely
$\left\{ K'_1\left(\dfrac{\partial f}{\partial r} - \phi'\right) + F'\dfrac{\partial f}{\partial F}\left(g' - K'_2\phi'\right)\right\}$, common to the expressions for all the D's, must be positive.

§ 4. Mathematical analysis shows further that, when
systems A and B differ in respect of the money rate of
wages and of the level of the money income function,
the numerators of the expressions for D_1 and D_2 are
the same as they are in Model II. D_1 is thus negative
and D_2 positive. But this is not so for the other D's.
Within their numerators for Model II we found the
expression $\left\{ \dfrac{d}{dx}\left(\dfrac{F}{F'}\right) - \dfrac{d}{dy}\left(\dfrac{\psi}{\psi'}\right)\right\}$, but within those for
Model III there stands a much more complicated
expression,

$$\frac{d}{dx}\left\{\frac{F}{F'} \cdot \left\{\frac{1}{1 - \dfrac{1}{\eta_1}}\right\}\right\} - \frac{d}{dy}\left\{\frac{\psi}{\psi'} \cdot \left\{\frac{1}{1 - \dfrac{1}{\eta_2}}\right\}\right\},$$

where η_1 is a function of $m_6 F(x)$ and η_2 of $m_4 \psi(y)$. In
this model, therefore, new elements being present, the
signs of the numerators for the D's other than D_1 and
D_2 are, so to speak, even more uncertain than in
Model II. As in that model, however, the introduction
of the restrictive proviso, that production and demand
conditions shall be exactly alike in the consumption
and in the investment industries, so that $K'_1 = K'_2$ makes

the numerators D_3 and D_5 unambiguous. D_3 is then positive, and D_5 negative. For D_4 to be positive and D_6 to be negative further restrictive conditions must, however, also be satisfied.

(b) *A banking policy directed to keep money income constant*

§ 5. As with a normal banking policy, D_1 is negative and D_2 is positive. In the general case all the other D's may be either positive or negative. If we introduce the restriction that $K'_1 = K'_2$, D_3 and D_5 reduce to 0. In order that D_4 and D_6 may reduce to 0, further restrictive conditions must also be satisfied.

(c) *A banking policy directed to keep the price of consumption goods constant*

§ 6. For a banking policy directed to keep the price of consumption goods constant, when the situation is determinate, D_1 is negative and D_2 positive. D_3 and D_4 are positive, provided that, other things being equal, a higher rate of interest evokes a larger supply of labour for investment. D_5 is positive ; but the sign of D_6 is uncertain. The situation is indeterminate, and the signs of all the D's consequently also indeterminate, not now, as in Model II, simply when constant physical returns rule in the consumption industries, but when

$$\frac{d}{dx}\left\{\left(1 - \frac{1}{\eta_1\{m_6 F(x)\}}\right)F'\right\} = 0.$$

There is nothing in the nature of things to prevent this condition — it means, of course, a different thing for D_6 from what it means for the other D's — from being satisfied over a substantial range, even though constant physical returns do not prevail. But, on the other hand, while, as was argued in Part II, Chapter II, § 5, there are definite grounds for expecting constancy of physical returns on certain occasions in real life, this cannot be said about the above highly complex and artificial-seeming condition.

CHAPTER VIII

EMPLOYMENT MULTIPLIERS

§ 1. THE term multiplier, for which Keynes secured wide currency, has been used in a variety of different senses.[1] In particular, it is necessary to distinguish employment multipliers and money multipliers. Employment multipliers are differences in aggregate employment divided by associated net differences in employment in the investment industries; money multipliers are differences in total money income divided by associated net differences in money investment: and these two sorts of multiplier, while they are equal in certain conditions, are not equal in others. In the present chapter I am concerned exclusively with employment multipliers, the relation between these and money multipliers being left for discussion in the next chapter.

§ 2. It is easy to see that, according to circumstances, employment multipliers for various types of difference between two systems may be found with values less than 0, equal to 0, equal to 1 or greater than 1. An employment multiplier less than 0 implies that, for a given excess of employment in the investment industries, as between systems B and A, there is a more than equal deficiency of employment in the consumption industries; one equal to 0 implies that there is an equal deficiency; one equal to 1 implies that an excess

[1] At the beginning of the century the term was widely used to express the relation between the total stock of private capital in the country and annual assessments to death duties.

or deficiency of employment in the investment industries is associated with no difference in employment in the consumption industries ; one greater than 1 implies that an excess (or deficiency) of employment in system B as against system A in the investment industries is associated with some excess (or deficiency) in the consumption industries also. Thus, in order that any employment multiplier shall be other than equal to 1, it is necessary that the cause which has modified the quantity of employment for investment shall also have modified — either increased or decreased — the quantity of employment in consumption industries. Clearly 0 and 1 are two critical values for employment multipliers.

§ 3. For real life, where the scales of different investment industries are free, as they are not in our models, to vary relatively to one another, a word of warning is appropriate here. As is explicitly stated in our definition, employment multipliers relate differences in aggregate employment to differences in *net* employment for investment. Hence from a knowledge of what these multipliers are we can learn nothing about the implications for aggregate employment of, say, a difference between two systems as regards investment in public works by the Government. For larger Government investment may in some circumstances entail smaller investment by private persons, either because the products resulting from Government investment compete with the products of particular private firms, so that the expectation of profit from investment in private industry is directly reduced — as would obviously happen, for example, if the Government invested in a public boot and shoe factory — or because it makes the rate of interest higher, and so indirectly discourages investment in all kinds of private industry. Before, therefore, the calculation of any employment multiplier can tell us the implications for aggregate employment of a given excess of employment in a particular field of investment, we must know how employment in other fields is affected.

§ 4. In some discussions of " the multiplier " it has been tacitly assumed that, when two systems differ in respect of employment in investment industries, the associated difference in aggregate employment is related to this difference by one single multiplier, *The Multiplier*, which is always the same regardless of the way in which the excess of employment in investment industries has been brought about. This view is completely erroneous. It is hoped that the discussion which follows, together with the relevant tables in the Appendix, will make the true position clear. As in the preceding chapters, it is necessary to distinguish what happens with a normal banking policy, with one that keeps money income constant, and with one that keeps the price of consumption goods constant. It is also necessary to distinguish what happens respectively in each of our several models. As with the D's, so here with the M's, I shall begin with Model I (A), or rather, since Models I (A) and I (B) function similarly, with Model I.

(a) Model I

§ 5. With a normal banking policy we find that the six multipliers are arranged in pairs, M_1 having the same value as M_2, M_3 as M_4, and M_5 as M_6. These pairs have all, in general, different values. In the special case where the quantity of labour supplied for investment is completely insensitive to variations in the rate of interest, the first two pairs do, indeed, coincide — a matter to which reference will be made presently. But in no circumstances can the first two pairs have the same value as the pair M_5 and M_6. On the contrary, while all the other multipliers must be positive, M_5 and

M_6 must be negative. The necessity for a difference in sign is easily seen when we recall what was said in Chapter IV about D_5 and D_6. We there saw that, whereas greater demand for labour in investment industries is associated with more employment for investment and more aggregate employment, greater readiness to supply employment for investment — greater " thriftiness " — is associated with more employment for investment but *less* aggregate employment. Thus, in the former case the multiplier is positive ; in the latter, negative. This is, of course, merely a particular illustration of the general statement made above. The actual values of all the M's are set out in Table VII of the Appendix.

§ 6. With a banking policy directed to keep money income constant, since in Model I the proportion of income going to wage-earners is constant, so long as the money rate of wage is fixed the aggregate quantity of employment must be fixed. It follows that all the multipliers, other than M_1 and M_2, reduce to 0. For M_1 the rate of money wages is higher in system B than in system A. Therefore, money income being the same in both systems, employment in each of our two types of industry is smaller in system B. Hence M_1 is positive and greater than unity. With a constant-income banking policy, in the sense that allows of different incomes in systems A and B, it is evident that, as with a normal banking policy, M_2 has the same value as M_1.

§ 7. There remains a banking policy directed to keep the price of consumption goods constant. In that special case of Model I (B) in which the D's are indeterminate all the M's are, of course, also indeterminate. Apart from this case, alike in Model I (B) and in Model I (A) the values of M_1 and M_2 are both equal to one another and the same as they are with a normal bank-

ing policy. This at first sight is surprising ; but algebraic analysis leaves no doubt on the matter. They are
always positive and greater than unity. If the supply
of employment for investment is completely insensitive
to variations in the rate of interest, the multipliers M_3
and M_4 are both $= \dfrac{0}{0}$; for difference in total employment
and difference in employment in the investment in-
dustries are both nil. If the supply of employment for
investment is not thus completely insensitive, the
quantity of employment for investment is larger, the
more expanded is the demand function or the supply
function of labour for investment. But the quantity
of employment in the consumption industries is rigidly
fixed. It follows that aggregate employment varies
as between two economic systems to the precise extent
to which employment in the investment industries
varies. Hence M_3 and M_4 are equal to unity. The
multiplier M_5 is in like manner equal to unity ; both
when the supply of employment for investment is and
when it is not completely insensitive to variations in
the rate of interest. M_6, like M_1 and M_2, is positive and
greater than unity ; for employment in the consumption
industries, as well as in the investment industries, is
larger, the more expanded is the productivity function of
labour in the investment industries. The precise values
of all these M's are set out in Table IX in the Appendix.

(b) Models II and III

§ 8. In the case of constant returns in the consumption industries, under Model II and in the sub-case of
Model III named in Part III, Chapter VII, § 6, a banking policy directed to keep the price of consumption
goods constant makes all the multipliers indeterminate.

Subject to this, the following results can be established. First, in Models II and III the multipliers M_1 and M_2 have the same value as they had in Model I ; this value being itself the same with all three types of banking policy. Secondly, with a normal banking policy, and also with one that keeps money income constant, in the sub-cases of Models II and III, where respectively $\frac{d}{dx}\left(\frac{F}{F'}\right)$ and $\frac{d}{dy}\left(\frac{\psi}{\psi'}\right)$ are equal and positive and K'_1 and K'_2 are equal and positive, the multipliers M_3 and M_5, though they need not have the same values as in Model I, necessarily have the same sign. Thirdly, in like conditions the same thing is true of M_4 and M_6 in Model II, but not necessarily in Model III. Fourthly, in the general cases of Models II and III it will be recalled that, with a normal banking policy and with one directed to keep money income constant, the signs of D_3 to D_6 are uncertain. It follows that the signs of the corresponding M's are also uncertain. Fifthly, with a banking policy that keeps the price of consumption goods constant, except in those cases when the analysis breaks down,[1] the multipliers M_3 . . . M_5 have the same signs and values that they have in Model I. M_6 has a different value and may have a different sign.

(c) *A special condition*

§ 9. Some writers have suggested that the quantity of labour supplied for investment — via saving — is completely, or so nearly completely as to make no difference, insensitive to variations in the rate of interest. Keynes appears to have been of this opinion. If it is correct, the formulae for our multipliers are greatly simplified. Not only in Models I (A) and I (B), but also in the more complex Models II and III, M_1 and M_2

---

[1] Cf. Appendix, § 7.

reduce to the value $\left\{1 + \dfrac{1}{F'\dfrac{\partial f}{\partial F}}\right\}$ with all three types of

banking policy — except in the cases where the third type makes all the multipliers indeterminate. Moreover, with a normal banking policy M_3 reduces to this value in all cases of all the models ; and M_4 reduces to it except in Model III. This, of course, is far from

saying that the value $\left\{1 + \dfrac{1}{F'\dfrac{\partial f}{\partial F}}\right\}$ can be regarded as *The*

Multiplier for all purposes. Even now under a normal banking policy M_5 and M_6 in all cases have different values, and in some cases have opposite signs from the others. Further, with a banking policy directed to keep money income constant, and equally with one directed — successfully — to keep the price of consumption goods constant, M_3 and, in the latter case, also M_4 become equal to $\dfrac{0}{0}$. That is to say, differences in the demand function for labour for investment and differences in the productivity of labour in investment industries carry with them no difference either in aggregate employment or in employment in investment industries. Thus, even when the special condition of which we have been speaking is satisfied, the idea that there is only one single employment multiplier applicable to all purposes is incorrect. Nevertheless, when that special condition is satisfied, the expression $\left\{1 + \dfrac{1}{F'\dfrac{\partial f}{\partial F}}\right\}$, which is obviously > 1, has a wide range and

occupies an important place among multipliers in general, and *a fortiori* among those that are determinate.

§ 10. The explanation of this fact is not difficult.

So long as, between two economic systems A and B, conditions of productive technique are the same, the supply functions of labour for investment are not different and the quantities supplied are insensitive to variations in the rate of interest, the quantity of employment in the investment industries and the quantity in the consumption industries are uniquely correlated. There can be no question, whatever happens to the other balancing factors, of the one quantity being modified without the other being modified; and, if the one is modified in a given degree, the other must be modified in another degree, which is the same irrespective of how the modification has been caused. Where, however, as between two systems, the cause of difference is that the supply functions of labour for investment are themselves different, even though supply is wholly insensitive to differences in the rate of interest, the unique correlation spoken of above does not exist. Aggregate employment is still, indeed, *in each given situation,* uniquely related to labour supplied in investment industries; but the unique relation is a different one in different situations. For the cases to which M_1, M_2 and M_3 refer, aggregate employment is the same function of labour supplied for investment; for those to which M_5 and M_6 refer, it is one function for system A and a different function for system B. Thus it happens that

M_1 and M_2 have the same value, namely $\left\{ 1 + \dfrac{1}{F'\dfrac{\partial f}{\partial F}} \right\}$,

with all three types of banking policy; that M_3 either has this value or is equal to $\dfrac{0}{0}$ in the way explained above; and that M_5 and M_6 have different values; while M_4 constitutes a peculiar intermediate case.

§ 11. Lest, however, the importance of the expression $\left\{1 + \dfrac{1}{F'\dfrac{\partial f}{\partial F}}\right\}$ should be exaggerated, a cautionary

word must be added. The assumption that the supply of labour for investment is wholly insensitive to the rate of interest, though, of course, we may make it, if we choose, for purposes of pure theory, cannot be made whole-heartedly in models which aim at simulating actual life. The assumption *cannot* be valid universally. For, if it were, when full employment prevailed, the amount of investment would remain the same no matter how greatly demand functions for investment differed unless, indeed, swings in them were accompanied by swings in the money income function.

CONCLUSION

§ 12. It should be added that every one of the several multipliers that we have been discussing may be expected to have a different value according to what the position is from which we start.[1] This follows from the fact that the second differentials of the functions involved are, in general, not nil. Moreover, our multipliers, whatever the position from which we start, refer directly only to differences in labour investment that approach the limit of smallness. The formulae must, therefore, be used with caution when applied to substantial differences.[2] The conclusions we have reached about the signs of the several multipliers and as to whether they are greater than 0 or than 1 may be expected, however, as a rule, to hold good for such differences.

[1] This implies that any multipliers we might succeed in constructing for the real world would, in general, have different values in respect of different parts of the trade cycle.

[2] Cf. *ante*, Part III, Chapter I, § 4.

CHAPTER IX

MONEY MULTIPLIERS

§ 1. IT is not easy to see without the help of mathematics precisely how the multipliers discussed in the last chapter are related to the corresponding money multipliers. Moreover, we are in danger of falling into a serious fallacy. We may be tempted to argue as follows. In Models I (A) and I (B), the proportion of income accruing to wage-earners being always the same, alike in consumption industries and in investment industries, the ratio which money investment bears to total money income must be always the same as the ratio which employment devoted to investment bears to total investment. *Therefore* in these models every money multiplier must be identical with the corresponding employment multiplier. But to argue so is to forget our definition of multipliers. These are, not income or employment divided by associated investment income or investment employment, but *difference* in income or employment divided by associated *difference* in investment income or investment employment. When this is held in mind, it is apparent that the above argument fails. We cannot prove in that direct and simple way — nor, as will appear in a moment, is it in fact true even in Model I (A) — that all the money multipliers coincide with the corresponding employment multipliers. A more difficult analysis is required.

190

Money multipliers, it will be remembered, are called N, as against M for employment multipliers. In what follows I shall ignore the special case — possible except in Model I (A) — in which the analysis breaks down. With this understanding, I shall, as in the last chapter, begin with Model I.

Model I

§ 2. Here there is considerable difficulty about N_1, the money multiplier associated with a difference in the money rate of wages. There is no ground for expecting that N_1 will ever be identical with its opposite number M_1, the employment multiplier. With a banking policy directed to keep money income constant it is obviously nil. Also with either of the other two banking policies it has a value quite different from M_1. Alike under a normal banking policy and under one directed to keep the price of consumption goods constant, the expression for it is very complicated ; and there is, moreover, little resemblance between the expressions proper to these two banking policies. Further, under both policies the sign of N_1 is uncertain. Thus in Model I the relation of this particular money multiplier N_1 to the corresponding employment multiplier is ambiguous. A little reflection shows, however, that this is not so with the other multipliers. Since in this model the proportionate share of income accruing to wage-earners is constant, provided that the rate of money wages and the money income function are the same as between system A and system B, money multipliers and employment multipliers must be identical. That is to say, for all three types of banking policy N_3, N_4, N_5 and N_6 are all identical with the corresponding M's. This, if it cannot be seen with the naked eye, is readily demonstrated

algebraically. Further, algebraic analysis shows — a
thing very far from obvious to the naked eye — that
for all three types of banking policy N_2 in Model I is
identical with M_2.[1]

Model II

§ 3. When we move forward to Model II, the complications noticed in the relation of N_1 to M_1 in Model I
are naturally still present with all three types of banking
policy. With all three the other N's are found to
coincide with the corresponding M's, provided that
$\left\{\dfrac{d}{dx}\left(\dfrac{F}{F'}\right) - \dfrac{d}{dy}\left(\dfrac{\psi}{\psi'}\right)\right\}$, which played an important part in
Chapter VI, is equal to 0. In the general case of Model
II there is nothing to be said of a clear-cut kind about
the relation of any N to any M with a normal banking
policy. But with that banking policy N_2, N_3 and N_4
are positive and N_5 and N_6 negative ; with a banking
policy directed to keep money income constant, all the
N's, except N_2, are nil ; while, with one directed to keep
the price of consumption goods constant, N_2, N_3, N_4, N_5
and N_6 are positive, N_3, N_4 and N_5 being equal to the
corresponding employment multipliers.

Model III

§ 4. In Model III with all three types of banking
policy the relation of N_1 to M_1 is even more complex
than in Model II. With all three types, provided that
$K'_1 = K'_2$, N_2, N_3 and N_5 coincide with the correspond-

[1] When the supply of employment for investment is completely insensitive
to variations in the rate of interest, N_3 (and N_4) are identical with M_3 (and
M_4), in the sense that both are equal to $\dfrac{0}{0}$. Thus mathematically $\dfrac{N_3}{M_3}$ and $\dfrac{N_4}{M_4}$
might be called indeterminate rather than equal to unity. The essential fact
is that investment employment, money investment, total employment and
total money income all remain unaltered when m_3 and m_4 vary.

ing M's. In the general case of Model III the conclusions set out in § 3 for the general case of Model II hold good except that, with a normal banking policy, the sign of N_4 is uncertain.[1]

[1] Cf. Appendix, Tables II and VI.

CHAPTER X

THE CASE OF A BANKING POLICY THAT KEEPS THE RATE OF INTEREST CONSTANT

§ 1. THE discussion of what happens to the values of the D's, M's and N's with a banking policy directed to keep the rate of interest constant, has been reserved, as was forecast in Chapter III, § 6, for a separate chapter. The reason is that, whereas with the other three kinds of banking policy the answers to the questions we had to ask were frequently different for different models and sub-cases of models, with this type all the D's and M's are the same in all circumstances and there is no need to draw any distinction between the models. Some of the N's are, indeed, different for different models, but, as will be seen, that matter can be disposed of in a brief space. I shall consider first the D's and M's together, then the N's. In general, apart from the case in which the money income function is different in systems A and B, the condition that the money rate of interest is held constant may be expressed by saying that $g'(r)$ is infinite.

D_1 and M_1

§ 2. The rate of interest being held constant, it is evident that, when the demand function for labour for investment, the supply function of labour for investment and the productivity functions of labour in the consumption and the investment industries are all given, the quantity of labour devoted to investment cannot vary, and, therefore (in view of the invariability of the rate of interest), the quantity devoted to consumption, which is a function of this, cannot vary either. This implies that a difference, as between systems B and A, in the money rate of wage carries with it no difference in aggregate employment. D_1 is nil. Thus, on this assumption about banking policy, those writers who affirm that differences in money wage-rates are associated with equi-proportionate differences in money incomes and money prices, leaving employment unvaried, are right. From what has been said it follows immediately that M_1 is equal to $\dfrac{0}{0}$.

D_2 *and* M_2

§ 3. When we say that in system A banking policy is directed to keep the rate of interest constant, this implies that *any* volume of money income is compatible with the given rate of interest. If, therefore, we interpret our condition to entail that the rate of interest is kept the same in system B as in system A, D_2 must be nil and M_2 must be $\dfrac{0}{0}$. Let us, however, interpret it otherwise. We want to know what difference there is in employment, and what the multiplier is, when in system A the fixed interest rate is one thing, and in system B a different thing. With a higher rate of interest there must be less employment in the investment industries and, therefore, also in the consumption industries. That is to say, D_2 is negative. M_2, on the other, hand is positive and greater than unity.[1]

D_3 *and* D_4 *and* M_3 *and* M_4

§ 4. If, all the other balancing factors being given, the demand function for labour for investment stands

---

[1] Cf. Appendix, Table III and footnote.

higher in system B than in system A, then, since the
rate of interest is held constant, there is necessarily
more employment in the investment industries in system
B than in system A ; and this implies that there is
also more employment in the consumption industries
there. Hence D_3 is positive. By parity of reasoning it
can be shown that D_4 is positive. It follows from what
was said above that M_3 and M_4 are greater than
unity. They are equal to one another, having the
value $\left\{ 1 + \dfrac{1}{F' \dfrac{\partial f}{\partial F}} \right\}$, with which we became familiar in
Chapter VIII.

D_5 and D_6 and M_5 and M_6

§ 5. If, all the other factors being given, the supply
function of labour for investment is more expanded in
system B than in system A, since the rate of interest is
held constant, the amount of labour demanded in investment industries cannot be different in the two systems.
Employment in the investment industries is, therefore,
not different. The different form of the supply function
of labour for investment in system B implies, however,
that, with the same employment in the investment industries in systems B and A, there must be less employment
in the consumption industries in system B. It follows
that D_5 is negative. By parity of reasoning D_6 is negative. It follows from what has been said that M_5 is
infinite ; and the same thing is easily proved of M_6.

The N's

§ 6. As was indicated in § 1, the values of all the
D's and M's are the same in all cases of all our models.
This is also true of N_5 and N_6, which are equal to the

corresponding M's and are infinite. N_1, N_2 and N_3 are positive and greater than unity in all the models ; but their values are different in different models.[1] N_4 may be either greater or smaller than N_3, and *may* be less than unity or even negative.

[1] For a summary statement of the contents of this chapter compare Table IV of the Appendix and the accompanying footnote.

CHAPTER XI

§ 1. Up to the present no account has been taken of the fact that persons who are unemployed generally receive payments, in part at all events, at the expense of non-wage-earners. This does not merely happen when legal systems of unemployment benefit and assistance have been established. In one way or another it happens everywhere, partly through private charity, partly through the Poor Law. Indeed it is conceivable, though unlikely, that an Unemployment Insurance Scheme might be so organised — a levy being made each year on all wage-earners in employment to provide a fund for those out of work — that it would cause the contributions of non-wage-earners to be *smaller* than it would have been had no legal scheme existed. However that may be, it is convenient for the purpose of our present discussion to suppose the contributions of non-wage-earners to be made through an organised system of some such type as is actually established in this country. A full study of the implications of the British scheme would, in view of the details about employers' and workpeople's contributions, be very complicated. The dominant characteristic of the scheme is, however, that under it substantial quantities of consumption goods are transferred from the command of non-wage-earners to that of unemployed persons, and that the total amount of the transfer is larger when unemployment is heavy than when it is light. Ignoring secondary matters, I shall concentrate attention upon this characteristic.

§ 2. Two questions have to be considered. First : In a given state of all the relevant functions referred to in the preceding chapters, what, if any, difference will there be in aggregate employment when some provision is made for the unemployed instead of none, or when a provision more costly, from the standpoint of non-wage-earners, is substituted for a less costly provision ? Secondly : When two economic systems differ from one another in each of the six ways whose implications were examined in this Part, how will the associated differences in aggregate employment be affected by the existence of a scheme of assistance to the unemployed ? Both of these questions have to be asked and answered in respect of each of the four principal types of banking policy that have been distinguished.

§ 3. As a preliminary to attacking either of them we have to note that the existence of unemployment benefit may induce some men, who could have obtained work and would have done so had there been no benefit, in one way or another to avoid it. It is conceivable that voluntary unemployment induced in this manner may be so large that, in spite of perfect mobility of labour, extensive unemployment, as recorded for insurance, and an extensive shortage of labour exist at the same time, employers having a larger number of vacancies than they are able to fill. If the rate of unemployment benefit were fixed at two or three times the rate of wages, this paradoxical situation would probably in fact establish itself ; until it was broken either by a rise in wage-rates or by a reduction in the rate of benefit. So long, however, as the existence of a benefit system does not create sufficient voluntary unemployment to entail a shortage of labour, any malingering that does occur

o

merely ensures that the particular people who choose to malinger shall be included among the unemployed ; it does not affect the aggregate numbers who are respectively employed and unemployed. I shall not, therefore, say anything more about this.

§ 4. So much being understood, for both our questions the first step in analysis is as follows. Hitherto we have expressed the supply of labour for investment as a function of the rate of interest and of the total income of consumption goods. Plainly, however, as was indicated in Part II, Chapter II, § 13, it is not *aggregate* income of consumption goods that is relevant here. For people with very small means are in receipt of income, but cannot save anything, and so cannot contribute anything towards hiring labour for investment. For our earlier discussions this did not matter, because *relevant* income of consumption goods itself is a straightforward function of total consumption income. Now, however, the point becomes significant. What is paid over to unemployed persons at the expense of non-wage-earners is clearly not *relevant* income of consumption goods. It follows that the establishment or the liberalising of a benefit system of the type in which we are interested entails that the relevant income of consumption goods is at all times smaller than it would otherwise have been, and is affected more adversely the more unemployment there is.

§ 5. With this analytical basis, let us turn more particularly to the first of our two questions. We suppose that, all the other balancing factors being the same, a system of unemployment benefit is present in system B but not in system A, or is more liberal in system B, in the sense that the transfer from non-wage-earners per unemployed man is larger. Since income of consumption goods so transferred is not relevant to investment, the broad effect of a transfer being made on the aggregate volume of employment must be similar to that of a lesser readiness to save on the part of the community as a whole in respect of a given rate of interest. Thus the answer to our question is already given by implication in what has been said in earlier chapters about the sign of D_5. Nevertheless, it will be convenient to collect together here the several parts of that answer.

§ 6. First, with a normal banking policy, *i.e.* where g' is positive but not infinite, in Model I the net effect of the provision, or of an increase in the rate, of unemployment benefit at the expense of non-wage-earners will be favourable to aggregate employment ; whatever damage may be done to employment for investment being more than offset by benefit to employment in the consumption industries. In Model II the effect may be either favourable or unfavourable, but, in accordance with the reasoning developed in Part III, Chapter VI, § 6, is more likely to be favourable. For Model III additional sources of uncertainty are present, and no general solution can be given.

Secondly, with a banking policy that keeps money income constant, in Model I, since the proportion of income accruing to employed wage-earners is fixed, it is clear that (so long as the money rate of wage is unaltered) transfers of income from non-wage-earners to unemployed wage-earners can make no difference to aggregate employment. The provision of unemployment benefit or the existence of a higher rate of benefit has, therefore, no effect on aggregate employment. In Model II it can be shown — by reference to Table VI of the Appendix — that aggregate employment will be affected favourably or unfavourably, according as $\left\{ \dfrac{d}{dx}\left(\dfrac{F}{F'}\right) - \dfrac{d}{dy}\left(\dfrac{\psi}{\psi'}\right) \right\}$ is negative or positive. This is the same condition that was found, in Chapter VI, to make D_5 and D_6 positive or negative. There is no general reason to suppose that $\dfrac{d}{dx}\left(\dfrac{F}{F'}\right)$ and $\dfrac{d}{dy}\left(\dfrac{\psi}{\psi'}\right)$ will differ appreciably from one another. We may, therefore, conclude that the provision of benefit, or an addition to the rate of benefit, for unemployed persons may affect aggregate employment either favourably or unfavourably. On the evidence, it is equally likely to affect it in either sense, but in any event is not likely to affect it much. In Model III no general solution can be given.

Thirdly, with a banking policy that keeps the price of consumption goods, and so the real wage-rate, fixed, the existence of a benefit system or of a more liberal scale of benefit, while — apart from indeterminate cases — it leaves the amount of employment in the consumption industries unaffected, entails a smaller amount of it in investment industries. Hence, contrary to what happens in Model I with a normal banking policy, it is unfavourable to aggregate employment. This is true of all our models.

Fourthly, with a banking policy that keeps the rate of interest constant, *i.e.* when g' is infinite, in all our models the existence of unemployment benefit is favourable to aggregate employment.

§ 7. At first glance it appears that our second question must need a lengthy answer. For, since we have distinguished six types of difference among balancing factors, there are six sub-heads to it. In fact, however, no very elaborate discussion is required. We start with the fact that, when, for any reason whatever, system B contains less unemployment than system A, there is in it less need for payment to unemployed persons. Hence, whatever induces more employment induces also, because there is more *relevant* income of consumption goods, greater readiness to supply labour for investment at a given rate of interest.

With a normal banking policy this means, certainly in Model I and probably in Model II, that, when provision for the unemployed exists, every influence that makes for enlarged (or for contracted) employment, calls into play a counteracting force, and one, moreover, which is more powerful the more liberal is the provision made. Thus, under a normal banking policy, the effect of a benefit scheme, certainly in Model I and probably in Model II, is to damp down differences in aggregate employment between two systems, no matter in what respect the two systems differ. $D_1 \ldots D_6$ are all made smaller than they would have been in the absence of a benefit scheme.[1] With Model III the answer to my second question, like that to my first, is uncertain.

With a banking policy directed to keep money income constant, in Model I, $D_3 \ldots D_6$ are nil. So far as they are concerned, therefore, there is nothing to damp down, and no damping-down takes place. For D_1 and D_2 there is obviously the same kind of damping-down, certainly in Model I and probably in Model II, as occurs with a normal banking policy.

With a banking policy directed to keep the price of consumption goods constant the effect of a benefit scheme is, for all our models, the opposite to what it is in Model I under a normal banking policy. The existence of such a scheme, instead of damping down differences in aggregate employment as between two systems, magnifies them. $D_1 \ldots D_6$ are all larger in all our models

[1] Throughout this analysis we have assumed that the money income function g is kept intact. Should it happen that, when unemployment becomes heavy, the Government finances itself by causing the banking system to create a larger volume of money at a given rate of interest, it will be causing the function g to be expanded. Evidently, if this function is to be expanded or contracted as unemployment grows or lessens, a new factor is introduced, as a consequence of which the damping-down process is further accentuated.

than they would have been in the absence of the benefit scheme.

Finally, with a banking policy directed to keep the rate of interest constant $D_1 = 0$, so that, in respect of it, no damping-down is possible. In all other cases in all our models, the establishment of a benefit scheme has a damping-down effect.

CHAPTER XII

PERIODS OF PRODUCTION

§ 1. Strictly, as was pointed out in Part II, Chapter II, alike in the consumption and the investment industries, the money rate of wage is a specifiable function of the value of the marginal product of labour, divided, so as to allow for discounting, in the one case by $(1 + rh_1)$, in the other by $(1 + rh_2)$; where r is the annual rate of interest and h_1 and h_2 the periods of production in the consumption industries and the investment industries respectively, expressed as fractions of a year. Throughout our discussions so far we have assumed that h_1 and h_2 are so small that $(1 + rh_1)$ and $(1 + rh_2)$ may both be regarded as equal to unity. We have now to enquire how far and in what respects the conclusions we have reached are modified when this assumption is removed and an alternative assumption more accurately reflecting the conditions of real life is substituted for it. I shall not trouble with the case where h_1 and h_2 are different, but shall be content with the simpler case in which they are identical and may both be written h.

§ 2. The essence of the matter is this. In all circumstances the formulae set out in the Appendix still stand. When $h = 0$ the function $g(r)$ measures aggregate money income, and what has been said in the preceding chapters on that basis is correct. But, when h is positive, the function $g(r)$ does not measure money income. Money income is measured by a different function, $\omega(r)$, which

205

is related to the function $g(r)$ by the equation $g(r)$ $= \frac{\omega(r)}{(1 + rh)}$ for all values of r. Consequently, the condition that g' is positive, nil, infinite, or such as to make the price of consumption goods constant, implies that these things are true of $\frac{d}{dr}\left(\frac{\omega(r)}{1 + rh}\right)$. Now, when ϵ is written for the elasticity of money income in respect of the rate of interest,

$$g' = \frac{d}{dr}\left(\frac{\omega(r)}{1 + rh}\right) = \frac{\omega(r)}{r(1 + rh)}\left(\epsilon - \frac{rh}{1 + rh}\right).$$

Of course, in real life h is different for different sorts of goods. But there is some reason for thinking that in this country and in the United States aggregate working capital — the value of goods in process — is equivalent to some five or six months' income, and aggregate liquid capital — the value of goods in warehouses and shops — to a few weeks' or possibly months' income.[1] This implies a period of production — in the sense of interval between the date when a representative man's work is done and the date when the product of that work is sold to final purchasers [2] — of a little over six months. Let us call it six months : and let us take the value of r initially, *i.e.* in system A, to be 4 per cent. In these conditions, for g' to be positive implies that $\epsilon > \frac{1}{51}$, and for g' to be nil implies that $\epsilon = \frac{1}{51}$. It follows that the signs for our several D's, M's and N's which were found to hold with a normal banking policy when $h = 0$, also hold, when $h = \frac{1}{2}$ and the initial value of r is 4 per cent, with a banking policy directed to make money income increase by more than $\frac{1}{51}$st of

---

[1] Cf. Keynes, *Treatise on Money*, vol. ii. pp. 107 and 134.

[2] The date of these sales, not the date of sales to wholesalers, is the proper one to take, since money income is, on our definition, equal to the expenditure of final purchasers.

itself should r increase by 1 per cent of itself. In like manner the signs which, with h nil, held for a banking policy that keeps money income constant, now hold for one that in these conditions makes money income increase by exactly $\frac{1}{51}$st of itself. Further, whenever in our expressions g enters, this now means, not money income, but money income divided by $(1 + rh)$, *i.e.* by 1·02.

§ 3. There remains the question, what now corresponds to a banking policy directed to keep the price level of consumption goods constant ? The policy, which, when h is finite, has the same effect that that policy has when h equals 0, is one directed to keeping constant, not exactly the price of consumption goods, but this price divided by $(1 + rh)$. Thus, in Model II, it is when this condition, not the condition, constancy of the price of consumption goods itself, is satisfied, that the existence of constant returns in the consumption industries now leaves the volume of employment indeterminate.

CHAPTER XIII

MONOPOLISTIC POLICY

§ 1. In Chapter I, § 2, of this Part it was proposed to leave out of account until the final chapter the implications of differences in the degree to which the economic system is subjected in different circumstances to monopolistic action. A little must now be said upon that subject.

§ 2. Throughout the main part of our discussion we have argued as though the supply of labour offered for investment depended simply on the rate of interest and on the aggregate income of consumption goods, without regard to the way in which these are distributed among people of different degrees of wealth. This simplification is warranted by the high measure of stability that has prevailed for a long time in the proportions of income accruing to wage-earners and non-wage-earners respectively.[1] It was shown, however, in Chapter II of this Part that real income controlled by better-to-do persons has much more relevance to the supply of labour for investment than equal amounts of real income controlled by relatively poor persons. Thus, in general, anything that increases the proportionate share of real income accruing to non-wage-earners has the effect of increasing the supply of labour for investment; so lowering the rate of interest; so lowering the amount of money income; and so lowering the volume of

[1] Cf. *ante*, Part III, Chapter III, § 3.

employment. Now monopolistic action in industry, by cutting the real rate of wages below the work-people's marginal product, carries with it a gain for non-wage-earners at the expense of wage-earners. It follows that the introduction of monopolistic activity into industry, or an intensification in the degree of it, must, other things being equal, reduce employment via a reduction of money income.

§ 3. Thus as regards employment — and this is also true as regards the employment multiplier — a growth in the degree of monopoly in industry has the same kind of effect as would have followed had other things remained equal but the money rate of wages had been raised. There will always be some addition to the degree of monopolistic activity that will offset a given decrease in the money rate of wages ; and conversely. In order to establish a given level of employment we must put money wage-rates lower if the degree of monopolisation is large than if it is small ; or alternatively we must put the degree of monopolisation lower if the money wage-rate is large than if it is small.

§ 4. There is, however, a tendency in industry for monopolistic pressure to be keener in bad times than in good ; so that, when, for example, aggregate money income is reduced in consequence of a fall in the demand for labour for investment leading to a fall in the rate of money interest, it is enhanced. Hence the fluctuations of employment associated with given fluctuations in the demand for labour to invest are made larger than they would be if either there were no monopolistic pressure at any time or if equal pressures were exercised at all times.

§ 5. One further point should be noted. At first sight it might seem that, since, when monopolistic pressure is being exercised, the wielders of that pressure are enjoying, on account of it, a special gain, there is a kind of cushion available to absorb the effect of additions to money wage-rates, so that these might be enforced without any consequential increase in prices or decrease in employment. This is a misconception. It is true that, if an increase in money wage-rates were accompanied by a cessation of monopolistic pressure, and if the increase in money wage-rates did not exceed a certain size, the two changes would cancel one another out. But, given that monopolistic pressure is still exercised, the mere fact that it provides for those who exercise it a special gain does not imply that money wage-rates can be pushed up even to a small extent without affecting prices or output. On the contrary, some increase in prices and some contraction of employment is sure to be brought about.

PART IV

DISTURBANCES OF SHORT-PERIOD
FLOW EQUILIBRIUM

CHAPTER I

INTRODUCTORY

§ 1. In Part II we were concerned predominantly with the conditions which must be satisfied in order that an economic system may stand in short-period flow equilibrium, and with the way in which these conditions are related to the volume of employment. In Part III a study was made of the way in which differences between two systems, in respect of each of the relevant functions, or balancing factors, which we have distinguished, are related to differences in the volume of employment, and into the ratio in various circumstances between differences in total employment and differences in employment in the investment industries — what Keynes calls multipliers. These investigations need to be supplemented by a twofold enquiry.

§ 2. First, granted that, when some given function in a system in short-period flow equilibrium *changes* in a given way, there results ultimately a new system, also in short-period flow equilibrium, exactly equivalent to a system *differing* from the original one only in respect of the difference in the given function, what happens during the process of change — a process necessarily covering an interval of short-period flow disequilibrium — before the new equilibrium situation is reached? Secondly, in what circumstances are we justified in believing that, when a given element in a system in short-period flow equilibrium is changed in a given way,

213

a new system differing from the original one in respect of that change alone unmodified by any cumulative reaction,[1] and, therefore, with a like implication for employment, will in fact emerge ?

§ 3. To answer these questions in respect of all types of change would be an intolerably unwieldy task, and would, moreover, involve a great deal of repetition. I propose, therefore, in this Part, to discuss them, not in general, but in respect of one type of change only, namely that arising out of variations, whether warranted or not, in business confidence. This, from the point of view of pure abstract theory, reduces what I have to say to the level of an illustrative particular case. It is, however, I think, the opinion of most economists that, over short periods, this type of disturbance plays a leading part in actual life. In the chapter that follows I shall try in some measure to justify that opinion. If it is correct, our enquiry will, from the standpoint of realism, be more than merely illustrative. Since, however, it is conducted within the framework of a model world, which not only postulates complete mobility of labour, but also requires the relative values of all sorts of consumption goods, and likewise of all sorts of investment goods, to stand constant, we shall *not* be discussing the great problem of industrial fluctuations. That is quite outside our scope.

[1] This sort of reaction, to be discussed in Chapter VI, is, of course, distinct from the sort set up when a change in one governing factor, *e.g.* the demand function for labour for investment, induces a change in another governing factor, *e.g.* the money rate of wages (cf. *ante*, Part III, Chapter I, § 3).

CHAPTER II

DOMINANT FACTORS OF CHANGE

§ 1. In my *Industrial Fluctuations*, 1927, I showed, with the help of a chart based on pre-1914 statistics, that for this country there was a close positive correspondence between employment and short money rates of interest.[1] This makes it clear that the dominant factor behind short-term changes did not consist in variations of physical productivity. It also shows, with still greater force, that it did not consist in movements " on the money side ". For, had it done so, whether via changes in the quantity of gold in the Central Bank's Reserve, or through variations in reserve policy, the correlation between short money rates and employment must have been negative, not positive. I concluded : " Thus, while recognising that the varying expectations of business men may themselves be in part a psycho-

---

[1] *Loc. cit.*, Chart facing p. 32. In statistics of this type there is reason to expect a *variable* lag of A behind B, and, indeed, situations where A sometimes follows and sometimes precedes B. In these conditions, correlation coefficients are apt greatly to underrate the essential intimacy of the relation between two series, while the comparison of charts may bring it into clear light. Still, as between short money rates and employment, the correlation coefficients are themselves substantial. Mr. Rothbarth worked them out for me as follows :

RATE OF DISCOUNT AND EMPLOYMENT

Period	Correlation Coefficient	Probable Error
1880–1895	0·53	..
1896–1913	0·43	..
1880–1913	0·48	0·15
1924–1936	0·55	0·16

215   P

logical reflex of such things as good and bad harvests — while not, indeed, for the present enquiring *how* these varying expectations themselves come about — we conclude definitely that they, and not anything else, constitute the immediate and direct causes or antecedents of industrial fluctuations ".[1] Since work paid for now is sold and yields its fruit in the future, sometimes in the far future, this conclusion seems fairly obvious. Of course, business men in making forecasts are shadowed by immense uncertainties. Political events, about which they can form no secure judgment, may upset all their plans ; and, in a less degree, inventions or changes in popular taste or in monetary policy may do the same. But the fact that their decisions rest on imperfect data and emerge from a morass of uncertainty does not prevent them from *being* decisions. The immediate cause lying behind general movements of employment consists in shifts in the expectations of business men about future prospects, or, if we prefer a looser term, business confidence.

§ 2. These movements of business confidence are not sporadic, but are found to wax and wane gradually over periods of several years. Moreover, in the light of the facts through which they manifest themselves, it is evident that, while after a downward turn the waning may sometimes be rapid, after an upward turn it is almost always slow. That this is likely to be so is made clear by Prof. Schumpeter's analysis. " Everyone ", he writes, " is an entrepreneur only when he actually carries out ' new combinations ', and loses that character as soon as he has built up his business, when he settles down to running it as other people run theirs." [2] Only a few people, he points out, possess the

---

[1] *Industrial Fluctuations*, 2nd edition, pp. 33-4.
[2] *The Theory of Economic Development*, p. 78.

quality of leadership — the quality of actually introducing and undertaking " new combinations " — which is quite a different thing from inventing them. " However, if one or a few have advanced with success, many of the difficulties disappear. Others can then follow these pioneers, as they will clearly do under the stimulus of the success now attainable. Their success again makes it easier . . . for more people to follow suit, until finally the innovation becomes familiar and the acceptance of it a matter of free choice. . . . Since, as we have seen, the entrepreneurial qualification is something which, like many other qualities, is distributed in an ethnically homogeneous group according to the law of error, the number of individuals who satisfy progressively diminishing standards in this respect continually increases. Hence, neglecting exceptional cases — of which the existence of a few Europeans in a negro population would be an example — with the progressive lightening of the task continually more people can and will become entrepreneurs ; wherefore the successful appearance of an entrepreneur is followed by the appearance, not simply of some others, but of ever greater numbers, though progressively less qualified. . . . Reality also discloses that every normal boom starts in one or a few branches of industry (railway building, electrical and chemical industries, and so forth), and that it derives its character from the innovations in the industry where it begins. But the pioneers remove the obstacles for the others, not only in the branch of production in which they first appear, but, owing to the nature of these obstacles, *ipso facto* in other branches too." [1]

§ 3. One further item of description may be added. For technical reasons there is bound to be a certain lag

[1] *The Theory of Economic Development*, pp. 228-9.

between the up-turn and the down-turn of business men's state of confidence and the full manifestation in physical fact of what has happened. The reason is that in many works of construction the earlier stages are of such a nature that they *can* only occupy a comparatively small number of men. Thus, when a ship is being built, the keel must be laid first, exposing only a small area on which work is possible. As the structure grows, a larger and larger area becomes available, and the number of men at work grows in sympathy. A relatively narrow spear-head advances first and the main body of the army follows after a road has been prepared. In like manner, if the rate of shipbuilding declines, the decline will at first only affect the relatively small number of men who would have been engaged on the beginning of new ships. How important in practice this consideration is, is a question for technical experts.

§ 4. It might perhaps be thought at first sight that, if the foregoing account is correct, the positive correlation between employment and short money rates ought to be substantially closer than it in fact is ; that there ought to be *no* occasions on which low employment is associated with high discount, and vice versa. This, however, would only be so if shifts in business confidence were, not merely the dominant, but the sole factor initiating industrial fluctuations in this country. Of course, in fact an upward movement may be initiated by, say, an influx of gold consequent upon some happening in the outside world. In this case, under the pre-1914 gold standard, the extra gold would entail an up-swing of the money income function, leading to improved employment quite independently of the state of demand for real investment, and the up-swing would, of course, be associated with abnormally low short money rates. Thus the broad conclusion set out at the end of § 1 remains intact. The dominant factor behind industrial fluctuations consists in variations in the expectations of business men — alias business confidence, alias again, if we like, the (expected) marginal efficiency of (given quantities of) capital.

§ 5. These movements in business confidence manifest themselves in swings of the demand function for labour for investment — chiefly for investment in works of construction. Thus a main feature of the boom culminating in 1825 was investment in Mexican mines and other enterprises in the South American countries recently freed from Spain. In 1833–36 there was large investment in railway building in England and in the United States. The crisis of 1847 was associated with a tremendous boom in English railway building ; the amount of money turned into railways rising from under £7 millions in 1844 to over £40 millions in 1847. Prior to the 1857 crisis we had made large investments in, and had exported much material for, American railways.[1] In the early 'sixties there was another British railway boom and in the early 'seventies another American one. The Baring crisis followed large investments in railways in Argentina. The beginning of the twentieth century witnessed a great expansion of electrical enterprise, especially in Germany, and the 1907 crisis, initiated in the United States, followed upon a similar development there. Thus industrial expansions have always been, in the main, expansions in the building of means of production. What means of production are selected depends upon circumstances. " At the beginning of the nineteenth century it was the means for sewing and spinning ; in a word, all kinds of textile

---

[1] As Mr. C. K. Hobson's study of nineteenth-century figures shows, " in the case of railways at any rate British foreign investments, over a wide portion of the globe, are very largely represented by orders to British manufacturers of railway materials and railway stock." (*The Export of Capital*, p. 15.)

machinery ; a little later it was the formidable apparatus of railways and railway material and of steel steamships to take the place of wooden sailing vessels ; in our own day it is electrical energy and its manifold industrial applications, tramways, electric railways, electric furnaces, electric light, and so on." [1] But always *some* form of construction dominates the stage. Thus Jevons wrote : " A characteristic of boom periods is that the proportion which the capital devoted to permanent and remote investment bears to that which is but temporarily invested soon to reproduce itself " [2] is increased. Thus, again, Prof. Robertson finds : " The most characteristic feature of an industrial boom is the utilisation of an abnormally large proportion both of past accumulations and of the current production of consumable goods to elicit the production, not of other consumable goods, but of constructional goods ".[3] Yet again, Prof. Röpke writes : " The history of cycles and crises teaches us further that the jumpy increases of investment characterising every boom are usually connected with some definite technical advance. In fact the beginnings of almost every modern technical achievement — the railway, the iron and steel industry, the electrical industry, the chemical industry and, most recently, the automobile industry — can be traced back to a boom. It seems as if our economic system reacts to the stimulus of some technical advance with the prompt and complete mobilisation of all its inner forces in order to carry it out everywhere in the shortest possible time." [4] Prof. Hansen strongly confirms these conclusions. He shows that in the United States from

---

[1] Cf. Lescure, *Les Crises générales et périodiques*, p. 413.
[2] Jevons, *Investigations in Currency and Finance*, p. 28.
[3] *A Study of Industrial Fluctuations*, p. 157. Down to this point the above section, § 5, with its citations is reproduced from my *Industrial Fluctuations*, Part I, chap. i, § 7.   [4] *Crises and Cycles*, p. 98.

1921 to 1937 ordinary business investment kept pace roughly with consumption, while non-business investment, notably in residential building and public construction, underwent large oscillations.[1] But it is not the shifts in type of investment which variations in business confidence, or expectations, bring about that chiefly concern us here. The essential fact is that variations in this confidence, or these expectations, manifest themselves powerfully in the form of shifts in the aggregate demand function for labour for investment.

§ 6. There is reason to believe that, with a normal banking policy, they also manifest themselves in upward and downward swings in the money income function. For improved confidence may be expected to lessen the desire to hold large real balances in the form of money; in other words, to reduce the desire for liquidity ; in yet other words, to increase the income velocity of money — at any given rate of interest.

§ 7. There is also a third tendency to bring into account. It is well known that in times of prosperity workpeople strive harder for, and are more likely to achieve, increases in rates of money wage than at other times. This implies that upward and downward variations in business confidence indirectly cause money rates of wages to vary in the same sense.

§ 8. Now in Chapter IV-VII and X of Part III the implications for employment, as between two systems in short-period flow equilibrium, of differences in the demand function for labour for investment, in the state of the money income function, and in the rate of money wages, were all studied at length. It was found that, whereas, other things being equal, a higher money wage-rate is in all circumstances associated with a smaller, and a higher money income function with a larger,

[1] *Full Recovery or Stagnation*, pp. 293 and 296.

volume of employment, a higher demand function for
labour for investment may in some circumstances be
associated with a larger and in others with a smaller
volume.   Thus no *a priori* generalisation is possible.
In the experience of this country, however, there is no
room for doubt that expansions of business confidence,
associated, as they have been, with an enhanced demand
for labour for investment, a heightened money income
function and a higher rate of money wage, have also
been associated with increased aggregate employment.
It is certain that the expansions of demand for labour
for investment have substantially increased employment ;   that the associated upward movement in the
money income function has reinforced this effect ; while,
per contra, the associated tendency of money wages to
rise has acted as a drag upon it.

§ 9. We may, if we are daring enough, suppose
that shifts in the money income function and shifts in
money wage-rates roughly compensate one another.
But there is no evidence that this very convenient sup-
position fits the facts.   We cannot, therefore, prove that
shifts in the demand function for labour for investment
have been the predominant factor behind short-period
changes of employment.   That, at all events in this
country, they have been an important factor is reasonably certain.   To treat them as the predominant one is
an act of faith.   Since, however, the essence of the
analysis is not altered, while exposition is made less
cumbrous, I shall in the two following chapters under-
take that act.

CHAPTER III

TRANSITIONS BETWEEN POSITIONS OF EQUILIBRIUM

§ 1. LET us suppose then, in accordance with the programme sketched in the introduction to this Part, that,
the economic system being initially in a state of short-
period flow equilibrium, the demand function for labour
for investment alters in a given way ; that no cumulative tendency manifests itself ; and that system A is
transformed into system B in such a way that the implications for employment and so on can be found by the
analysis developed in Part III. It is evident that, even
so, system A is not converted into system B instantaneously. There is necessarily a process of transition. We
have here to consider how that process works. It is
assumed that the banking policy in vogue, as is almost
certainly the case in this country, is what I have called
normal.

§ 2. The demand function for labour for investment
swings up or down — to the right or to the left. Apart
from the special case of a down-swing so marked that
it would carry the rate of interest below the permissible
minimum as described in Part II, Chapter IX, § 7-8,
market equilibrium between quantity demanded and
quantity supplied must still hold at every moment. *A
priori* this can be achieved, when the demand is altered,
by an alteration either in the rate of interest or in real
income or in both. Thus, in response to a rise in the
demand function for labour for investment, the quantity

of investment supplied would presumably go up if there were more employment, and so more real income, leading people at any given rate of interest to make more real saving. It would also presumably (though not certainly) go up if the money rate of interest on long loans were raised, provided that prices were not expected to rise so far as to wipe out any gain to lenders, to which high interest rates would otherwise lead. Unless one or other, or both, of these two things happened, there would be no tendency for the required increase in the supply of real investment to take place. Therefore one or other, or both of them, *must* happen. If initially employment is full, adjustment *cannot* be brought about by increased employment, and, therefore, must be brought about via the rate of interest.[1] In actual life, indeed, except near the peak of the boom, employment is never full ; so that this kind of compulsion hardly operates. In general, we may expect adjustment to be made through movements in the same direction both in the volume of employment *and* in the rate of interest.

§ 3. In the last section I spoke of *the* money rate of interest. But in the present connection this is not proper. As has already been observed, there is an important distinction between short and long rates of interest.[2] It is true, of course, that the trends of the two rates must run together. As Wicksell wrote : "The long-term rate of interest (*the bond rate of interest*) must correspond somewhat closely to the short-term rate of interest (*the bank rate of interest*), or, at any rate, a certain connection must be maintained between them. It is not possible for the long-term rate to stand much

---

[1] In these conditions if *less* real investment were supplied at a higher than at a lower rate of interest, no new state of equilibrium would be attainable except through a shift in the money rate of wages.

[2] Cf. *ante*, p. 45.

higher than the short-term rate, for otherwise entrepreneurs would run their businesses on bank credit :
— this is usually feasible, at any rate by indirect means.
Similarly, it cannot stand lower than the short-term
rate, for otherwise most capitalists would prefer to
leave their money at the Bank (or to use it in discounting bills of exchange)." [1] But — and this is the
crucial point — in conditions of flow disequilibrium
there is not, as there is in conditions of flow equilibrium, a rigid connection between short and long rates
of interest of such a sort that it is proper to speak
of one rate of interest as *the* rate. On the contrary,
long rates and short rates may vary relatively to one
another.

§ 4. At this point we may appeal to history ; despite
the fact that, since in practice shifts in the demand
function for labour for investment are often accompanied by other changes, its witness is not conclusive.
A study of the facts shows that there is practically no
correlation between the volume of employment and the
yield on Consols, which may fairly be taken as representative of the rate of interest on long loans. A natural
inference is that the required adjustment of the supply
to the demand for investment, when the demand
function is expanded, is not brought about through
movements in this rate. On the other hand, as is shown
in a chart in my *Industrial Fluctuations*,[2] the short
rate of interest varies very closely in correspondence
with the volume of employment. When employment
is good the short rate for money is high ; in converse
conditions, low. Moreover, as a careful study of the
chart shows, the turning points in interest rates tend
to lag a year or so behind the turning points in the
employment percentage. This is in agreement with

---

[1] *Interest and Prices*, p. 75.   [2] *Loc. cit.* Chart facing p. 32.

Mr. Snyder's findings for the U.S.A. There the upward turns in business activity, as inferred from bank clearings, usually anticipate the upward turns of interest by from ten to fifteen months, while the interval for the downward turns is still longer. We may, I think, reasonably conclude from these facts that an expansion of the demand function for real investment would cause employment to increase, even though the long rate of interest remained unaltered, by raising the short rate of interest and, along with it, the provision of bank money, and so money income.[1] This suggestion is confirmed by other charts in *Industrial Fluctuations*, on which there is shown a distinct positive correlation between annual additions to credits outstanding and the short rate of interest.[2]

§ 5. Thus, even if there were no reaction on the desire for liquidity, money income would expand and employment would be enhanced sufficiently to maintain market equilibrium between demand and supply of investment. Obviously, however, if the desire for liquidity were unaffected, the short rate of interest would need, in order that this should happen, to vary more widely than it does in fact vary.

§ 6. This, however, is not all. Money is usually provided by the banks only to finance working capital, not fixed capital. But it is certain that expansions in the demand for real investment entail increases in demand for both sorts of capital. How is the financing of unusually large amounts of new fixed capital accomplished without an immediate rise in the long-term rate

---

[1] This conclusion is not, of course, inconsistent with the fact that in panics, as is well known, high money rates go with low money incomes. The reason for this is that in panics enhanced desire for liquidity exercises a strong downward pressure on the money income function. Consequently this function falls.

[2] *Industrial Fluctuations*, Charts facing pp. 144 and 146.

of interest ; and conversely, how does it happen that
the financing of unusually small amounts of new fixed
capital is not associated with an immediate fall in this
long-term rate ? The explanation is, I suggest, that
expansions of business confidence entail in the first
instance an enhancement in the demand for investment on long term ; the extra demand is met by money,
which private persons and institutions would otherwise have been lending short, being attracted by the
improvement in business expectations into long loans ;
so that the supply of these loans is enhanced sufficiently to restore equilibrium without any rise in long-
term interest in sympathy with short term ; while, for
short loans themselves, the balance between demand
and the now deficient supply is maintained through
short money rates being raised. Contractions in business confidence operate in the same manner, but in the
opposite direction.[1]

§ 7. The process just described is, moreover, associated with another. We have agreed that in short-
period flow equilibrium the actual and the expected
prices, alike of consumption and of investment goods,
must coincide. Consequently, when an entrepreneur
engages labour in such quantities as to make the money
rate of wages equal to the discounted expected value
of $\left(1 - \dfrac{1}{\eta}\right)$ times the marginal cost of production, actual
value, when the product comes to be sold, coincides
with this expected value. Therefore the employer finds
that it has in fact been worth his while to engage the
amount of labour that he has engaged ; and the money
income that he receives at any time is what he was
expecting to receive. Thus the fact that, whereas the

---

[1] This explanation is suggested in substance in a different connection in
Mr. A. K. Grant's *A Study of the Capital Market*.

workers' share of the proceeds of what is being produced at any time comes to them at once, the entrepreneur's share comes to him later on, is immaterial. Apart from the element of discount, everything works in exactly the same way as it would do if the period of production of commodities was nil. When, however, equilibrium is disturbed by, say, a rise in the demand function for labour for investment, this — even though it is not accompanied by a rise in the money income function — entails a rise in the rate of interest, and so an expansion in money income available for expenditure. This means that the prices of goods are higher, and that employers get a larger return of money than they had expected to get when they hired their labour. Thus, so long as the movement of the demand function for labour for investment continues, they are making windfall gains in respect of some of their previous investments, and, consequently, the quantity of labour from which they expect a given marginal return in money, when its product comes to be sold, undergoes a constant rise. Evidently processes converse to the above are set in motion if the demand function for labour for investment falls. In either case, unless cumulative movements, about which something will be said in Chapter VI, are started, all the processes that have been described stop when the upward or downward shift in the demand function for labour for investment, which we suppose to have initiated them, is fully accomplished. Then once more expected prices of commodities coincide with actual prices, and there is no secondary reinforcement of the initial change. In what sense and in what degree employment will differ in the new position of short-period equilibrium from what it was in the old depends, of course, on the extent to which the demand function for labour for investment has shifted and on the forms of the several relevant functions.[1]

§ 8. It should be added that, after a rise in the demand function for labour for investment has taken place, entrepreneurs will for some time be turning over their balances more quickly and borrowing more from banks in order to take advantage of the new openings available to them ; and so, since the money wage-rate is sticky, will be bringing about more and more employment and production. This process, so long as it continues, is associated with the process, as it is sometimes called, of dis-hoarding; or, in the converse case, with the process of hoarding. So long as either process is going on, adjustment is not complete, and the state of flow equilibrium proper to the new state of demand for labour for investment has not been attained.

[1] In the case of a downward movement it is possible for entrepreneurs to avoid a fall in prices at the expense of piling up unsold stocks. But this does not affect the substance of our argument. Cf. *post*, Chapter VI, § 10.

CHAPTER IV

TRANSITIONS BETWEEN POSITIONS OF DISEQUILIBRIUM

§ 1. In Part III it was shown how, as between two economic systems both in short-period flow equilibrium, which differ as regards the demand function for investment, aggregate employment will differ; and what the relation is between the difference in aggregate employment and the difference in employment directed to investment. In the preceding chapter of this Part we have enquired what will happen when a change in the demand function for labour for investment is imposed on a system standing in short-period flow equilibrium. What, if any, light does our analysis throw on the consequences for employment of a change in the demand function for labour for investment imposed on a system that is not initially in short-period flow equilibrium ? On the assumption that no cumulative movement takes place — a matter to be discussed in the next chapter but one — we may fairly expect that the *effect* of a push will be the same for a man in movement as it is for a man at rest. Thus, when the price of something is falling at an unknown rate and a tax is imposed on it, we cannot possibly tell what the price afterwards will be ; but we can, with adequate data about elasticities, tell how the actual price afterwards will differ from what it would have been had there been no tax. On the same principle, I suggest, we are entitled to conclude that, when a shift in the demand function for labour for investment is imposed on an economic system which is in motion, the effect on employment in the future (*i.e.* the difference between what it is and what it would otherwise have been) is substantially the same as if the system had initially stood in a position of short-period flow equilibrium. Thus the analysis of Part III is not without relevance to the problems of a continually changing world.

CHAPTER V

THE EVALUATION OF MULTIPLIERS

§ 1. In Chapters VIII and IX of Part III an account was given of the various employment and money multipliers which are associated with several kinds of difference between two economic systems in short-period flow equilibrium. If by an act of faith [1] we agree that swings in the demand function for labour for investment constitute the dominant factor of change in industrial activity, it is reasonable to speak of the employment or the money multiplier associated with these swings as *the* employment or *the* money multiplier. The other multipliers that were distinguished will not play an important part. We are thus *prima facie* justified in attempting a numerical evaluation of *the* employment multiplier from employment statistics, and of *the* money multiplier from comparative statistics of income changes and investment changes.

§ 2. It was shown, however, in the chapters cited, that *the* employment and *the* money multiplier, in the above sense, are both expressed by formulae which are not only different with different types of banking policy, but also, with all types, embody elements whose values are liable to vary at the several stages of the trade cycle. Since, for this reason, neither multiplier has a single unambiguous value, no statistical manipulation can possibly determine what that value is. The best that can be hoped for is some rough indication of the

---

[1] Cf. *ante*, Part IV, Chapter II, § 9.

average order of magnitude.

§ 3. It is in the light of these considerations that Mr. Colin Clark's attempt to determine the value of the money multiplier for this country must be examined. In his *National Income and Outlay* he prints a diagram [1] depicting alongside of one another differences in the values of investment and in the values of national income between 1924 and 1936. As between 1929–35 this diagram suggests that variations in investment were accompanied throughout by variations in income about twice as large, *i.e.* that the multiplier was stable at about 2. But Mr. Clark states — though the statement hardly seems to accord with the diagram — that " during the period 1924–29 income rose considerably at a time of stationary investment ", and " in 1935 investment again stood at about the 1929 level, while income was substantially higher ".[2]

§ 4. This type of calculation is unfortunately rendered highly dubious by the fact that both the income and the investment figures are based on estimates subject to substantial error. Since, moreover, income in this country is, on a rough average, say, ten times as large as investment, a very small error in the estimates of income, unless it was common to all the estimates, would completely destroy the statistical case for a money multiplier stable at about 2, even over the period 1929–35.[3]

---

[1] *Loc. cit.* p. 249.   [2] *Ibid.* p. 250.

[3] Mr. Clark calls attention to the fact that, over the period 1924–35, of each additional £ of the income of companies, whether we start from a low level or a high one, about one-half has been put to reserve and the other half distributed in dividends (*loc. cit.* p. 255). In this country a very large part of total investment — before the war from one-third to one-half — consists of the undistributed profits of companies. Since these profits have varied widely, Mr. Clark suggests that the custom of putting half of them to reserve " probably explains the closeness with which the multiplier 2 is adhered to in the relation between investment and national income " (*ibid.* p. 255). It will be noticed, however, that, while this custom on the part of companies prevailed over the whole period 1924–35, it is only for the period 1929–35 that Mr. Clark thinks the multiplier was close to 2.

§ 5. Mr. Champernowne has published a chart of the employment figures in industries predominantly making goods for immediate consumption, durable goods, coal-mining and textiles, and goods for deferred consumption respectively.[1] *Prima facie*, this chart suggests a value for the employment multiplier in the neighbourhood of unity. But here inference is rendered insecure by the difficulty of making a satisfactory division between people working at consumption goods and capital goods respectively. Moreover, in an actual community, as distinct from the isolated community we have been mainly studying in this book, some investment may be made abroad. So far as this happens, the labour engaged in making *any* sort of exported good may be regarded as labour devoted to investment. This implies that any value for *the* employment multiplier derived from employment statistics is subject to large error.

[1] Cf. *Review of Economic Studies*, February 1939, p. 116. Mr. Champernowne, it should be made clear, does not profess to derive from his chart any value for the employment multiplier.

CHAPTER VI

CUMULATIVE MOVEMENTS

§ 1. In the introductory chapter to this Part it was indicated that the implications for employment of *differences* between the state of one or another balancing factor in two economic systems standing side by side are not necessarily identical with those of *changes* in the state of balancing factors in the same economic system as between one time and another. The reason for this is that in certain circumstances the fact of change may set up a cumulative process. The business world may, for one reason or another, be in a state so unstable that a small push will not merely produce its normal physical effect, but will start up an internal mechanism which impels it forward at a run. When this happens — and that it should happen implies that the equations we have been using do not exhaust the facts — the *implications of differences*, which were worked out in Part III, are obviously not equivalent to the *effects of changes*. The conclusions of Chapters III and IV of this Part are then not valid. Hence, it is very important to determine how far, and in what conditions, processes of cumulation may be looked for. I shall consider first what we may call mechanical cumulation and, thereafter, cumulation via psychology, or, perhaps better, via expectations.

§ 2. There are three principal forms of mechanical cumulation theory. The first has its source in a well-known passage in Bagehot's *Lombard Street*. He wrote: "There is a partnership in industries. No single large industry can be depressed without injury to other industries ; still less can any great group of industries. Each industry, when prosperous, buys and consumes the produce, probably of most (certainly of very many) other industries, and, if industry A fail and is in difficulty, industries B and C and D, which used to sell to it, will not be able to sell that which they had produced in reliance on A's demand ; and in future they will stand idle until industry A recovers, because, in default of A, there will be no one to buy the commodities which they create. Then, as industry B buys of C, D, etc., the adversity of B tells on C, D, etc., and, as these buy of E, F, etc., the effect is propagated throughout the whole alphabet. *And in a certain sense it rebounds. Z feels the want caused by the diminished custom of A, B and C, and so it does not earn so much ; in consequence, it cannot lay out as much on the produce of A, B and C, and so these do not earn as much either. In all this, money is but an instrument.*" [1] The unitalicised part of this passage does not, of course, suggest cumulation, and I have no quarrel with it. But the part which I have italicised does suggest it. Mr. Hawtrey, as I read him, in substance adopts this suggestion — though, unlike Bagehot, he does not regard money as merely an instrument — and founds upon it his conception of the "vicious circles" of depression and of activity. But I am not certain that I have properly understood Mr. Hawtrey. In any case the view which I wish to examine amounts, in the last analysis, to this. If one of two groups of persons, A, pays less than hitherto for purchases from B, B, being impoverished, will in turn pay less for purchases from A ; this will further impoverish

---

[1] *Lombard Street*, pp. 127-8.

A ; which causes A to pay still less for purchases from B ; and so on for ever.[1] This surely is a mistake. To realise that, it is enough to consider the highly simplified case in which (i) money consists exclusively of metal pieces, and (ii) each of these pieces, so long as it stands in the income-expenditure circuit, moves round at the same pace, manifesting itself as income at intervals of, say, one week. Initially A has been handing over, say, £10,000 weekly to B in payment for B's product, and B has been handing back, one week later, each £10,000 that he has received in payment for A's product. The total stock of money is thus £10,000, and the bi-weekly income of each of A and B is £10,000. In a particular week A, instead of paying out £10,000 to B, pays out £9000, puts the other £1000 into a stocking, and subsequently keeps it there. B's income in that week is then £9000. No cause has been introduced to make what he pays out one week later in purchases from A less than £9000. If he pays out this sum, after a further week A has only £9000 to pay out in purchases from B ; and so on for ever. The net effect of A's action is that the joint bi-weekly income of A and B is £18,000 instead of £20,000. There is nothing cumulative about this. Indeed there may well be some tendency towards self-correction. For, B's bi-weekly income being cut down from £10,000 to £9000, he is likely presently to cut down his holding of savings deposits, if he holds any, more or less in the same proportion. This will enable him to pay out in purchases from A rather more than £9000 ; so that the bi-weekly income of each of the parties is ultimately contracted by rather less than £1000, and of both parties together by rather less than £2000. But with that secondary matter we are not here concerned. I have merely tried to show that the concept of a

[1] Cf. Hawtrey, *Trade Depressions and the Way Out*, pp. 2 and 3.

mechanical cumulation on this pattern is not valid.

§ 3. The second principal form of mechanical cumulation — this one definitely sponsored by Mr. Hawtrey
— may be summarised thus. If the short-term rate of
interest rises, this will induce shopkeepers, wholesalers
and so on to contract their holding of stocks. These
persons will then reduce their orders to manufacturers.
Manufacturers thereupon will either reduce money wage-
rates or reduce employment, each of which things entails
a reduction in money income. This in turn induces
dealers to contract their stocks still further, and the
cumulative process is set up.

In considering this view, we must grant that, if the
rate of interest rises, dealers will be inclined to hold
smaller stocks and their orders to manufacturers will,
consequently, be reduced ; thus entailing a reduction
in aggregate money income and (the money rate of
wages being taken as fixed) a fall in the volume of employment. *This, however, is a once-for-all affair.* When
the rate of interest is given, dealers' holdings of stocks
depend on the rate of turnover of their stocks in conjunction with conditions of business convenience. The
essential fact is that a raised rate of interest (with a
normal banking policy) entails lessened money income,
so to speak, permanently. It also entails *at the moment*
a cut in the aggregate quantity of investment demanded
by dealers. Apart from the consequences of an upset
in expectations, which for the present we are excluding,
there is no tendency whatever towards cumulation. It
is true that, if stocks were always nil, the immediate
consequence for employment of a downward swing of
the money income function would be smaller than it
actually is. But, so soon as dealers' stocks have adapted
themselves, the situation is stable, just as it would have
been had no such stocks normally been carried.

§ 4. The third principal form of the mechanical cumulation view is associated chiefly with the name of Mr. Harrod. His argument takes for its starting point the obvious fact that, if for any reason the output of consumption goods is to be expanded beyond a certain measure, additional investment in machinery and plant will become necessary. This additional investment, he argues, will then indirectly evoke more employment in the consumption industries ; this will react and make necessary more investment in machinery ; and so on cumulatively. In like manner, if for any reason the output of consumption goods is contracted beyond a certain measure, mechanical equipment will be allowed to run down ; that is to say, there will be disinvestment in equipment, with the result that a downward cumulation is set up.[1] Let us consider this argument.

§ 5. If we start from a situation in which there is substantial unemployment and a large part of a country's equipment is lying idle, a considerable expansion in the output of consumption goods may take place without any stimulus being given to the demand for machinery and so on. Moreover, if we start from that situation, it is not likely, human psychology being what it is, that a moderate, as distinct from a large, contraction in the demand for consumption goods will entail an appreciable amount of disinvestment, in the sense of equipment being allowed to run down through lapse of adequate repairs and renewals. Thus there is a wide range over which the type of cumulation on which Mr. Harrod lays stress cannot occur. But large shifts in the demand for consumption goods, or shifts, even though small, which occur when industry is fully extended near the peak of a

---

[1] Since in Part III we assumed, for convenience, that equipment lasts for ever, this side of Mr. Harrod's thesis cannot touch anything that was said there. For real life, however, this side of it is just as important as the other.

boom, do *prima facie* set up reactions in the machine-
making industries. Thus, when, say, a railway boom
has evoked an expansion in the consumption industries,
a secondary demand for labour to make the machinery
used in consumption industries may well be called out ;
and so, it appears, a cumulative process may be set up.

§ 6. It may seem *prima facie* that this analysis fails
in exactly the same way as Mr. Hawtrey's. When the
rate of output of consumption goods is lifted in a given
proportion, the *stock* of equipment may need to be lifted
in an equivalent proportion. But this lifting is a once-
for-all affair. Such-and-such an increase in the annual
investment in railways may require an extra provision
of equipment for making consumption goods. Consequently, a swing-up in the rate of demand for railway-
making may entail immediately a new demand for that
equipment. Hence aggregate employment at the
moment is bigger than it would have been if the manufacture of consumption goods were normally carried on
without the use of any equipment. But, as I have said,
the secondary boom is a once-for-all affair and there
is no cumulative movement.[1] On this view Mr. Harrod's
type of mechanical cumulation fares no better than
Mr. Hawtrey's. Moreover, both types are in the last
analysis exactly the same. They both look for cumulation via additions to capital associated with additional
output of consumption goods. The only difference is
that the capital in which Mr. Hawtrey is interested
consists of dealers' stocks ; that in which Mr. Harrod
is interested, of manufacturers' machines.

 [1] Mr. Harrod in his book on *The Trade Cycle* is contemplating an economy
in process of expansion, so that after each short interval there is a higher
demand for investment (*e.g.* in railways) apart altogether from the secondary
once-for-all induced demand for equipment in consumption industries. In
such an economy, of course, there will be a sequence of secondary once-for-all
demands for investment associated with the sequence of swings-up in the rate
of primary demand. But this is not cumulation.

§ 7. Believers in Mr. Harrod's type of cumulation may, however, reply that the above argument begs the question. It is not denied, they may say, that system A will be in equilibrium with so much consumption and such-and-such a stock of equipment, and system B will be in equilibrium with a larger consumption and a correspondingly larger stock of equipment. But it does not follow that, if we start from system A and increase employment for consumption by so much, we shall in fact be led on to system B. Indeed, the essence of the argument is that we shall not be led on to this, but, on the contrary, landed in a cumulative process. All that the argument of the preceding paragraph shows, they may say, is that, *if we are not so landed,* system B will be reached; and that is irrelevant to the question whether we *shall* be so landed. This, I think, should be granted. That being so, the question whether there is cumulation or not depends, it would seem, on a matter of fact. Thus, suppose that initially the stock of capital goods (as measured by the labour employed in making them) is four times as large as annual income, *e.g.* 4000 units as against 1000. A railway boom evokes, say, 100 more units of employment in making consumption goods. If capital and output in the consumption industries are to maintain their original proportion, this will entail an investment in making new capital of 400 units. This may evoke either more or less than 100 units of additional employment in the consumption industries. If it evokes less, we have a convergent series, which does not, if it evokes more, a divergent series which does, imply cumulation. Hence the issue turns on whether the series is, in fact, convergent or divergent. This, though the implications of a divergent series are extremely paradoxical, we cannot, I think, know for certain.

§ 8. In sum then, while we may be satisfied that the mechanical type of cumulation does not occur in ordinary times — in the middle ranges of an upward or downward oscillation in industrial activity — we must allow that it may occur in the upper reaches of a boom and near the nadir of a depression. Subject to this qualification, the argument of this chapter has led us to conclude that mechanical cumulation, as described in § 1, does not occur in the real world.

§ 9. There remains, what is a much more important matter, cumulation via psychology or expectations. The equations with which we worked in Part III were built on the assumption that people at each instant expect that prices and rates of interest will be the same in the future as they are at that instant. For the type of comparison with which we were engaged in Part III this was well enough. But, in considering the implications of *changes*, we must remember that the fact of prices or rates of interest having fallen (or risen) may create an expectation that they are going to fall (or rise) further.

§ 10. Thus suppose that the demand for labour for investment falls off, with the result that the rate of interest, and so money income, and so the money demand for consumption goods, contracts. This implies that the actual amount of money available to buy consumption goods is less than entrepreneurs had expected it to be. As a consequence the output of these goods which is due to come on the market now, but the labour engaged on which has been paid for previously, cannot all find purchasers at a price sufficient to cover marginal prime cost. Either the goods must be all sold for less than this, or — provided they are not immediately perishable or liable to vagaries of fashion — the sellers, hoping that prices will presently improve, may hold out for the price they had expected ; in which case unsold stocks must accumulate. In either event entrepreneurs are injured. As a result of this injury, particularly if it is repeated several times, they may well come to look at facts through less rosy glasses. Instead of expecting that future demand will continue at the level to which it has fallen, they may well expect it to fall still further.

§ 11. Thus, when the demand function for labour for investment changes, the new situation immediately created may differ from the original one, not only in that this demand function is different, but also in that, whereas, before, future prices of consumption goods were expected to be the same as actual prices, they are now expected to be different from actual prices. So long as any expectation of this kind is present, the system is not in short-period flow equilibrium.[1] Moreover, such shifts in expectation due to actual upward or downward price movements as have happened may themselves cause further movements in actual prices ; which in turn cause further shifts in expectation. Thus, instead of the initial movement simply transforming system A into system B, it may set up a cumulative process of change. A new system in short-period flow equilibrium is not attained until prices and rates of interest have reached a level at which an upward or downward movement no longer creates an expectation of further movements. As regards upward movements, there is not necessarily any ceiling ; it may be that a new state of equilibrium will never be attained. As regards downward movements, there must be a bottom, since nobody can expect prices or rates of interest to

[1] The existence of this expectation *implies* that the money and the real rates of interest are different. We may, therefore, say indifferently that the existence of this expectation or that a difference between the money and the real rate of interest is incompatible with short-period flow equilibrium.

become appreciably negative. In either case, if there is a new position of short-period flow equilibrium, it may be far distant from the original position.

§ 12. It follows that great care must be exercised in applying the analysis of Part III to determine what happens when any balancing factor in a system in short-period flow equilibrium, and *a fortiori* in a system in disequilibrium, is changed. That analysis is directly applicable if the change leaves intact the condition that prices (and interest rates) actual in any instant are expected also to be actual in the future. But, if this is not so, a cumulative process is set up. When and how that process will reach its term, whether, when it does so, stability may be expected, or an inevitable rebound, are questions that lie beyond the scope of this volume.

APPENDIX

SECTION I

THE principal problems investigated in Part III can be set out mathematically thus :

§ 1. We are given the three general equations :

$$m_3\phi\left(\frac{r}{m_4}\right) = m_5 f\{r, m_6 F(x)\} \qquad . \qquad . \qquad . \quad \text{(I)}$$

$$y = m_5 f\{r, m_6 F(x)\} \qquad . \qquad . \qquad . \quad \text{(II)}$$

$$m_2 g(r) = m_1\{K_1(x, m_6) + K_2(y, m_4)\} . \qquad . \quad \text{(III)}$$

where x, y and r are functions of the six m's and ϕ, f, F, g, K_1 and K_2 are functions of the variable or variables within the brackets. The money wage-rate w is embedded in the right-hand side of the third equation, but does not appear, since we can write $w = 1$.

§ 2. For Model III :

$$K_1(x, m_6) = \frac{1}{1 - \dfrac{1}{\eta_1\{m_6 F(x)\}}} \cdot \frac{F(x)}{F'(x)},$$

$$K_2(y, m_4) = \frac{1}{1 - \dfrac{1}{\eta_2\{m_4 \psi(y)\}}} \cdot \frac{\psi(y)}{\psi'(y)}.$$

For Model II :

$$K_1(x) = \frac{F(x)}{F'(x)},$$

$$K_2(y) = \frac{\psi(y)}{\psi'(y)}.$$

For Model I (B) :

$$K_1(x) = \frac{1}{1 - \dfrac{1}{\eta_1\{F(x)\}}} \cdot \frac{F(x)}{F'(x)} = Cx,$$

$$K_2(y) = \frac{1}{1 - \dfrac{1}{\eta_2\{\psi(y)\}}} \cdot \frac{\psi(y)}{\psi'(y)} = Cy.$$

R

For Model I (A) :

$$K_1(x) = \frac{F(x)}{F'(x)} = C_1 x,$$

$$K_2(y) = \frac{\psi(y)}{\psi'(y)} = C_1 y.$$

Dashes will denote differentiation with respect to the variable under the bracket after the m's have been put equal to 1 ; e.g. $F'(x) = \frac{d}{dx} F(x)$ and

$$K'_1 = \frac{d}{dx} \left\{ \frac{1}{1 - \dfrac{1}{\eta_1\{F(x)\}}} \cdot \frac{F(x)}{F'(x)} \right\}.$$

§ 3. It might be thought at first sight that for Model I (B), K_1 should have been written

$$K_1(x, m_6) = \frac{1}{1 - \dfrac{1}{\eta_1\{m_6 F(x)\}}} \cdot \frac{F(x)}{F'(x)} = Cx.$$

But, if we differentiate $K_1(x, m_6)$, so defined, to x, we obtain

$$\frac{dK_1}{dx} = \left\{ \frac{1}{1 - \dfrac{1}{\eta_1}} - \frac{F}{(\eta_1 - 1)^2} \cdot \frac{d\eta_1}{dF} \right\} + \frac{xF}{(\eta_1 - 1)^2} \cdot \frac{d\eta_1}{dF} \cdot \frac{dm_6}{dx}.$$

The presence of the element $\frac{dm_6}{dx}$ makes it impossible for this to be a constant unless either $\frac{dm_6}{dx}$ or $\frac{d\eta_1}{dF} = 0$; each of which conditions reduces $\frac{1}{\eta_1\{m_6 F(x)\}}$ to a constant. Thus, in order that the definition of Model I (B) may be satisfied, K_1 must be written as it has been written for that model in the last section ; and the same thing is true of K_2.

§ 4. We write :
(1) for the difference in aggregate employment when any one m, say m_n, varies, while the others remain constant and equal to unity and m_n is put equal to unity after the differentiation has been performed,

$$\frac{d(x+y)}{dm_n} = D_n ;$$

(2) for the difference in aggregate employment divided by the difference in employment for investment, *i.e.* the employment multiplier, when any one m varies,

$$\left(\frac{d(x+y)}{dy}\right)_n = M_n \; ;$$

(3) for the difference in money income divided by the difference in money investment when any one m varies,

$$\frac{\dfrac{d}{dm_n}(gm_2)}{\dfrac{d}{dm_n}(K_2m_1)} = N_n.$$

§ 5. We require :

(i) The values and signs of D_1, D_2, etc., in respect of each model (*a*) when g' is positive and finite, (*b*) when g' is positive and finite and also $\frac{\partial f}{\partial r} = 0$, (*c*) when $g' = 0$, (*d*) when g' is infinite, (*e*) when there is superimposed the condition

$$\frac{d}{dm_n}\left(\frac{K_1m_1}{Fm_2m_6}\right) = 0 :$$

(ii) The values of M_1, M_2, etc., in like circumstances :
(iii) The values of N_1, N_2, etc., in like circumstances.

We postulate for reasons given in the text that $(-\phi')$ and $F'\frac{\partial f}{\partial F}$ are positive ; that $\left(\frac{\partial f}{\partial r} - \phi'\right)$ is positive ; and that, with a normal monetary and banking policy, as also with one directed to keeping money income constant, K'_1 and K'_2 are positive ; while, with a policy directed to keeping the price level of consumption goods constant,

$$\left(\frac{K'_1}{K_1} - \frac{F'}{F}\right) = > 0.$$

Further, in the formulae into which they enter, as displayed in the heading to Table I, η_1 and η_2 are both positive and greater than unity. The signs of $\frac{d\eta_1}{dF}$ and $\frac{d\eta_2}{d\psi}$ and, therefore, also the signs of λ_1 and λ_2, as defined in that heading, must be regarded as uncertain. Further, since it is impossible that the whole of the product of any industries shall accrue to the wage-earners in those industries, $\left(\dfrac{K_1}{x}-1\right)$ and $\left(\dfrac{K_2}{y}-1\right)$ must both be positive. This implies that, in Model I (B), $(C-1)$ and, *a fortiori*, $\left\{C-\left(1-\dfrac{1}{\eta_1}\right)\right\}$ are positive, and that, in Model I (A), (C_1-1) is positive.

§ 6. The values required are set out in Tables II–IX. These are preceded by a general table (Table I), which forms the basis of the mathematical analysis.

Tables

I. General Table.

II. Form of Model III when g' is positive and finite.

IIB. Form of Model III when g' is positive and finite and

$$\frac{\partial f}{\partial r}=0.$$

III. Form of Model III when $g'=0$.

IV. Form of Model III when g' is infinite.

V. Form of Model III when

$$\frac{d}{dm_n}\left(\frac{K_1 m_1}{F m_2 m_6}\right)=0.$$

VB. Form of Model III when

$$\frac{d}{dm_n}\left(\frac{K_1 m_1}{F m_2 m_6}\right)=0 \text{ and } \frac{\partial f}{\partial r}=0.$$

VI. Form of Model II when g' is positive and finite.

VII. Form of Model I when g' is positive and finite.

VIIB. Form of Model I when g' is positive and finite and

$$\frac{\partial f}{\partial r}=0.$$

VIII. Form of Model I when $g'=0$.

IX. Form of Model I when

$$\frac{d}{dm_n}\left(\frac{K_1 m_1}{F m_2 m_6}\right)=0.$$

Note.—In line 4 of each of Tables I-IX and in the differentiations of D_4 in Tables X-XI, ϕ' stands for $\dfrac{d\phi\left(\dfrac{r}{m_4}\right)}{d\dfrac{r}{m_4}}$, with m_4 put equal to 1 after the differentiation has been performed, not, as elsewhere, for $\dfrac{d\phi(r)}{dr}$. In either meaning ϕ' is negative. Similarly in line 6 of each of Tables I-IX and in the differentiations of D_6 in Tables X-XI $\dfrac{\partial f}{\partial F}$ stands for $\dfrac{\partial f\{r, m_6 F(x)\}}{\partial m_6 F(x)}$, with m_6 put equal to 1 after the differentiation has been performed, not, as elsewhere, for $\dfrac{\partial f\{r, F(x)\}}{\partial F(x)}$. In either meaning $\dfrac{\partial f}{\partial F}$ is positive.

In like manner in the heading to Table I, in the case where m_4 is allowed to vary, $\dfrac{d\eta_2}{d\psi}$ stands for $\dfrac{d\eta_2(m_4\psi)}{d(m_4\psi)}$ with m_4 put equal to 1 after the differentiation ; and in the case where m_6 is allowed to vary $\dfrac{d\eta_1}{dF}$ stands for $\dfrac{d\eta_1(m_6 F)}{d(m_6 F)}$ with m_6 put equal to 1 after the differentiation.

TABLE I

GENERAL TABLE OF MODEL III

$$K_1 = \frac{1}{1-\dfrac{1}{\eta_1\{m_a F(x)\}}} \cdot \frac{F}{F'}; \quad K_2 = -\frac{1}{1-\dfrac{1}{\eta_2\{m_a\psi(y)\}}} \cdot \frac{\psi}{\psi'}; \quad dK_1 = \left\{\frac{\eta_1}{\eta_1-1} \cdot \frac{d}{dz}\left(\frac{F}{F'}\right)\right\} dz + \frac{F}{F'}\cdot\frac{d\eta_1}{dF}\cdot\frac{dz + \lambda_1 K_1 F dm_a}{(\eta_1-1)^2}.\; F dm_a = K_1' dz - \frac{d\eta_1}{dF}K_1 F dm_a = K_1' dx + \lambda_1 K_1 F dm_a, \text{ where } -\frac{d\eta_1}{dF}\eta_1 = (\eta_1-1)\eta_1 \Rightarrow \lambda_1$$

$$\frac{d\eta_2}{d\psi} = \lambda_2 \qquad -(\eta_2-1)\eta_2$$

Similarly $dK_2 = K_2' dy + \lambda_2 K_2\psi\, dm_a$, where $-\dfrac{1}{\eta_2\{m_a\psi(y)\}} = \lambda_2$

Denominator $A = K_1'\left(\dfrac{\partial f}{\partial r} - \phi'\right) + F'\dfrac{\partial f}{\partial F}(g' - K_2'\phi')$

	m_1 varies	m_2 varies	m_3 varies	m_4 varies
$\dfrac{dx}{dm_n}$	$-\left(\dfrac{\partial f}{\partial r}-\phi'\right)\dfrac{g}{A}$	$-\dfrac{dx}{dm_1}$	$\left(g'-K_2'\dfrac{\partial f}{\partial r}\right)\dfrac{\phi}{A}$	$\left\{\left(g'-K_2'\dfrac{\partial f}{\partial r}\right)(-r\phi')-\left(\dfrac{\partial f}{\partial r}-\phi'\right)\lambda_2 K_2\psi\right\}\Big/A$
$\dfrac{dy}{dm_n}$	$\phi'F'\dfrac{\partial f}{\partial F}\cdot\dfrac{g}{A}$	$-\dfrac{dy}{dm_1}$	$\left(K_1'\dfrac{\partial f}{\partial r}+g'F'\dfrac{\partial f}{\partial F}\right)\dfrac{\phi}{A}$	$\left\{\left(K_1'\dfrac{\partial f}{\partial r}+g'F'\dfrac{\partial f}{\partial F}\right)(-r\phi')+\phi'F'\dfrac{\partial f}{\partial F}\lambda_2 K_2\psi\right\}\Big/A$
$\dfrac{dr}{dm_n}$	$F'\dfrac{\partial f}{\partial F}\cdot\dfrac{g}{A}$	$-\dfrac{dr}{dm_1}$	$\left(K_1'+K_2'F'\dfrac{\partial f}{\partial F}\right)\dfrac{\phi}{A}$	$\left\{\left(K_1'+K_2'F'\dfrac{\partial f}{\partial F}\right)(-r\phi')+F'\dfrac{\partial f}{\partial F}\lambda_2 K_2\psi\right\}\Big/A$
$\dfrac{d(x+y)}{dm_n}$	$-\left\{\left(\dfrac{\partial f}{\partial r}-\phi'\right)-\phi'F'\dfrac{\partial f}{\partial F}\right\}\dfrac{g}{A}$	$-\dfrac{d(x+y)}{dm_1}$	$\left\{g'\left(1+F'\dfrac{\partial f}{\partial F}\right)+\left(K_1'-K_2'\dfrac{\partial f}{\partial r}\right)\right\}\dfrac{\phi}{A}$	$\left[\left\{g'\left(1+F'\dfrac{\partial f}{\partial F}\right)+\left(K_1'-K_2'\dfrac{\partial f}{\partial r}\right)\right\}(-r\phi')-\left(\dfrac{\partial f}{\partial r}-\phi'-\phi'F'\dfrac{\partial f}{\partial F}\right)\lambda_2 K_2\psi\right]\Big/A$
$\left[\dfrac{dz}{dy}\right]_{m_n}$	$\dfrac{\dfrac{\partial f}{\partial r}-\phi'}{(-\phi')F'\dfrac{\partial f}{\partial F}}$	$\left[\dfrac{dz}{dy}\right]_{m_1}$	$\dfrac{g'-K_2'\dfrac{\partial f}{\partial r}}{K_1'\dfrac{\partial f}{\partial r}+g'F'\dfrac{\partial f}{\partial F}}$	$\dfrac{\left(g'-K_2'\dfrac{\partial f}{\partial r}\right)(-r\phi')-\left(\dfrac{\partial f}{\partial r}-\phi'\right)\lambda_2 K_2\psi}{\left(K_1'\dfrac{\partial f}{\partial r}+g'F'\dfrac{\partial f}{\partial F}\right)(-r\phi')+\phi'F'\dfrac{\partial f}{\partial F}\lambda_2 K_2\psi}$
$\left[\dfrac{d(z+y)}{dy}\right]_{m_n}$	$\dfrac{\left(\dfrac{\partial f}{\partial r}-\phi'\right)-\phi'F'\dfrac{\partial f}{\partial F}}{(-)F'\dfrac{\partial f}{\partial F}}$	$\left[\dfrac{d(z+y)}{dy}\right]_{m_1}$	$\dfrac{g'\left(1+F'\dfrac{\partial f}{\partial F}\right)+\left(K_1'-K_2'\dfrac{\partial f}{\partial r}\right)}{K_1'\dfrac{\partial f}{\partial r}+g'F'\dfrac{\partial f}{\partial F}}$	$\dfrac{g'\left(1+F'\dfrac{\partial f}{\partial F}\right)+\left(K_1'-K_2'\dfrac{\partial f}{\partial r}\right)(-r\phi')-\left(\dfrac{\partial f}{\partial r}-\phi'-\phi'F'\dfrac{\partial f}{\partial F}\right)\lambda_2 K_2\psi}{\left(K_1'\dfrac{\partial f}{\partial r}+g'F'\dfrac{\partial f}{\partial F}\right)(-r\phi')+\phi'F'\dfrac{\partial f}{\partial F}\lambda_2 K_2\psi}$

TABLE I—*contd:*

	m_5 varies	m_8 varies
$\dfrac{dx}{dm_n}$	$-(g' - K'_8\phi')\cdot\dfrac{\phi}{\Delta}$	$\left\{-(g' - K'_8\phi')_1F\dfrac{\partial f}{\partial F} - \left(\dfrac{\partial f}{\partial r} - \phi'\right)\lambda_1 K_1 F\right\}\Big/\Delta$
$\dfrac{dy}{dm_n}$	$-K'_1\phi'\cdot\dfrac{\phi}{\Delta}$	$\left(-K'_1\phi'F\dfrac{\partial f}{\partial F} + \phi'F''\dfrac{\partial f}{\partial F}\cdot\lambda_1 K_1 F\right)\Big/\Delta$
$\dfrac{dr}{dm_n}$	$-K'_1\dfrac{\phi}{\Delta}$	$\left(-K'_1\cdot F\dfrac{\partial f}{\partial F} + F''\dfrac{\partial f}{\partial F}\cdot\lambda_1 K_1 F\right)\Big/\Delta$
$\dfrac{d(x+y)}{dm_n}$	$-\{g' + (K'_1 - K'_2\phi')\phi'\}\dfrac{\phi}{\Delta}$	$-\left[\{g' + (K'_1 - K'_2\phi')_1F\dfrac{\partial f}{\partial F} + \left(\dfrac{\partial f}{\partial r} - \phi - \phi F''\dfrac{\partial f}{\partial F}\right)\lambda_1 K_1 F\right]\Big/\Delta$
$\left[\dfrac{dx}{dy}\right]_{m_n}$	$\dfrac{g' - K'_8\phi'}{K'_1\phi'}$	$\dfrac{(g' - K'_2\phi')_1F\dfrac{\partial f}{\partial F} + \left(\dfrac{\partial f}{\partial r} - \phi'\right)\lambda_1 K_1 F}{K'_1\phi'F\dfrac{\partial f}{\partial F} - \phi F''\dfrac{\partial f}{\partial F}\cdot\lambda_1 K_1 F}$
$\left[\dfrac{d(x+y)}{dy}\right]_{m_n}$	$\dfrac{g' + (K'_1 - K'_2\phi')\phi'}{K'_1\phi'}$	$\dfrac{\{g' + (K'_1 - K'_2\phi')_1F\dfrac{\partial f}{\partial F} - \left(\dfrac{\partial f}{\partial r} - \phi' - \phi F''\dfrac{\partial f}{\partial F}\right)\lambda_1 K_1 F}{K'_1\phi F\dfrac{\partial f}{\partial F} - \phi'F''\dfrac{\partial f}{\partial F}\cdot\lambda_1 K_1 F}$

TABLE II

FORM OF MODEL III WHEN g' IS POSITIVE AND FINITE

Denominator $A = K'_1\left(\dfrac{\partial f}{\partial \tau} - \phi'\right) + F'\dfrac{\partial f}{\partial F}(g' - K'_2\phi')$

		Sign			Sign
D_1	$-\left\{\left(\dfrac{\partial f}{\partial \tau} - \phi'\right) - \phi F'\dfrac{\partial f}{\partial F}\right\}\dfrac{g}{A}$	$-$	M_1	$\dfrac{\left(\dfrac{\partial f}{\partial \tau} - \phi'\right) - \phi'F'\dfrac{\partial f}{\partial F}}{(-\phi')F'\dfrac{\partial f}{\partial F}}$	$+$
D_2	$-D_1$	$+$	M_2		$\pm$
D_3	$\left\{g'\left(1+F'\dfrac{\partial f}{\partial F}\right) + \left(K'_1 - K'_2\dfrac{\partial f}{\partial \tau}\right)\right\}\dfrac{\phi}{A}$	$\pm$	M_3	$\dfrac{g'\left(1+F'\dfrac{\partial f}{\partial F}\right) + \left(K'_1 - K'_2\dfrac{\partial f}{\partial \tau}\right)}{K'_1\dfrac{\partial f}{\partial \tau} + g'F'\dfrac{\partial f}{\partial F}}$	$\pm$
D_4	$\left[\left\{g'\left(1+F'\dfrac{\partial f}{\partial F}\right) + \left(K'_1 - K'_2\dfrac{\partial f}{\partial \tau}\right)\right\}(-\tau\phi') - \left(\dfrac{\partial f}{\partial \tau} - \phi' - \phi F'\dfrac{\partial f}{\partial F}\right)\lambda_2 K_2\psi\right]\Big/ A$	$\pm$	M_4	$\dfrac{\left\{g'\left(1+F'\dfrac{\partial f}{\partial F}\right) + \left(K'_1 - K'_2\dfrac{\partial f}{\partial \tau}\right)\right\}(-\tau\phi') - \left(\dfrac{\partial f}{\partial \tau} - \phi' - \phi F'\dfrac{\partial f}{\partial F}\right)\lambda_2 K_2\psi}{\left(K'_1\dfrac{\partial f}{\partial \tau} + g'F'\dfrac{\partial f}{\partial F}\right)(-\tau\phi') + \phi'F'\dfrac{\partial f}{\partial F}\lambda_2 K_2\psi}$	$\pm$
D_5	$-\left\{g'+(K'_1 - K'_2\phi')\right\}\dfrac{\phi}{A}$	$\pm$	M_5	$\dfrac{g'+(K'_1 - K'_2)\phi'}{K'_1\phi'}$	$\pm$
D_6	$-\left[\left\{g'+(K'_1 - K'_2\phi')\right\}F'\dfrac{\partial f}{\partial F} + \left(\dfrac{\partial f}{\partial \tau} - \phi' - \phi F'\dfrac{\partial f}{\partial F}\right)\lambda_1 K_1 F\right]\Big/ A$	$\pm$	M_6	$\dfrac{\left\{g'+(K'_1 - K'_2\phi')\right\}F'\dfrac{\partial f}{\partial F} + \left(\dfrac{\partial f}{\partial \tau} - \phi' - \phi'F'\dfrac{\partial f}{\partial F}\right)\lambda_1 K_1 F}{K'_1 F'\dfrac{\partial f}{\partial F} - \phi'F'\dfrac{\partial f}{\partial F}\lambda_1 K_1 F}$	$\pm$

TABLE II—*contd.*

		Sign
N_1	$\dfrac{\mathrm{K}'_1 \mathrm{K}_2 \left(\frac{\partial f}{\partial \tau} - \phi'\right) + \mathrm{F}' \frac{\partial f}{\partial \mathrm{F}} (\mathrm{K}_2 g' + \mathrm{K}_1 \mathrm{K}_2 \phi')}{\mathrm{F}' \frac{\partial f}{\partial \mathrm{F}} g g'}$	±
N_2	$\dfrac{\mathrm{K}'_1 \left(\frac{\partial f}{\partial \tau} - \phi'\right) - \mathrm{K}'_2 \phi' \mathrm{F}' \frac{\partial f}{\partial \mathrm{F}}}{-\mathrm{K}'_2 \phi' \cdot \mathrm{F}' \frac{\partial f}{\partial \mathrm{F}}}$	+
N_3	$\dfrac{\mathrm{K}'_1 + \mathrm{K}_2 \mathrm{F}' \frac{\partial f}{\partial \mathrm{F}}}{\mathrm{K}'_1 \frac{\partial f}{\partial \tau} + g \mathrm{F}' \frac{\partial f}{\partial \mathrm{F}}} \quad \dfrac{g'}{\mathrm{K}'_2}$	+*
N_4	$\dfrac{\left(\mathrm{K}'_1 + \mathrm{K}'_2 \mathrm{F}' \frac{\partial f}{\partial \mathrm{F}}\right)(-g'\phi') + g'\mathrm{F}' \frac{\partial f}{\partial \mathrm{F}} \lambda_2 \mathrm{K}_2 \psi}{\left(\mathrm{K}'_1 \frac{\partial f}{\partial \tau} + g \mathrm{F}' \frac{\partial f}{\partial \mathrm{F}}\right)(-\mathrm{K}'_2 \phi') + \left\{\mathrm{K}'_1 \left(\frac{\partial f}{\partial \tau} - \phi'\right) + g' \mathrm{F}' \frac{\partial f}{\partial \mathrm{F}}\right\} \lambda_2 \mathrm{K}_2 \psi}$	±
N_5 N_6	$\dfrac{g'}{\mathrm{K}'_2 \phi'}$	—

* On the assumption that $\frac{\partial f}{\partial \tau}$ is not negative.

TABLE II B

FORM OF MODEL III WHEN g' IS POSITIVE AND FINITE AND $\frac{\partial f}{\partial r}=0$

Denominator $A = -\left(K'_1+K'_2F'\frac{\partial f}{\partial F}\right)\phi' + g'F'\frac{\partial f}{\partial F}$

	Sign			Sign	
D_1	$-$	$\left(1+F'\frac{\partial f}{\partial F}\right)\phi'\cdot\frac{g}{A}$	M_1, M_2	$+$	$\dfrac{1+F'\frac{\partial f}{\partial F}}{F'\frac{\partial f}{\partial F}}\phi'$
D_2	$+$	$-D_1$			
D_3	$+$	$\left(1+F'\frac{\partial f}{\partial F}\right)g'\cdot\frac{\phi}{A}$	M_3	$+$	$\dfrac{1+F'\frac{\partial f}{\partial F}}{F'\frac{\partial f}{\partial F}}\phi'$
D_4	$\pm$	$\left[\left(1+F'\frac{\partial f}{\partial F}\right)(-g'\phi'+\phi'\lambda_2 K_2\psi)\right]/A$	M_4	$\pm$	$\dfrac{g'\left(1+F'\frac{\partial f}{\partial F}\right)(-r\phi')-\left(1+F'\frac{\partial f}{\partial F}\right)\phi'\lambda_2 K_2\psi}{g'F'\frac{\partial f}{\partial F}-r\phi')+\phi'F'\frac{\partial f}{\partial F}\lambda_2 K_2\phi}$
D_5	$\pm$	$-\{g'+(K'_1-K'_2)\phi'\}\phi'_1\frac{\phi}{A}$	M_5	$\pm$	$\dfrac{g'+(K'_1-K'_2)\phi'}{K'_1\phi'}$
D_6	$\pm$	$-\left[\{g'+(K'_1-K'_2)\phi'\}F'\frac{\partial f}{\partial F}+\left(1+F'\frac{\partial f}{\partial F}\right)\phi\lambda_1 K_1 F\right]/A$	M_6	$\pm$	$\dfrac{\{g'+(K'_1-K'_2)\phi'\}F'\frac{\partial f}{\partial F}-\left(1+F'\frac{\partial f}{\partial F}\right)\phi'\lambda_1 K_1 F}{\phi'K'_1F'\frac{\partial f}{\partial F}-\phi F'\frac{\partial f}{\partial F}\lambda_1 K_1 F}$

TABLE II B—*contd.*

		Sign
N_1	$\dfrac{F'\frac{\partial f}{\partial F}gg'}{K_2g'F'\frac{\partial f}{\partial F}+K_1K'_2\phi'F'\frac{\partial f}{\partial F}-K'_1K_2\phi'}$	++
N_2	$\dfrac{K'_1+K'_2F'\frac{\partial f}{\partial F}}{K'_2F'\frac{\partial f}{\partial F}}$	+
N_3	$\dfrac{K'_1+K'_2F'\frac{\partial f}{\partial F}}{K'_2F'\frac{\partial f}{\partial F}}$	+
N_4	$\dfrac{\left(K'_1+K'_2F'\frac{\partial f}{\partial F}\right)(-g'\phi'+g'F'\frac{\partial f}{\partial F})K_2\phi}{K'_2F'\frac{\partial f}{\partial F}-g'\phi'+\left(-K_1\phi'+g'F'\frac{\partial f}{\partial F}\right)\lambda_2\phi}$	+
N_5 N_6	$\dfrac{g'}{K'_2\phi'}$	-

TABLE III

FORM OF MODEL III WHEN $g' = 0$

$$\text{Denominator } A = K'_1\left(\frac{\partial f}{\partial r}-\phi'\right)-K'_2\phi'F'\frac{\partial f}{\partial F}$$

	Sign		Sign		Sign
$D_1 = -\left\{\left(\dfrac{\partial f}{\partial r}-\phi'\right)-\phi'F'\dfrac{\partial f}{\partial F}\right\}\dfrac{g}{A}$	$-$	$M_1 = \left(\dfrac{\partial f}{\partial r}-\phi'\right)-\phi'F'\dfrac{\partial f}{\partial F}$		$N_1 = 0$	$+$
$D_2 = -D_1$	$+$	$M_2 = \dfrac{(-\phi')F'\dfrac{\partial f}{\partial F}}{}$	$+$	$N_2 = \dfrac{K'_1\left(\dfrac{\partial f}{\partial r}-\phi'\right)-K'_2\phi'F'\dfrac{\partial f}{\partial F}}{-K'_2\phi'F'\dfrac{\partial f}{\partial F}}$	
$D_3 = (K'_1-K'_2)\dfrac{\partial f}{\partial r}\cdot\dfrac{\phi}{A}$	$\pm$	$M_3^{*} = \dfrac{K'_1-K'_2}{K'_1}$	$\pm$	$N_3 = 0$	
$D_4 = \left[(K'_1-K'_2)\left(\dfrac{\partial f}{\partial r}-r\phi'\right)-\left(\dfrac{\partial f}{\partial r}-\phi'-\phi'F'\dfrac{\partial f}{\partial F}\right)\lambda_2K_2\mu\right]/A$	$\pm$	$M_4 = \dfrac{(K'_1-K'_2)\left(\dfrac{\partial f}{\partial r}-r\phi'\right)-\left(\dfrac{\partial f}{\partial r}-\phi'-\phi'F'\dfrac{\partial f}{\partial F}\right)\lambda_2K_2\mu}{K'_1\dfrac{\partial f}{\partial r}(-r\phi')+\phi'F'\dfrac{\partial f}{\partial F}\lambda_2K_2\mu}$	$\pm$	$N_4 = 0$	
$D_5 = -(K'_1-K'_2)\phi'\cdot\dfrac{\phi}{A}$	$\pm$	$M_5 = \dfrac{K'_1-K'_2}{K'_1}$	$\pm$	$N_5 = 0$	
$D_6 = -\left[(K_1-K'_2)\phi'F'\dfrac{\partial f}{\partial F}+\left(\dfrac{\partial f}{\partial r}-\phi'-\phi'F'\dfrac{\partial f}{\partial F}\right)\lambda_1K_1F\right]/A$	$\pm$	$M_6 = \dfrac{(K'_1-K'_2)\phi'F'\dfrac{\partial f}{\partial F}+\left(\dfrac{\partial f}{\partial r}-\phi'-\phi'F'\dfrac{\partial}{\partial F}\right)\lambda_1K_1F}{K'_1\phi'F'\dfrac{\partial f}{\partial F}-\phi'F'\dfrac{\partial f}{\partial F}\lambda_1K_1F}$	$\pm$	$N_6 = 0$	

* When $\dfrac{\partial f}{\partial r}$ also $= 0$, $M_3 = \dfrac{0}{0}$. (Cf. Table II.)

TABLE IV

FORM OF MODEL III WHEN g' IS INFINITE

		Sign			Sign			Sign
D_1	0		M_1	$\dfrac{0}{0}$		N_1	$\dfrac{g}{K_2}$	$+$
D_2^*	0		M_2^*	$\dfrac{0}{0}$		N_2^*	$\dfrac{0}{0}$	
D_3	$\dfrac{1+F''\frac{\partial f}{\partial F}}{F''\frac{\partial f}{\partial F}}\cdot\phi$	$+$	M_3	$\dfrac{1+F''\frac{\partial f}{\partial F}}{F''\frac{\partial f}{\partial F}}$	$+$	N_3	$\dfrac{K'_1+K'_2F''\frac{\partial f}{\partial F}}{K'_2F''\frac{\partial f}{\partial F}}$	$+$
D_4	$\dfrac{1+F''\frac{\partial f}{\partial F}}{F''\frac{\partial f}{\partial F}}(-r\phi')$	$+$	M_4			N_4	$\dfrac{\left(K'_1+K'_2F''\frac{\partial f}{\partial F}\right)(-r\phi')}{F''\frac{\partial f}{\partial F}(-K_2r\phi'+\lambda_2K_2\mu')}$	$\boxplus$
D_5	$-\dfrac{\phi}{F''\frac{\partial f}{\partial F}}$	$-$	M_5	∞	$+$	N_5	∞	$+$
D_6	$-\dfrac{F}{F''}$	$-$	M_6			N_6		

* In the interpretation of Part III, Chapter X, § 3, $D_2 = -\dfrac{\left(\frac{\partial f}{\partial r}-\phi'\right)-\phi F''\frac{\partial f}{\partial F}}{F''\frac{\partial f}{\partial F}}$, which is negative; while $M_2 = \dfrac{\left(\frac{\partial f}{\partial r}-\phi'\right)-\phi F''\frac{\partial f}{\partial F}}{-\phi F''\frac{\partial f}{\partial F}}$, and

$N_2 = \dfrac{K'_1\left(\frac{\partial f}{\partial r}-\phi'\right)-K'_2\phi F''\frac{\partial f}{\partial F}}{-K'_2\phi F''\frac{\partial f}{\partial F}}$, both of which are positive.

TABLE V

FORM OF MODEL III WHEN $\dfrac{d}{dm_n}\left(\dfrac{K_1 m_1}{Fm_2 m_6}\right)=0$

$$\frac{dx}{dm_1} = -\frac{1}{\frac{K_1'}{K_1}-\frac{F'}{F}} = -\frac{dx}{dm_2}\ ;\quad \frac{dx}{dm_3}=\frac{dx}{dm_4}=\frac{dx}{dm_5}=0\ ;\quad \frac{dx}{dm_6}=\frac{1-\lambda_1 F}{\frac{K_1'}{K_1}-\frac{F'}{F}}$$

		Sign			Sign
D_1	$-\dfrac{\left(\frac{\partial f}{\partial r}-\phi'\right)-\phi T'\frac{\partial f}{\partial F}}{\frac{\partial f}{\partial r}-\phi'}\cdot\dfrac{1}{\frac{K_1'}{K_1}-\frac{F'}{F}}$	−	$\dfrac{\left(\frac{\partial f}{\partial r}-\phi'\right)-\phi T'\frac{\partial f}{\partial F}}{-\phi T'\frac{\partial f}{\partial F}}$	$\Big\}\ M_1$	+
D_2	$-D_1$	+		M_2	
D_3^{*}	$\dfrac{\frac{\partial f}{\partial r}}{\frac{\partial f}{\partial r}-\phi'}\cdot\phi$	+	1	$\Big\}\ M_3$	+
D_4^{*}	$\dfrac{\frac{\partial f}{\partial r}}{\frac{\partial f}{\partial r}-\phi'}\cdot(-r\phi')$	+		M_4	
D_5	$\dfrac{-\phi'}{\frac{\partial f}{\partial r}-\phi'}\cdot\phi$	+	1	M_5	+
D_6	$\dfrac{\left(\frac{\partial f}{\partial r}-\phi'\right)-\frac{K_1'}{K_1}\phi T\frac{\partial f}{\partial F}-\left(\frac{\partial f}{\partial r}-\phi'-\phi T'\frac{\partial f}{\partial F}\right)\lambda_1 F}{\frac{\partial f}{\partial r}-\phi'}\cdot\dfrac{1}{\frac{K_1'}{K_1}-\frac{F'}{F}}$	±	$\dfrac{\left(\frac{\partial f}{\partial r}-\phi'\right)-\frac{K_1'}{K_1}\phi T\frac{\partial f}{\partial F}-\left(\frac{\partial f}{\partial r}-\phi'-\phi T'\frac{\partial f}{\partial F}\right)\lambda_1 F}{\frac{K_1'}{K_1}\phi T\frac{\partial f}{\partial F}+\phi T'\frac{\partial f}{\partial F}-\frac{K_1'}{K_1}\phi T'\frac{\partial f}{\partial F}\lambda_1 F}$	M_6	±

* The signs of D_3 and D_4 are, of course, only positive on the assumption that $\partial f/\partial r$ is positive.

TABLE V —*contd.*

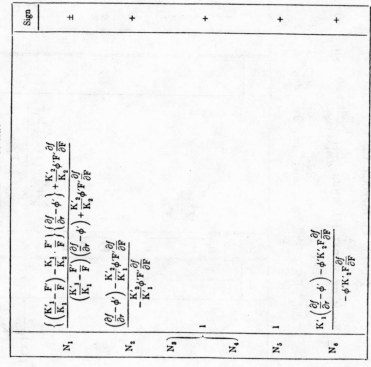

		Sign
N_1	$\dfrac{\left\{\left(\dfrac{K'_1}{K_1}-\dfrac{F'}{F}\right)-\dfrac{K_1}{K_2}\cdot\dfrac{F'}{F}\right\}\left(\dfrac{\partial f}{\partial \tau}-\phi'\right)+\dfrac{K'_2}{K_2}\phi'F'\dfrac{\partial f}{\partial F}}{\left(\dfrac{K'_1}{K_1}-\dfrac{F'}{F}\right)\left(\dfrac{\partial f}{\partial \tau}-\phi'\right)+\dfrac{K'_2}{K_2}\phi F'\dfrac{\partial f}{\partial F}}$	$\pm$
N_2	$\dfrac{\left(\dfrac{\partial f}{\partial \tau}-\phi'\right)-\dfrac{K'_2}{K'_1}\phi F'\dfrac{\partial f}{\partial F}}{-\dfrac{K'_2}{K'_1}\phi F'\dfrac{\partial f}{\partial F}}$	$+$
$\left.\begin{array}{c}N_3\\N_4\end{array}\right\}$	1	$+$
N_5	1	$+$
N_6	$\dfrac{K'_1\left(\dfrac{\partial f}{\partial \tau}-\phi'\right)-\phi'K'_2F'\dfrac{\partial f}{\partial F}}{-\phi'K'_2F'\dfrac{\partial f}{\partial F}}$	$+$

TABLE Vb (Special Case of Table V)

Form of Model III when $\dfrac{d}{dm_n}\left(\dfrac{K_1 m_1}{F m_2 m_6}\right) = 0$ and $\dfrac{\partial f}{\partial r} = 0$

$$\frac{dx}{dm_1} = -\frac{1}{\frac{K_1'}{K_1} - \frac{F'}{F}} \quad ; \quad \frac{dx}{dm_2} = -\frac{dx}{dm_2} \quad ; \quad \frac{dx}{dm_3} = \frac{dx}{dm_4} = \frac{dx}{dm_5} \quad ; \quad \frac{dx}{dm_6} = \frac{1 - \lambda_1 F}{\frac{K_1'}{K_1} - \frac{F'}{F}}$$

	D	Sign		M	Sign		N	Sign
D_1	$-\left(1 + F'\dfrac{\partial f}{\partial F}\right)\dfrac{1}{\frac{K_1'}{K_1} - \frac{F'}{F}}$	±	M_1	$\dfrac{1 + F'\frac{\partial f}{\partial F}}{F'\frac{\partial f}{\partial F}}$	+	N_1	$\dfrac{\left(\frac{K_1'}{K_1} - \frac{F'}{F}\right) - \frac{K_1}{K_2}\cdot\frac{F'}{F} - \frac{K_2'}{K_2}F'\frac{\partial f}{\partial F}}{\left(\frac{K_1'}{K_1} - \frac{F'}{F}\right)}$	±
D_2	$-D_1$	±	M_2			N_2	$\dfrac{1 + \frac{K_1'}{K_1}F\frac{\partial f}{\partial F}}{\frac{K_2'}{K_2}\cdot F'\frac{\partial f}{\partial F}}$	+
D_3	0		M_3	$\dfrac{0}{0}$		N_3	$\dfrac{0}{0}$	
D_4	0		M_4			N_4		
D_5	ϕ	+	M_5	1	+	N_5	1	+
D_6	$\left\{1 + \dfrac{K_1'F}{K_2}\dfrac{\partial f}{\partial F} - \left(1 + F'\dfrac{\partial f}{\partial F}\right)\lambda_1 F\right\}\dfrac{1}{\frac{K_1'}{K_1} - \frac{F'}{F}}$	±	M_6	$\dfrac{1 + \frac{K_1'F}{K_1}\frac{\partial f}{\partial F} - \left(1 + F'\frac{\partial f}{\partial F}\right)\lambda_1 F}{\frac{K_1'}{K_1}F\frac{\partial f}{\partial F} - F'\frac{\partial f}{\partial F}\lambda_1 F}$	±	N_6	$\dfrac{K_1' + K_2'F\frac{\partial f}{\partial F}}{K_2'F\frac{\partial f}{\partial F}}$	÷

TABLE VI

FORM OF MODEL II WHEN g' IS POSITIVE AND FINITE

$$\text{Denominator } A = \left(\frac{\partial f}{\partial r} - \phi'\right)\frac{d}{dx}\left(\frac{F}{\bar{F}}\right) + F'\frac{\partial f}{\partial \bar{F}}\left\{g' - \phi'\frac{d}{dy}\left(\frac{\psi}{\psi'}\right)\right\}$$

	S	Sign		M	Sign		N	Sign
D_1	$-\left\{\left(\dfrac{\partial f}{\partial r} - \phi'\right) - \phi'F'\dfrac{\partial f}{\partial \bar{F}}\right\}\cdot\dfrac{g}{A}$	$-$	M_1	$\left(\dfrac{\partial f}{\partial r} - \phi'\right) - \phi'F'\dfrac{\partial f}{\partial \bar{F}}$	$-$	N_1	$\dfrac{\dfrac{\psi}{\psi'}\left(\dfrac{\partial f}{\partial r} - \phi'\right)\dfrac{d}{dx}\left(\dfrac{F}{\bar{F}}\right) + F'\dfrac{\partial f}{\partial \bar{F}}\left\{0 - \phi'\dfrac{\psi}{\psi'} + \phi'\dfrac{F}{\bar{F}}\dfrac{d}{dy}\left(\dfrac{\psi}{\psi'}\right)\right\}}{F'\dfrac{\partial f}{\partial \bar{F}}gg'}$	$+$
D_2	$-D_1$	$+$	M_2	$-\phi'F'\dfrac{\partial f}{\partial \bar{F}}$	$+$	N_2	$\dfrac{\left\{\dfrac{\partial f}{\partial r} - \phi'\right\}\dfrac{d}{dx}\left(\dfrac{F}{\bar{F}}\right) - \phi'F'\dfrac{\partial f}{\partial \bar{F}}\dfrac{d}{dy}\left(\dfrac{\psi}{\psi'}\right)}{-\phi'F'\dfrac{\partial f}{\partial \bar{F}}\dfrac{d}{dx}\dfrac{d}{dy}\left(\dfrac{\psi}{\psi'}\right)}$	$+$
D_3	$\left[g'\left\{1 + F'\dfrac{\partial f}{\partial \bar{F}}\right\} + \dfrac{\partial f}{\partial r}\left\{\dfrac{d}{dx}\left(\dfrac{F}{\bar{F}}\right) - \dfrac{d}{dy}\left(\dfrac{\psi}{\psi'}\right)\right\}\right]\cdot\dfrac{\phi}{A}$	$\pm$	M_3	$g'\left\{1 + F'\dfrac{\partial f}{\partial \bar{F}}\right\} + \dfrac{\partial f}{\partial r}\left\{\dfrac{d}{dx}\left(\dfrac{F}{\bar{F}}\right) - \dfrac{d}{dy}\left(\dfrac{\psi}{\psi'}\right)\right\}$	$\pm$	N_3	$\dfrac{\dfrac{d}{dx}\left(\dfrac{F}{\bar{F}}\right) + F'\dfrac{\partial f}{\partial \bar{F}}\dfrac{d}{dy}\left(\dfrac{\psi}{\psi'}\right)}{\dfrac{\partial f}{\partial r}\dfrac{d}{dx}\left(\dfrac{F}{\bar{F}}\right) + g'F'\dfrac{\partial f}{\partial \bar{F}}}$	$+$
D_4	$\left[g'\left\{1 + F'\dfrac{\partial f}{\partial \bar{F}}\right\} + \dfrac{\partial f}{\partial r}\left\{\dfrac{d}{dx}\left(\dfrac{F}{\bar{F}}\right) - \dfrac{d}{dy}\left(\dfrac{\psi}{\psi'}\right)\right\}\right]\dfrac{(-r\phi')}{A}$	$\pm$	M_4	$\dfrac{\partial f}{\partial r}\dfrac{d}{dx}\left(\dfrac{F}{\bar{F}}\right) + g'F'\dfrac{\partial f}{\partial \bar{F}}$	$\pm$	N_4		
D_5	$-\left[g' + \phi'\left\{\dfrac{d}{dx}\left(\dfrac{F}{\bar{F}}\right) - \dfrac{d}{dy}\left(\dfrac{\psi}{\psi'}\right)\right\}\right]\cdot\dfrac{\phi}{A}$	$\pm$	M_5	$g' + \phi'\left\{\dfrac{d}{dx}\left(\dfrac{F}{\bar{F}}\right) - \dfrac{d}{dy}\left(\dfrac{\psi}{\psi'}\right)\right\}$	$\pm$	N_5	$\dfrac{\dfrac{g'}{\dfrac{d}{dy}\left(\dfrac{\psi}{\psi'}\right)}}{\dfrac{1}{\phi'}}$	$-$
D_6	$-\left[g' + \phi'\left\{\dfrac{d}{dx}\left(\dfrac{F}{\bar{F}}\right) - \dfrac{d}{dy}\left(\dfrac{\psi}{\psi'}\right)\right\}\right]\dfrac{F'\dfrac{\partial f}{\partial \bar{F}}}{A}$	$\pm$	M_6	$\phi'\left\{\dfrac{d}{dx}\left(\dfrac{F}{\bar{F}}\right) - \dfrac{d}{dy}\left(\dfrac{\psi}{\psi'}\right)\right\}$	$\pm$	N_6	$\dfrac{g'}{\dfrac{d}{dy}\left(\dfrac{\psi}{\psi'}\right)}$	

TABLE VII

FORM OF MODEL I WHEN g' IS POSITIVE AND FINITE

Model I (B). $\quad K_1 = \left(1 - \frac{1}{\eta_1}\right)\frac{F}{F'}, \quad F = Cx \quad \therefore K'_1 = C.$ Denominator $A = C\left(\frac{\partial f}{\partial r} - \phi'\right) + F'\frac{\partial f}{\partial F}(g' - C\phi')$

Model I (A). $\quad K_1 = \frac{F}{F'} = C_1 x,$ obtained from Model I (B) when $\eta_1 \to \infty$

$\therefore$ the form of Model I (A) is identical with that of Model I (B) save that C_1 must be substituted for C

		Sign			Sign			Sign
D_1	$-\left\{\left(\dfrac{\partial f}{\partial r} - \phi'\right) - \phi'F'\dfrac{\partial f}{\partial F}\right\}\dfrac{g}{A}$	$-$	M_1	$\dfrac{\left(\dfrac{\partial f}{\partial r} - \phi'\right) - \phi'F'\dfrac{\partial f}{\partial F}}{-\phi'F'\dfrac{\partial f}{\partial F}}$	$+$	N_1	$\dfrac{F'\dfrac{\partial f}{\partial F}gg'}{C^2y\left(\dfrac{\partial f}{\partial r} - \phi'\right) + CF'\dfrac{\partial f}{\partial F}\{yg' + Cx\phi'\}}$	$\dashv\vdash$
D_2	$-D_1$	$+$	M_2			N_2	$\dfrac{\left(\dfrac{\partial f}{\partial r} - \phi'\right) - \phi'F'\dfrac{\partial f}{\partial F}}{-\phi'F'\dfrac{\partial f}{\partial F}}$	$+$
D_3	$g'\left(1+F'\dfrac{\partial f}{\partial F}\right)\dfrac{\phi}{A}$	$+$	M_3	$\dfrac{\left(1+F'\dfrac{\partial f}{\partial F}\right)g'}{C\dfrac{\partial f}{\partial r} + g'F'\dfrac{\partial f}{\partial F}}$	$+$	N_3	$\dfrac{\left(1+F'\dfrac{\partial f}{\partial F}\right)g'}{C\dfrac{\partial f}{\partial r} + g'F'\dfrac{\partial f}{\partial F}}$	$+$
D_4	$g'\left(1+F'\dfrac{\partial f}{\partial F}\right)\cdot\dfrac{(-r\phi')}{A}$	$+$	M_4			N_4		
D_5	$-g'\cdot\dfrac{\phi}{A}$	$-$	M_5	$\dfrac{g'}{C\phi}$	$-$	N_5	$\dfrac{g'}{C\phi}$	$-$
D_6	$-g'\cdot\dfrac{F'\dfrac{\partial f}{\partial F}}{A}$	$-$	M_6			N_6		

TABLE VIIb (SPECIAL CASE OF TABLE VII)

FORM OF MODEL I WHEN g' IS POSITIVE AND FINITE AND $\frac{\partial f}{\partial r}=0$

In Model I(B) $K'_1 = K'_3 = C$. Denominator $A = -C\phi'\left(1+F'\frac{\partial f}{\partial F}\right)+g'F'\frac{\partial f}{\partial F}$

In Model I(A) C_1 is substituted for C

	Expression	Sign		Expression	Sign		Expression	Sign
D_1	$\left(1+F'\frac{\partial f}{\partial F}\right)\phi'\cdot\frac{g}{A}$	−	M_1	$\dfrac{1+F'\frac{\partial f}{\partial F}}{F'\frac{\partial f}{\partial F}}$	+	N_1	$\dfrac{F'\frac{\partial f}{\partial F}gg'}{Cyg'F'\frac{\partial f}{\partial F}+C\phi'\left(zF'\frac{\partial f}{\partial F}-y\right)}$	±
D_2	$-D_1$	+	M_2			N_2	$\dfrac{1+F'\frac{\partial f}{\partial F}}{F'\frac{\partial f}{\partial F}}$	+
D_3	$\left(1+F'\frac{\partial f}{\partial F}\right)g'\cdot\frac{\phi}{A}$	+	M_3	$\dfrac{1+F'\frac{\partial f}{\partial F}}{F'\frac{\partial f}{\partial F}}$	+	N_3	$\dfrac{1+F'\frac{\partial f}{\partial F}}{F'\frac{\partial f}{\partial F}}$	+
D_4	$\left(1+F'\frac{\partial f}{\partial F}\right)g'\cdot\frac{(-r\phi')}{A}$	+	M_4			N_4		
D_5	$-\dfrac{g'\phi}{A}$	−	M_5	$\dfrac{g'}{C\phi'}$	−	N_5	$\dfrac{g'}{C\phi'}$	−
D_6	$-g'\ \dfrac{F\frac{\partial f}{\partial F}}{A}$	−	M_6			N_6		

TABLE VIII

FORM OF MODEL I WHEN $g' = 0$

In Model I (B) $K'_1 = K'_2 = C$

In Model I (A) $K'_1 = K'_2 = C_1$

		Sign
D_1	$-\dfrac{g}{C}$	$-$
D_2	$-D_1$	$+$
D_3		
D_4	0	
D_5		
D_6		

		Sign
M_1	$\dfrac{\left(\dfrac{\partial f}{\partial r} - \phi'\right) - \phi T' \dfrac{\partial f}{\partial F}}{-\phi T' \dfrac{\partial f}{\partial F}}$	$+$
M_2		
M_3		
M_4	0	
M_5		
M_6		

		Sign
N_1	0	$+$
N_2	$\dfrac{\left(\dfrac{\partial f}{\partial r} - \phi'\right) - \phi T' \dfrac{\partial f}{\partial F}}{-\phi T' \dfrac{\partial f}{\partial F}}$	
N_3		
N_4	0	
N_5		
N_6		

TABLE IX: FORM OF MODEL I WHEN $\dfrac{d}{dm_1}\left(\dfrac{K_1 m_1}{Fm_2 m_6}\right) = \dfrac{d}{dm_n}\left(\dfrac{Cxm_1}{Fm_2 m_6}\right) = 0$

In Model I(B) $K_1 = \dfrac{F}{\left(1-\frac{1}{\eta_1}\right)F'} = Cx$ $\therefore K_1' = C$ and $\left\{\dfrac{K_1'}{K_1} - \dfrac{F'}{F}\right\} = \dfrac{C-\left(1-\frac{1}{\eta_1}\right)}{Cx}$

$$\frac{dx}{dm_1} = -\frac{Cx}{C-\left(1-\frac{1}{\eta_1}\right)} ;\quad \frac{dx}{dm_2} = -\frac{dx}{dm_3} ;\quad \frac{dx}{dm_3} = \frac{dx}{dm_4} = \frac{dx}{dm_5} = 0 ;\quad \frac{dx}{dm_6} = \frac{Cx}{C-\left(1-\frac{1}{\eta_1}\right)}$$

We know (cf. ante, § 5) that $(C-1)$ is positive : hence, a fortiori $\left\{C-\left(1-\frac{1}{\eta_1}\right)\right\}$ is positive

Model I(A) is obtained from Model I(B) when C is replaced by C_1 and $1/\eta_1 = 0$

		Sign			Sign			Sign
D_1	$-\left(\frac{\partial f}{\partial r} - \phi'\right) - \phi_F\frac{\partial f}{\partial F} \cdot \dfrac{Cx}{C-\left(1-\frac{1}{\eta_1}\right)}$	$-$	M_1	$\dfrac{\left(\frac{\partial f}{\partial r} - \phi'\right) - \phi_F \frac{\partial f}{\partial F}}{-\phi_F \frac{\partial f}{\partial F}}$	$+$	N_1	$\dfrac{\left[\left\{C-\left(1-\frac{1}{\eta_1}\right)\right\}y - x\right]\left(\frac{\partial f}{\partial r} - \phi'\right) + Cx\phi_F\frac{\partial f}{\partial F}}{\left\{C-\left(1-\frac{1}{\eta_1}\right)\right\}y\left(\frac{\partial f}{\partial r} - \phi'\right) + Cx\phi_F\frac{\partial f}{\partial F}}$	$\pm$
D_2	$-D_1 \cdot \dfrac{\partial f}{\partial r}$	$+$	M_2	$\dfrac{\left(\frac{\partial f}{\partial r} - \phi'\right) - \phi_F \frac{\partial f}{\partial F}}{-\phi_F \frac{\partial f}{\partial F}}$	$+$	N_2	$\dfrac{\left(\frac{\partial f}{\partial r} - \phi'\right) - \phi_F \frac{\partial f}{\partial F}}{-\phi_F \frac{\partial f}{\partial F}}$	$+$
D_3^{*}	$\dfrac{\frac{\partial f}{\partial r}}{\left(\frac{\partial f}{\partial r} - \phi'\right)} \cdot \phi$	$+$	M_3	$\Big\}\,1$		N_3	$\Big\}\,1$	
D_4^{*}	$\dfrac{\frac{\partial f}{\partial r}}{\left(\frac{\partial f}{\partial r} - \phi'\right)} \cdot (-r\phi')$	$+$	M_4		$+$	N_4		$+$
D_5	$\dfrac{-\phi'}{\left(\frac{\partial f}{\partial r} - \phi'\right)} \cdot \phi$	$+$	M_5	1	$+$	N_5	1	$+$
D_6	$\dfrac{\left(\frac{\partial f}{\partial r} - \phi'\right) - \frac{1}{x}\phi_F\frac{\partial f}{\partial F}}{x} \cdot \dfrac{Cx}{C-\left(1-\frac{1}{\eta_1}\right)}$	$+$	M_6	$\dfrac{x\left(\frac{\partial f}{\partial r} - \phi'\right) - \phi_F\frac{\partial f}{\partial F}}{-\phi_F\frac{\partial f}{\partial F}}$	$+$	N_6	$\dfrac{x\left(\frac{\partial f}{\partial r} - \phi'\right) - \phi_F\frac{\partial f}{\partial F}}{-\phi_F\frac{\partial f}{\partial F}}$	$+$

* The signs of D_2 and D_4 are, of course, only positive on the assumption that $\partial f/\partial r$ is positive.

NOTE TO TABLES V AND IX

§ 7. Given the condition that $\dfrac{d}{dm_n}\left(\dfrac{K_1 m_1}{F m_2 m_6}\right) = 0$, *i.e.* that $\dfrac{d}{dx}\left(\dfrac{K_1}{F}\right)$ $= 0$, or, what is equivalent, that $\dfrac{K'_1}{K_1} - \dfrac{F'}{F} = 0$, the analysis breaks down for all the ratios.

For *Model III* this happens when

$$\frac{d}{dx}\left\{\frac{1}{\left(1 - \dfrac{1}{\eta_1}\right)F'}\right\} = 0,$$

since

$$K_1 = \frac{F}{\left(1 - \dfrac{1}{\eta_1}\right)F'}\,;$$

i.e. when

$$F'' = -\frac{\dfrac{d\eta_1}{dF}(F')^2}{(\eta_1 - 1)\eta_1}.$$

For *Model II* the condition is

$$\frac{d}{dx}\left(\frac{1}{F'}\right) = 0,$$

since

$$K_1 = \frac{F}{F'}.$$

i.e. when

$$F'' = 0.$$

For *Model I* (B) the condition is

$$\frac{d}{dx}\left(\frac{Cx}{F}\right) = 0.$$

Since

$$K_1 = \frac{F}{\left(1 - \dfrac{1}{\eta_1}\right)F'} = Cx$$

we have

$$\frac{F}{xF'} = C\left(1 - \frac{1}{\eta_1}\right) = 1.$$

Now, we have seen in § 5 that, since C measures total income divided by wage income, C must be > 1. But it does not follow that

$C\left(1 - \dfrac{1}{\eta_1}\right) > 1$. Hence the above equality is possible. It gives, as the condition for a breakdown, $F'' = 0$ and $\dfrac{d\eta_1}{dF} = 0$, and η_1 is not infinite.

For *Model I* (A) the condition is that

$$\frac{C_1 F'}{F} - \frac{F'}{F} = 0. \quad \textit{i.e.} \text{ that either } C_1 = 1, \text{ or } F'' = 0.$$

But C_1 is necessarily > 1 and F' is necessarily positive. Hence in Model I (A) the above condition cannot be satisfied, and a breakdown cannot occur.

SECTION II

§ 8. On the assumption that

$$(-\phi'), \frac{\partial f}{\partial r}, F'\frac{\partial f}{\partial F}, K'_1, \text{ and } K'_2$$

are positive, we wish to know, for Model I (A), how the numerical magnitudes of the several D's are affected by differences in the magnitudes of g', $\frac{\partial f}{\partial r}$, $(-\phi')$ and $F'\frac{\partial f}{\partial F}$.

In the following tables the D's are differentiated with respect to

$$g', \frac{\partial f}{\partial r}, (-\phi') \text{ and } F'\frac{\partial f}{\partial F}$$

in the cases (a) when g' is positive and finite, (b) when

$$\frac{d}{dm_n}\left(\frac{C_1 x m_1}{F m_2 m_6}\right) = 0.$$

Tables

X. Table of Differentiations for the form of Model I (A) with respect to $\frac{\partial f}{\partial r}$, $(-\phi')$, g', $F'\frac{\partial f}{\partial F}$, when g' is positive and finite.

XI. Table of Differentiations for the form of Model I (A) with respect to $\frac{\partial f}{\partial r}$, $(-\phi')$ and $F'\frac{\partial f}{\partial F}$ when

$$\frac{d}{dm_n}\left(\frac{C_1 x m_1}{F m_2 m_6}\right) = 0.$$

TABLE X

DIFFERENTIATIONS FOR MODEL I (A) WHEN g' IS POSITIVE AND FINITE

$$A = C_1\left(\frac{\partial f}{\partial r} - \phi'\right) + F'\frac{\partial f}{\partial F}(g' - C_1\phi')$$

		Sign			Sign
$\dfrac{\partial D_1}{\partial\left(\frac{\partial f}{\partial r}\right)}$	$-F'\dfrac{\partial f}{\partial F}\cdot\dfrac{gg'}{A^2}$	−	$\dfrac{\partial D_1}{\partial(-\phi')}$	$-\left(1+F'\dfrac{\partial f}{\partial F}\right)F'\dfrac{\partial f}{\partial F}\cdot\dfrac{gg'}{A^2}$	−
$\dfrac{\partial D_2}{\partial\left(\frac{\partial f}{\partial r}\right)}$	$-\dfrac{\partial D_1}{\partial\left(\frac{\partial f}{\partial r}\right)}$	+	$\dfrac{\partial D_2}{\partial(-\phi')}$	$-\dfrac{\partial D_1}{\partial(-\phi')}$	+
$\dfrac{\partial D_3}{\partial\left(\frac{\partial f}{\partial r}\right)}$	$-\left(1+F'\dfrac{\partial f}{\partial F}\right)\cdot\dfrac{C_1 g'\phi}{A^2}$	−	$\dfrac{\partial D_3}{\partial(-\phi')}$	$-\left(1+F'\dfrac{\partial f}{\partial F}\right)^2\cdot\dfrac{C_1 g'\phi}{A^2}$	−
$\dfrac{\partial D_4}{\partial\left(\frac{\partial f}{\partial r}\right)}$	$-\left(1+F'\dfrac{\partial f}{\partial F}\right)\cdot\dfrac{C_1 g'(1-r\phi')}{A^2}$	−	$\dfrac{\partial D_4}{\partial(-\phi')}$	$-\left(1+F'\dfrac{\partial f}{\partial F}\right)\left(C_1\dfrac{\partial f}{\partial r}+g'F'\dfrac{\partial f}{\partial F}\right)\cdot\dfrac{g'r}{A^3}$	−
$\dfrac{\partial D_5}{\partial\left(\frac{\partial f}{\partial r}\right)}$	$\dfrac{C_1 g'\phi}{A^2}$	+	$\dfrac{\partial D_5}{\partial(-\phi')}$	$\left(1+F'\dfrac{\partial f}{\partial F}\right)\cdot\dfrac{C_1 g'\phi}{A^2}$	+
$\dfrac{\partial D_6}{\partial\left(\frac{\partial f}{\partial r}\right)}$	$\dfrac{C_1 g'F'\dfrac{\partial f}{\partial F}}{A^3}$	+	$\dfrac{\partial D_6}{\partial(-\phi')}$	$\left(1+F'\dfrac{\partial f}{\partial F}\right)\cdot\dfrac{C_1 g'F'\dfrac{\partial f}{\partial F}}{A^2}$	+

$\dfrac{\partial D_1}{\partial \left(F'\frac{\partial f}{\partial F}\right)}$	$\left\{\left(\dfrac{\partial f}{\partial r}-\phi'\right)g'+C_1\phi'\left(\dfrac{\partial f}{\partial r}-\phi'-\phi F'\dfrac{\partial f}{\partial F}\right)\right\}\cdot\dfrac{g}{A^3}$	$\mp$
$\dfrac{\partial D_2}{\partial \left(F'\frac{\partial f}{\partial F}\right)}$	$-\dfrac{\partial D_1}{\partial \left(F'\frac{\partial f}{\partial F}\right)}$	$\mp$
$\dfrac{\partial D_3}{\partial \left(F'\frac{\partial f}{\partial F}\right)}$	$\left\{-g'+C_1\phi'\left(\dfrac{\partial f}{\partial r}-\phi'-\phi F'\dfrac{\partial f}{\partial F}\right)\right\}\cdot\dfrac{g'\phi}{A^3}$	$-$
$\dfrac{\partial D_4}{\partial \left(F'\frac{\partial f}{\partial F}\right)}$	$\left\{-g'+C_1\phi'\left(\dfrac{\partial f}{\partial r}-\phi'-\phi F'\dfrac{\partial f}{\partial F}\right)\right\}\cdot\dfrac{g'(-r\phi')}{A^2}$	$-$
$\dfrac{\partial D_5}{\partial \left(F'\frac{\partial f}{\partial F}\right)}$	$\dfrac{(g')^2\phi}{A^2}$	$+$
$\dfrac{\partial D_6}{\partial \left(F'\frac{\partial f}{\partial F}\right)}$	$-\dfrac{(g')^3 F\frac{\partial f}{\partial F}}{A^2}$	$+$

$\dfrac{\partial D_1}{\partial g'}$	$\left\{\left(\dfrac{\partial f}{\partial r}-\phi'\right)-\phi F'\dfrac{\partial f}{\partial F}\right\}F'\dfrac{\partial f}{\partial F}\cdot\dfrac{g}{A^2}$	$+$
$\dfrac{\partial D_2}{\partial g'}$	$-\dfrac{\partial D_1}{\partial g'}$	$-$
$\dfrac{\partial D_3}{\partial g'}$	$\left\{\left(\dfrac{\partial f}{\partial r}-\phi'\right)-\phi F'\dfrac{\partial f}{\partial F}\right\}\left\{1+F'\dfrac{\partial f}{\partial F}\right\}\cdot\dfrac{C_1(-r\phi')}{A^2}$	$+$
$\dfrac{\partial D_4}{\partial g'}$	$\left\{\left(\dfrac{\partial f}{\partial r}-\phi'\right)-\phi F'\dfrac{\partial f}{\partial F}\right\}\left\{1+F'\dfrac{\partial f}{\partial F}\right\}\cdot\dfrac{C_1\phi}{A^2}$	$+$
$\dfrac{\partial D_5}{\partial g'}$	$-\left\{\left(\dfrac{\partial f}{\partial r}-\phi'\right)-\phi F'\dfrac{\partial f}{\partial F}\right\}\cdot\dfrac{C_1\phi}{A^2}$	$-$
$\dfrac{\partial D_6}{\partial g'}$	$-\left\{\left(\dfrac{\partial f}{\partial r}-\phi'\right)-\phi F'\dfrac{\partial f}{\partial F}\right\}\dfrac{C_1 F\frac{\partial f}{\partial F}}{A^2}$	$-$

TABLE XI

DIFFERENTIATIONS FOR MODEL I (A) WHEN $\dfrac{d}{dm_n}\left(\dfrac{C_1 x m_1}{F m_2 m_6}\right) = 0$

Derivative	Expression	Sign	Derivative	Expression	Sign	Derivative	Expression	Sign
$\dfrac{\partial D_1}{\partial\left(\frac{\partial f}{\partial r}\right)}$	$-\phi' F' \frac{\partial f}{\partial F} \cdot \dfrac{1}{\left(\frac{\partial f}{\partial r}-\phi'\right)^2}\cdot\dfrac{C_1 x}{C_1-1}$	+	$\dfrac{\partial D_1}{\partial(-\phi')}$	$\frac{\partial f}{\partial r}\cdot F'\frac{\partial f}{\partial F}\cdot\dfrac{1}{\left(\frac{\partial f}{\partial r}-\phi'\right)^2}\cdot\dfrac{C_1 x}{C_1-1}$	−	$\dfrac{\partial D_1}{\partial\left(F'\frac{\partial f}{\partial F}\right)}$	$\dfrac{\phi'}{\left(\frac{\partial f}{\partial r}-\phi'\right)}\cdot\dfrac{C_1 x}{C_1-1}$	−
$\dfrac{\partial D_2}{\partial\left(\frac{\partial f}{\partial r}\right)}$	$-\dfrac{\partial D_1}{\partial\left(\frac{\partial f}{\partial r}\right)}$	−	$\dfrac{\partial D_2}{\partial(-\phi')}$	$-\dfrac{\partial D_1}{\partial(-\phi')}$	+	$\dfrac{\partial D_2}{\partial\left(F'\frac{\partial f}{\partial F}\right)}$	$-\dfrac{\partial D_1}{\partial\left(F'\frac{\partial f}{\partial F}\right)}$	+
$\dfrac{\partial D_3}{\partial\left(\frac{\partial f}{\partial r}\right)}$	$\dfrac{-\phi'}{\left(\frac{\partial f}{\partial r}-\phi'\right)^2}\cdot\phi$	+	$\dfrac{\partial D_3}{\partial(-\phi')}$	$\dfrac{\frac{\partial f}{\partial r}}{\left(\frac{\partial f}{\partial r}-\phi'\right)^2}\cdot\phi$	−	$\dfrac{\partial D_3}{\partial\left(F'\frac{\partial f}{\partial F}\right)}$	0	
$\dfrac{\partial D_4}{\partial\left(\frac{\partial f}{\partial r}\right)}$	$\dfrac{-\phi'(-r\phi')}{\left(\frac{\partial f}{\partial r}-\phi'\right)^2}$	+	$\dfrac{\partial D_4}{\partial(-\phi')}$	$\dfrac{\left(\frac{\partial f}{\partial r}\right)^2}{\left(\frac{\partial f}{\partial r}-\phi'\right)^2}$	+	$\dfrac{\partial D_4}{\partial\left(F'\frac{\partial f}{\partial F}\right)}$	0	
$\dfrac{\partial D_5}{\partial\left(\frac{\partial f}{\partial r}\right)}$	$\dfrac{\phi'}{\left(\frac{\partial f}{\partial r}-\phi'\right)^2}\cdot\phi$	−	$\dfrac{\partial D_5}{\partial(-\phi')}$	$\dfrac{\frac{\partial f}{\partial r}}{\left(\frac{\partial f}{\partial r}-\phi'\right)^2}\cdot\phi$	+	$\dfrac{\partial D_5}{\partial\left(F'\frac{\partial f}{\partial F}\right)}$	0	
$\dfrac{\partial D_6}{\partial\left(\frac{\partial f}{\partial r}\right)}$	$\dfrac{\phi' F'\frac{\partial f}{\partial F}}{\left(\frac{\partial f}{\partial r}-\phi'\right)^2}\cdot\dfrac{C_1}{C_1-1}$	−	$\dfrac{\partial D_6}{\partial(-\phi')}$	$\dfrac{\frac{\partial f}{\partial r}\cdot F'\frac{\partial f}{\partial F}}{\left(\frac{\partial f}{\partial r}-\phi'\right)^2}\cdot\dfrac{C_1}{C_1-1}$	+	$\dfrac{\partial D_6}{\partial\left(F'\frac{\partial f}{\partial F}\right)}$	0	+

The signs of the differentials obtained for Model I (A) on the assumptions set out in the first sentence of this section are written in the tables. It must be borne in mind that, when any D is negative and its differential in respect of any element positive, this means that its magnitude, while larger absolutely, is smaller numerically, the larger that element is.

When g' is positive and finite all the signs are unambiguous ; except those of the differentials with respect to $F'\frac{\partial f}{\partial F}$ of the first two D's. Thus, the distinction between the numerical and absolute magnitudes being remembered, since in this case D_1, D_5 and D_6 are negative,

(i) D_1 and D_2 are numerically smaller and the other D's numerically larger, the larger is g'.

(ii) D_1 and D_2 are numerically larger and the other D's numerically smaller, the larger is $\frac{\partial f}{\partial r}$.

(iii) D_1 and D_2 are numerically larger and D_3, D_4, D_5 and D_6 numerically smaller, the larger is $(-\phi')$.

(iv) D_3, D_4, D_5 and D_6 are numerically smaller, the larger is $F'\frac{\partial f}{\partial F}$.

When $g' = 0$ in this model all the D's are always nil (which implies that the differentials relevant to them are nil), except D_1 and D_2. These two D's are independent of $\frac{\partial f}{\partial r}$ and $(-\phi')$; so that their differentials with respect to these variables are also nil. D_1 and D_2 are numerically larger, the larger is $F'\frac{\partial f}{\partial F}$.

When $$\frac{d}{dm_n}\Big(\frac{C_1 x m_1}{F m_2 m_6}\Big) = 0$$

D_5 and D_6 are positive instead of negative, D_3 and D_4 being still positive provided that $\frac{\partial f}{\partial r}$ is positive. Hence we learn from Table XI that D_1, D_2, D_5 and D_6 are numerically smaller and the other D's numerically larger, the larger is $\frac{\partial f}{\partial r}$; all the D's are numerically larger, the larger is $(-\phi')$; D_1 and D_2 are numerically larger, the larger is $F'\frac{\partial f}{\partial F}$, the other D's being independent of this element.

NOTE TO PART III, CHAPTER 3, § 3

THE PROPORTIONATE SHARES OF LABOUR AND CAPITAL WHERE THERE ARE NO OTHER FACTORS OF PRODUCTION

When the stock of capital is given, and also the (marginal) productivity function of labour and the degree of monopoly in industry, in order that the proportionate share of income accruing to labour shall be unchanged when employment grows, it is necessary that, over the relevant range, the elasticity of this (marginal) productivity function of labour shall be negative and numerically equal to the reciprocal of the proportionate share of income initially accruing to capital. For write x for the quantity of labour, F for this productivity function and e_t for this elasticity. The required condition is $\dfrac{d}{dx}\left\{\dfrac{x\mathrm{F}'}{\mathrm{F}}\right\}=0$: $i.e.$ $-\dfrac{x\mathrm{F}''}{\mathrm{F}'}=\dfrac{\mathrm{F}-x\mathrm{F}'}{\mathrm{F}}$; $i.e.$ $e_t=\dfrac{\mathrm{F}}{\mathrm{F}-x\mathrm{F}'}$. (Cf. *The Economics of Welfare*, p. 665 footnote).

It is sometimes thought that there is an inconsistency between this and the generally accepted proposition that the proportionate shares of product enjoyed by two co-operating factors of production (when there are no others) will be constant provided that the elasticity of substitution between them = 1. This is a mistake.

Let x represent the quantity of labour, y the quantity of capital and $\mathrm{F}(x, y)$ the quantity of product. Write η for the elasticity of substitution, e_t, as before, for the (partial) elasticity of demand for labour in terms of product when the stock of capital is given ; e_c for the corresponding (partial) elasticity of the demand for capital when the stock of labour is given.

These elasticities being written positive, it can be shown that $\dfrac{1}{\eta}=\dfrac{1}{e_t}+\dfrac{1}{e_c}$. For, putting a and b for the quantities and p_a and p_b for the marginal products of labour and capital respectively, we have, by definition $e_t=\dfrac{\partial a}{\partial p_a}\cdot\dfrac{p_a}{a}$ and $e_c=\dfrac{\partial b}{\partial p_b}\cdot\dfrac{p_b}{b}$. Further, the usual definition of the elasticity of substitution yields

$$\eta=\frac{p_a}{a\left\{\dfrac{\partial p_a}{\partial a}-\dfrac{p_a}{pb}\cdot\dfrac{\partial p_b}{\partial a}\right\}}.$$

But, since, with a homogeneous function of the first degree, the marginal product of any factor is unaltered by an equi-proportionate change in the quantities of all the factors,

$$\frac{\partial p_b}{\partial b} + \frac{a}{b} \cdot \frac{\partial p_b}{\partial a} = 0.$$

$$\therefore \eta = \frac{p_a}{a\left\{\dfrac{\partial p_a}{\partial a} + \dfrac{p_a}{pa} \cdot \dfrac{b}{a} \cdot \dfrac{\partial p_b}{\partial b}\right\}} = \frac{1}{\dfrac{\partial p_a}{\partial a} \cdot \dfrac{a}{p_a} + \dfrac{\partial p_b}{\partial b} \cdot \dfrac{b}{p_b}} = \frac{1}{\dfrac{1}{e_\iota} + \dfrac{1}{e_o}}$$

$$\therefore \frac{1}{\eta} = \frac{1}{e_\iota} + \frac{1}{e_o}.$$

(Cf. my article " The Elasticity of Substitution ", *Economic Journal*, June 1934.)

In accordance with what was said at the beginning of this note, the condition for the proportionate share accruing to labour to be constant when the stock of labour varies and the stock of capital is constant is $\dfrac{d}{dx}\left\{\dfrac{x\dfrac{\partial F}{\partial x}}{F}\right\} = 0 :$ *i.e.* $\dfrac{1}{e_\iota} = \dfrac{1 - x\dfrac{\partial F}{\partial x}}{F}$; which is the initial proportionate share of product accruing to capital. In like manner the condition for the proportionate share of capital to be constant when the stock of capital varies and the stock of labour is constant is, $\dfrac{1}{e_o} = \dfrac{1 - y\dfrac{\partial F}{\partial y}}{F}$: that is to say $\dfrac{1}{e_o} =$ the initial proportionate share of product accruing to labour.

Now obviously the initial proportionate shares of product accruing to the two factors of production added together must be equal to unity.

$$\therefore \frac{1}{e_\iota} + \frac{1}{e_o} = 1.$$

$$\therefore \frac{1}{\eta} = 1.$$

Thus the condition for the proportionate share of labour to be constant in the face of changes in the stock either of labour *or* of capital is that the elasticity of substitution $= 1$. This proposition is supplementary to, not inconsistent with, the proposition that, for the proportionate share of labour to be constant when the stock of capital is constant and the stock of labour changes, $\dfrac{1}{e_\iota}$ must be equal to the initial proportionate share accruing to capital.

INDEX

Allen, Prof., on expenditure, 83 *n*.
Annual Abstract of Statistics, 1935–46, 25

Bagehot on cumulation, 236
Bank loans as income, 30
Banking : and monetary policy, four types distinguished, 62-65 ; models, the, and, 150 *ff*. ; policies and unemployment benefit, 199-204 ; policy designed to keep price of consumption goods constant, 69, 77, 145, 162-6, 169, 175-6, 179-80, 184-5, 191-2 ; policy directed (successfully) to keeping money income constant, 156, 161-2, 169, 179, 183-184, 187, 191, 192 ; policy keeping interest rate constant, 194-7 ; policy, normal, 156-61, 168-9, 171-175, 177-9, 183, 186, 187, 191, 192
Banks, credit balances in, 23
Booms, industrial : Prof. Robertson on, 220 ; Prof. Röpke on, 220
Bowley, Dr. : money-wage index of, 92 ; on expenditure, 83 *n*. ; on sharing of income, 151
Business confidence : movements in, 216-22 ; operation of contractions in, 227 ; operation of expansions of, 227 ; Prof. Schumpeter on movements of, 216-17

Capital : accumulation, effects of, on interest rate, 127-8 ; constitution of earnings of working and liquid, 67 *n*. ; effects of accumulation on investment, 127 ; equipment, Keynes on, 135-6 ; proportionate share of, and income, 276-7 ; quantity of labour devoted to creating, 29
Champernowne, Mr., on income and saving, 110 ; chart of employment figures by, discussed, 234
Change, dominant factors of, 215-16
Cheques : as means of transferring bank money, 24 ; definition of, 24

Clark, Mr. Colin, 51 *n*. 3 : on investment and income, 233 ; on multipliers, 233 *nn*. 1, 2, 3
" Classical School " and employment, 86
Classical view : v, 85-98 ; and public works, 86 ; definition of, 86-8 ; Keynes' definition, 85 ; tested by British statistics, 95-8
Consumption : and investment, distinction between, 28 *n*. 2 ; definition of, 28 *n*. ; goods, 4-5 ; banking policy designed to keep price constant, 69, 145, 162-6, 175-6, 179-80, 184-5, 191, 192 ; quantity of labour devoted to, 29 ; utility curve, elasticity of parts of, 114-15
Cost : in " industry ", average and marginal, Colin Clark on, 51 *n*. 3 ; marginal, 42, 52
Cost-of-living sliding-scale for wages in Great Britain, adoption of, 93
Crises and Cycles, 220 *n*. 4
Crises générales et périodiques, Les, 220
Cumulation : Bagehot on, 236 ; mechanical, principal forms of, 235-242 ; Mr. Harrod on, 239-41 ; Mr. Hawtrey on, 236-8 ; via psychology or expectations, 242-4
Cumulative movements, 235-44

" Day of Judgment ", Keynes', examined, 135-6
Demand : and supply, equilibrium between, 39-42 ; elasticity of, 52 *ff*. ; function for investment for labour and movements in business confidence, 218-19
Deposits : active, 26 ; inactive, 26
Difference : in aggregate employment associated with small difference in labour demand function for investment, 158-9, 164 ; in aggregate employment associated with small difference in labour productivity in investment industries, 156-7, 163 ; in aggregate employment associ-

ated with small difference in labour productivity in consumption industries, 160-61, 165-6 ; in aggregate employment associated with small difference in labour supply function for investment, 159-60, 165 ; in aggregate employment associated with small difference in money income function, 157-8, 163-164 ; in aggregate employment associated with small difference in money wage-rate, 156, 163

Disequilibrium : 36, 46 ; flow disequilibrium, 46 ; transitions between positions of, 230-31

Dominant factors of change, 215-22

Economic History of England, 136
Economic Journal, 56 n., 79 n., 111
Economics of Stationary States, 133 n. 2

Employment : v-vi ; aggregate, 9 ; difference in, associated with small difference in money wage-rate, 156-7, 163 ; and money wages, classical view of relation between, 86, 87-88 ; and real wages under monopolistic conditions, 91 ; equilibrium level, Keynes' definition, 43-4 ; full, v, 85-7 ; full, definition of, 85-6 ; in post-1918 years, 97-8 ; money wages and volume of, vi, 9, 90 *ff.* ; monopolistic policy and, 209-10 ; multipliers, 147, 181-93 ; multipliers defined, 145 ; quantity of, functional relation between quantity of output per annum and, 49-52, 66 *ff.* ; statistical survey (1853–1913), 96

Entrepreneur's money income, definition of, 19

Equilibrium : conditions of, 74-80 ; distinctions between stable and unstable positions of, 74-80 ; dynamic, 47 ; flow, 39 *ff.* ; stable, 73-80 ; transitions between positions of, 223-29

Essays in the Theory of Economic Fluctuations, 152 n.

Expectations, cumulation via, 243-4

Expenditure, Prof. Allen and Dr. Bowley on, 83 n.

Export of Capital, The, 219 n.

Family Expenditure, 83 n.

Flow equilibrium : 19, 36-9 ; and market equilibrium compared, 41-42 ; difference between long-period and short-period, 42-4 ; differences among positions of short-period, 139-210 ; disturbances of short-period, 213-44 ; economic system in short-period, 66-72 ; long-period, 43, 123-34 ; market equilibrium compared with, 41-2 ; meaning of, 39-47 ; relation between long-period and short-period, v, 36, 42-44 ; short-period, 66-72 ; defined, 44 ; the special case of long-period, 123-34

Frisch, Prof. Ragnar, and measurement of elasticity of income utility curve, 116-17

Full Recovery or Stagnation, 221 n.

Functional relations, classification, 48-9

General Theory of Employment, Interest and Money, The, v, 28, 43, 128, 134, 135

Gilboy, Mrs. : criticism of Keynes by, 121 nn. 1, 2, 3 ; on relation of income to savings, 121, 122

Government interference with prices, 41 n.

Great Britain : money income, 25 ; unemployment in, 15-16, 96-8

Hansen, Prof., on investment and consumption in U.S.A., 220

Harrod, Mr. R., 4-5 ; on cumulation, 239-41 ; on saving and investment, 8, 39 n.

Hawtrey, Mr., on cumulation, 236-238

High-level full employment stationary state, 127-33

Income : American statistical survey of relation between savings and, 120-22 ; Dr. Bowley on proportionate share of, going to manual workers, 151, 276-7 ; Dr. Bowley on proportionate share of, going to property, 151 ; expenditure circuit, 27 ; factors *prima facie* relevant to proportion saved, 107 *ff.* ; function, money, difference in aggregate employment associated with small difference in, 157-8, 163-4 ; money, 18 *ff.*, 29 ; money, as function of interest rate, 64-5 ; banking policy keeping constant, 161-2, 174-5, 179, 184, 187, 191, 192 ; money, definition of, 18 *ff.*, 21 ; money, effect on existing stock of money of contracting, 132-3 ; money, function of, 60-65 ; money, of Great Britain, 25 ; money, Prof. Robertson on, 34 ; real, 18 *ff.*, 21, 29 ; real, definition of, 18, 28 ; real, effect of contracting money income on, 132-3 ; utility curve, Prof. Ragnar Frisch's method for measuring, 116-17, 119

Incomes : annual money, definition of, 18, 20 ; annual real, definition of, 18, 20 ; indirect taxation and, 104 ; proportions saved, 103-22 ; sizes of available real, and proportions saved, 103-22

Industrial Fluctuations, 215, 216 *n.* 1, 225, 226

Industry and Trade, 42

Interest : in money in relation to interest in consumption goods, 58-59 ; Marshall on the rate of, 81 ; Keynes on, 92-5, 99-102, 128 ; rate constant, banking policy keeping, 194-7 ; rate, and saving, 81-4 ; rate, effects of accumulation of capital on, 127-8 ; rate, money income as function of, 64-5 ; rate, Wicksell on long-term and short-term, 224 ; rates of, in relation to labour for investment, 58-9

Interest and Prices, 225

Investigations in Currency and Finance, 220 *n.* 2.

Investment : 28 - 36 ; aggregate money, definition of, 29-30 ; and consumption, distinction between, 28 *n.* 2 ; and consumption in U.S.A., Prof. Hansen on, 220 ; and income, Mr. Colin Clark on, 233 ; demand function for labour for, characteristics of, 53-5 ; effects of accumulation of capital on, 127-8 ; movements in business confidence and, 218-21 ; Mr. Harrod on, 5, 39 *n.* ; Keynes' definition of net, 28 ; quantity of labour, demanded for, 53 *ff.* ; quantity of labour devoted to, 29 ; quantity of labour supplied for, 53 *ff.* ; real, and real savings identical, 28 ; real, definition of, 28 ; supply function of labour for, 58-60

Investments, Keynes on, 135-6

Kalecki, Mr., on share of income going to labour, 151-2

Keynes, Lord : v, 5, 28, 43, 99, 101 ; classical view and, 85 ; definition of employment equilibrium level by, 43-4, and 44 *n.* ; definition of net investment by, 28 ; note on theory of, 135-6 ; on interest, 101 ; on interest rate, 128 ; on Marshall's *Principles*, 99-102

Labour : 51-2 ; demand function for investment, difference in aggregate employment associated with small difference in, 158-9, 163 ; demanded for investment, quantity of, 58-60 ; effect of larger productivity of, in investment industries, 144-5 ; for investment, characteristics of demand function of, 56-8 ; for investment in relation to rates of interest, 58-9 ; for investment, supply function of, 58-60, 208-10 ; income accruing to, 151, 276-7 ; Mr. Kalecki on proportionate share of gross home-produced income going to, 151-2 ; productivity in consumption industries, difference in aggregate employment associated with small difference in, 160-61, 165-6 ; productivity in investment industries, difference in aggregate employment associated with small difference in, 159, 164-5 ; quantity of, devoted to investment and saving similar, 29 ; quantity of, supplied for investment, 53 *ff.* ; supply function difference in aggregate employment associated with small difference in, 159-60, 163

Labour Gazette, the, on the Unemployment Insurance scheme, 12 ; on unemployment statistics, 16

Loans from banks as income, 30

Lombard Street, 236 *n.*

Long-period flow equilibrium, 123-134

Man, representative, definition of, 127 *n.* 1

Manual workers, Dr. Bowley on proportionate share of income going to, 151

Market equilibrium : 41 ; and flow equilibrium compared, 41-2

Mendershausen, Mr., on relation between income and savings, 121-122

Model I (A): 155-67, 183-5, 191-2; equations, 248; tables, 264, 266-7, 269, 272-5

Model I (B): 168-9, 183-5, 191-2; equations, 247; tables, 264, 266-7

Model II: 170-76, 185-6, 192; difference between I (A) and, 171-2; tables, 256-7, 263-5

Model III, 150, 177-80, 185-6, 192-3; tables, 252-5, 258-62

Models, The, 150-54

Monetary policy, normal, stability conditions and, 76-7

Monetary system in relation to banking policy and, 155 *ff.*; price levels, 94-5

Money: bank, 23, 25; circulation of, 20-22; circulation of command over bank, 24, 25; demand, money wages and falling, 92; income function, 60-65; income velocity of, 25-6; method for recording circulation of, 22-3; multipliers, 147-8, 190-93, 232-3; multipliers, definition of, 148, 181, 190; Prof. Robertson on hoarding, 35 *n.*, 46; rates, relation between high and low, in panics, 226 *n.*; statistical check-up, 21-23; transfer of command over bank, 24; wage-rates in relation to real wage-rates, 94; wage-rates, non-rigidity of, 88; wage-rates, trade unions and, 88-9; wages and downward movement of prices, 92, 95-6; wages and falling money demand, 92-3; wages and volume of employment, 87, 92; wages, Dr. Bowley's index of, 92; wages, monetary system in relation to cuts in, 94; wages, *Statistical Journal* on reduction of, 93 *n.*

Monopolistic policy, 4, 91, 208-10

Multiplier, definition of, 181

Multipliers: employment, 147-8, 181-189, 191, 232-4; evaluation of, 232-4; money, 147-8, 190-93, 232-233; money, definition of, 190; money, Mr. Colin Clark on, 233 *n.* 3

National Income and Outlay, 51 *n.* 3, 233

New Methods of Measuring Marginal Utility, 116 *n.* 2

Output, quantity of, functional relation between quantity of employment and, 49-51

Pension funds as savings, 104

Prices: effect of contracting money income on, 132-3, money wages and downward movement of, 91-2, 94

Principles (Marshall), 81-2, 99-102

Production, periods of, 205-7

Property, Dr. Bowley on proportionate share of income going to, 151

Psychology, cumulation via, 242-4

Quantities and functions, relevant, 48-65; fundamental, classification of, 48

Ramsey, Frank, on " The Mathematical Theory of Savings ", 111

Real wage-rates: in relation to money wage-rates, 94; and unemployment under monopolistic conditions, 95

Robertson, Prof. D. H.: on industrial boom, 220; on money hoarding, 35 *n.*, 46; on money savings, 34-6

Röpke, Prof., on booms, 220

Saving: 28-36; Mr. Harrod on, 39 *n.*; quantity of labour devoted to, 29

Savings: 103-22; American statistical survey of relation between income and, 120-22; definition of, 29-30; factors *prima facie* relevant to proportion of income as, 107-9; interest, rate of, and, 81-4; money, definition of, 30-31 and *n.*, 32 *ff.*; money, Prof. D. H. Robertson's definition examined, 34-6; real, and real investment, identical, 28

Schumpeter, Prof., on movements of business confidence, 216-17

Short-period flow equilibrium, 42-4, 123-34, 139-210, 213-44

Stability conditions, 73-84

Stocks, money, 20-27

Study of Industrial Fluctuations, A, 220 and *n.* 3

Study of the Capital Market, A, 227 *n.*

Technique, the formal, 144-9

Theory of Economic Development, The, 217

Theory of Unemployment, vii, 87, 90 *n.*, 166

Trade Cycle, The, 4, 39 *n.*, 83 *n.*, 240 *n.*

Trade Depressions and the Way Out, 236-7

Trade unions and money wage-rates, 93

Transitions : between positions of disequilibrium, 230-31 ; between positions of equilibrium, 223-9

Treatise on Money, 206 *n.* 1

Unemployment : 1-2, 9 - 17, 89 ; aggregate percentage, inquiries about, 15-16 ; benefit, 198-204 ; benefit and banking policies, 199-204 ; benefit, dominant characteristics of British, 199-200 ; definition of, 9 *ff.* ; factors causing, 1-2 ; individuals and, 9-11, 16-17 ; in post-War years, 97 ; percentage of, 15-16 ; in post-1918 period, reasons for excess, 97 ; statistical survey of average (1853–1913), 96 ; three facts essential to, 9-11 ; wages and, 13

Wage policy and employment, 88-90

Wage-rate, money, difference in aggregate employment associated with small difference in, 13, 157, 163-4 ; monopolistic policy and, 209-10 ; relations between quantity of labour and real, 66 *ff.*

Wages and Income since 1860, 92, 151 *n.*

THE END

PRINTED BY R. & R. CLARK, LTD., EDINBURGH